The
NATURAL LAW

HEINRICH A. ROMMEN

The

NATURAL LAW

A STUDY IN LEGAL AND SOCIAL HISTORY AND PHILOSOPHY

Heinrich A. Rommen

Dr. Rer. Pol. (Muenster) Dr. Jur. Utr. (Bonn)

Translated by
Thomas R. Hanley, O.S.B., Ph.D.

Introduction and Bibliography by
Russell Hittinger

LIBERTY FUND

INDIANAPOLIS

This book is published by Liberty Fund, Inc., a foundation
established to encourage study of the ideal of a society of free
and responsible individuals.

𒂼𒄄

The cuneiform inscription that serves as our logo and as the
design motif for our endpapers is the earliest-known written
appearance of the word "freedom" (*amagi*), or "liberty." It is
taken from a clay document written about 2300 B.C. in the Sumerian
city-state of Lagash.

First published as *Die ewige Wiederkehr des Naturrechts* in 1936
by Verlag Jakob Hegner. Translated and revised in 1947
by B. Herder Book Co.
Frontispiece by Bob Young, Jr.,
Georgetown University News Service

00	01	02	03	04	C	6	5	4	3	2
00	01	02	03	04	P	6	5	4	3	2

Library of Congress Cataloging-in-Publication Data
Rommen, Heinrich Albert, 1897–1967.
   [Ewige Wiederkehr des Naturrechts. English]
   The natural law : a study in legal and social history and philosophy /
by Heinrich A. Rommen ; translated by Thomas R. Hanley.
      p. cm.
   Includes bibliographical references and index.
   ISBN 0-86597-160-9 (hardcover : alk. paper). —ISBN 0-86597-161-7
(pbk. : alk. paper) 1. Natural law.   I. Title.
K415.R6513 1998   97-26334
340′.112—dc21

Liberty Fund, Inc.,
8335 Allison Pointe Trail, Suite 300
Indianapolis, IN 46250-1684

NIHIL OBSTAT
Matthaeus Britt, O.S.B.

IMPRIMI POTEST
✠ Raphael Heider, O.S.B.
Abbas S. Martini de Lacey

NIHIL OBSTAT
Ioannes McCorkle, S.S.
Censor Librorum

IMPRIMATUR
✠ Geraldus Shaughnessy, S.M.
Episcopus Seattlensis

Die 15 Ianuarii, 1946

Contents

Introduction

Heinrich Rommen is known in the United States primarily as the author of two widely read books on political philosophy, *The State in Catholic Thought: A Treatise in Political Philosophy* (1945) and *The Natural Law* (1947), and as a professor at Georgetown University (1953–67). Yet, before 1938, when he fled the Third Reich for the United States, Rommen was neither a scholar nor a university professor, but a professional lawyer—trained in civil and canon law—who had devoted considerable energies to Catholic social action during the dissolution of the Weimar Republic and the rise of the Nazi Party. The two books that secured his academic reputation in the United States were written in Germany in the midst of his legal and political work, for which he was imprisoned by the Nazis.[1]

Although *The Natural Law* displays erudition in a number of academic specialties (law, philosophy, history, theology), the reader will appreciate that the book was written by a lawyer in response to a political and legal crisis.[2] As a practicing lawyer, Rommen watched with alarm as the Nazi party deftly used German legislative, administrative, and judicial institutions to impose totalitarian rule. "Our modern dictators," he remarked, "are masters of legality."[3] "Hitler," Rommen concluded, "aimed not a revolution, but at a legal grasp of power according to the formal democratic processes."

---

1. *Der Staat in der katholischen Gedankenwelt* (1935) and *Die ewige Wiederkehr des Naturrechts* (1936).

2. Despite copious references to the works of great philosophers and jurisprudents, Rommen's original text contained no footnotes. The notes in the present volume were supplied later by his English translator.

3. *The State in Catholic Thought: A Treatise in Political Philosophy* (St. Louis: B. Herder, 1945), p. 212 (hereafter abbreviated *SCT*).

Every generation, it is said, finds a new reason for the study of natural law. For Rommen and many others of his generation, totalitarianism provided that occasion.[4] As he put it in his book on the state, "When one of the relativist theories is made the basis of a totalitarian state, man is stirred to free himself from the pessimistic resignation that characterizes these relativist theories and to return to his principles."[5] Rommen's writings were prompted by the spectacle of German legal professionals, who, while trained in the technicalities of positive law, were at a loss in responding to what he called *"Adolf Légalité."*[6]

What caused this loss of nerve, if not loss of moral perspective? Rommen points to the illusion that legal institutions are a sufficient bulwark against government by raw power—as though a system of positive law takes care of itself, requiring only the superintendence of certified professionals. "Forgotten is the fact that legal institutions themselves can be made the object of the non-legal power struggle. Who does not know that in a nation the courts or the judges themselves are subject to the power strife, showing itself in the public propaganda of contradictory social ideals?"[7]

The reader will find that Rommen is relentlessly critical of legal positivism. He distinguishes between two different kinds of positivism.[8] The first, he calls world view positivism. A world view positivist holds that human law is but a projection of force—proximately, legal force is the command of a sovereign; ultimately, however, the sovereign's decree replicates the force(s) of nature, history, or class. Whereas the world view positivist makes metaphysical, scientific, or ideological claims about law, the second kind of positivism is methodological, and its adherents are committed to the seemingly more modest project of studying and describing the law just as it is, without recourse to metaphysical or even moral analysis.

---

4. The original German title of *The Natural Law* is *Die ewige Wiederkehr des Naturrechts* (1936). Literally translated, "The Eternal Return of the Natural Right."

5. *SCT*, p. 48.

6. *SCT*, p. 212. For a recent study of the Nazi legal system, see Ingo Müller, *Hitler's Justice: The Courts of the Third Reich*, trans. D. L. Schneider (Cambridge: Harvard University Press, 1991).

7. *SCT*, p. 718.

8. Infra p. 110.

It is important to note that Rommen is not entirely critical of methodological positivism. He allows that so-called analytical jurisprudence
can be subtle and refined.[9] After all, lawyers should study law *as it is*—
in the statute books, judicial decrees, and policies of the state. Yet, by
consigning the moral predicates of law (good, bad, just, unjust) to a
realm of ethics that is separated, rather than merely distinguished, from
jurisprudence of the positive laws, the methodic positivists can become
world view positivists by default. In Germany, their "tired agnosticism"
with respect to the moral bases and ends of positive law left the German
legal profession intellectually defenseless in the face of National Socialism.[10]

In *The Natural Law,* Rommen traces the historical and philosophical
roots of this "tired agnosticism." He wants to show that the disrepair
of constitutional democracy is the result of skepticism and agnosticism,
which themselves are the cultural effects of disordered philosophy.
The idea that the project of constitutional democracy suffered from
philosophical neglect was a lesson drawn not only by Rommen but also
by a number of other influential European émigrés to the United States.
In 1938, the year that Rommen arrived in the United States, three
other important émigrés debarked on these shores: the French political
theorist Yves R. Simon, the Austrian legal philosopher Eric Voeglin,
and the German philosopher Leo Strauss. The most famous Catholic
thinker of the century, Jacques Maritain, arrived in New York in 1940,
one year before Hannah Arendt. These émigré intellectuals explained
the European problem to Americans and proposed also to explain
America to itself.

Beginning in the late 1930s and through the 1950s, there was a
renascence of interest in natural law—one that corresponded almost
exactly to the American careers of the European intellectuals who had
fled the chaos of Europe. The extraordinary talents of these émigrés
were almost immediately recognized. Consequently, they were able to
introduce Americans to a more classically oriented philosophy and
taught a new generation of students in law and political philosophy to

9. Infra p. 136.
10. Infra p. 113.

ask questions and to look for answers in places long forgotten by American schools. Arguably, they rescued the American departments of political science from positivism and behavioralism.

After stints at small Catholic colleges, Heinrich Rommen became a member of the faculty at Georgetown. The rest of the cohort of Europeans tended to cluster at three other universities. Dr. Alvin Johnson, President of the New School for Social Research in New York City, recruited Leo Strauss, Hannah Arendt, and other European-trained social theorists. At the University of Chicago, Robert Hutchins, Mortimer Adler, and John Nef, head of the Committee on Social Thought, also recruited Europeans, many of whom (Simon, who came by way of Notre Dame, Strauss, and Arendt) would eventually hold posts at Chicago. Ninety miles away, in South Bend, Indiana, Notre Dame's president, John F. O'Hara, began building what was called "the Foreign Legion." Most of the émigrés were either Catholic or Jewish, and Father O'Hara took full advantage of the Catholic connection to build the faculty at Notre Dame. Waldemar Gurian and F. A. Hermans came to the University of Notre Dame in 1937. Although compared with Maritain and Strauss they were lesser lights in the constellation of émigré scholars, Gurian and Hermans founded the *Review of Politics,* which led to the foundation of the *Natural Law Forum* (today, the *American Journal of Jurisprudence*).[11] Both journals quickly became important media for both Catholic and Jewish émigrés.

In the brief course of five years, therefore, the New School, the University of Chicago, and Notre Dame became, in a curious way, sister institutions. Political philosophy was pursued in the light of the ancient and medieval traditions, with a multidisciplinary breadth that was distinctively continental. It would be anachronistic to characterize this group of thinkers as "conservative." In their respective European contexts, they rejected the various species of nineteenth-century romanticism that formed the staple of European conservatism in fin-de-siècle Europe. In hindsight we see that the advent of a conservative intellectual

11. While still in Germany, Gurian allegedly threw the fascist legal philosopher Carl Schmitt down some stairs during a philosophical argument.

movement in the United States would have been unthinkable without these Europeans. Among other contributions, for present purposes, they called attention to the perennial debate over natural law.

With respect to the problem of natural law, what did these Europeans find upon their arrival? The answer is that, in the first decades of this century, American thinkers had given relatively little attention to natural law. If natural law was ever mentioned, it was usually in the context of theories of jurisprudence (rather than philosophy or political philosophy) and even then in a derisive or dismissive tone. In his brief but nonetheless influential 1918 essay "Natural Law," Oliver Wendell Holmes declared, "The jurists who believe in natural law seem to me to be in that naive state of mind that accepts what has been familiar and accepted by them and their neighbors as something that must be accepted by all men everywhere."[12]

It is a historical fact that ideas of natural law and natural rights shaped the Founding of the United States and in the 1860s its refounding. Nonetheless, American academicians and jurisprudents generally regarded natural law as an antique metaphysical ghost—an abstraction drawn from an obsolete philosophical conception of nature and the human mind's place within it. At the turn of the twentieth century, the educated classes thought of "nature" not according to the classical conception of an ordered cosmos of ends, nor even according to the Enlightenment understanding of fixed physical "laws of nature"; rather, nature was conceived according to one or another evolutionary scheme within which the human mind exercises creative, pragmatic adjustments.

At the same time, American legal theorists and jurisprudents resisted the pure positivism entrenched in England and in some legal cultures on the Continent.[13] They recognized that neither laws nor a legal system as a whole could be explained simply on the basis of the will of the

12. Oliver W. Holmes, "The Natural Law" (1918), in *Collected Legal Papers* (New York: Harcourt, Brace and Howe, 1920), p. 312.

13. For a comparison of English and American law, emphasizing the American dissatisfaction with formalism, see P. S. Atiyah and R. S. Summers, *Form and Substance in Anglo-American Law* (Oxford: Oxford University Press, Clarendon Press, 1987).

sovereign. Nor for that matter were the Americans satisfied with a formalistic treatment of legal rules. Having jettisoned both the classical and modern theories of natural law, the American legal mind was forced to turn elsewhere for an account of the extralegal bases of law. Such advocates of "sociological jurisprudence" as Louis Brandeis urged judges to set aside mechanistic and formalistic logic of "rules," and to interpret law in the light of economic and social facts. While not fully reducing law to social policy, sociological jurisprudence took the first step in that direction. Legal realists, including Karl Llewellyn and Benjamin Cardozo, took the argument further, contending that judges make law (*ius facere*) rather than merely discovering it (*ius dicere*). To them, law is to be made after considering multiple social, economic, and political facts. The tag "legal realism" thus conveyed the notion that a proper account of law is less a matter of explicating legal doctrines than of observing what judges actually do when they interpret and apply law, namely, contribute to the formation of social policy.

Although it might be doubted that these schools of jurisprudence rescued American law from the clutches of positivism, certainly they depicted the law as something more complicated and dynamic than the command of a sovereign; at least temporarily, these schools of jurisprudence satisfied the quest to have positive law rooted in something more than itself. The theories were tailor-made for a people agnostic about metaphysical truths but irrepressibly earnest in pursuing the tasks of progress and social reform.

There were, of course, notable exceptions to this rule. Edward S. Corwin's 1928–29 articles in the *Harvard Law Review*, eventually published as *The "Higher Law" Background of American Constitutional Law* (1955), traced both the theory and practice of American constitutional law to ideas of natural justice implicit in the English common law tradition, and beyond that to the ancient concept of *ius naturale*. It is worth noting, however, that Corwin's work was not widely read until it was assembled into a monograph in 1955, after the natural law renascence was well under way. In the early 1930s, Charles Haines's *The Revival of Natural Law Concepts* (1930) and Benjamin Wright's *American Interpretations of Natural Law* (1931) also investigated the role of natural law in American jurisprudence.

Still, Corwin, Haines, and Wright were not especially interested in the philosophical grounds of natural law. Like the advocates of sociological jurisprudence and the legal realists, they were interested primarily in what judges do. To be sure, until the 1890s there was relatively little reason for judicial review to ignite debates over natural law. For example, in federal cases adjudicated during the early years of the Republic, the theme of natural law arose infrequently and even then only indirectly. Admittedly, the federal courts of the nineteenth century did face problems of natural justice in connection with slavery. Even so, most federal judges enforced the written terms of the fugitive slave clause.[14] The *Dred Scott* case in 1857 was perhaps a premonition of a debate as to whether judges should avail themselves of moral theories in adjudicating constitutional cases, but the problem was settled by Congress after the Civil War. Abolitionist enthusiasm for natural justice found expression in the legislative rather than the judicial arena.

Corwin, Haines, and Wright's interest in natural law was piqued by judicial events that began to transpire three decades after the Civil War. In the 1890s the Supreme Court embarked on a new interpretation of the due process clause of the Fourteenth Amendment. Due process guarantees were invested with "substantive" meanings and purposes, especially with regard to rights of property and contract. Over the next two decades, federal courts struck down hundreds of state laws under the rubric of "substantive due process." Both partisans and critics of this new jurisprudence understood that the courts were using something like natural law reasoning.[15]

In varying degrees, Corwin, Haines, and Wright approved of what seemed to be a fresh "revival" (to cite Haines's term) of natural law, especially in defense of individual liberty against government.[16] But this

14. On the conduct of judges in the antebellum Republic, see Robert M. Cover, *Justice Accused: Antislavery and the Judicial Process* (New Haven: Yale University Press, 1975).

15. Even today, "natural law" often means any species of moral theory used by appellate judges when they interpret and apply law. See, for example, John Hart Ely, *Democracy and Distrust* (Cambridge: Harvard University Press, 1980).

16. Corwin wrote, "Invested with statutory form and implemented by judicial review, higher law, as with renewed youth, entered upon one of the greatest periods of its history, and juristically the most fruitful one since the days of Justinian." *The "Higher*

attitude was not widely shared, and it certainly did not represent a significant movement in the universities or law schools, not to mention the wider public. This is easily explained. At that time, the judicial discovery of natural rights was perceived not only as antipopulist but as contrary to social reform. By their advocates, these newly discovered rights were deemed to be bulwarks of individual economic liberty, upheld against the policies of social reform enacted by state legislatures in the early part of this century, and then by the New Deal Congress during the Depression. In defending individual property rights from the bench during a time of economic crisis and dislocation, the Court made natural law appear contrary to the common good. Here, of course, we are not passing judgment on that jurisprudence (natural law theory, after all, is typically used to check legislative will, whether of kings or of democratic majorities); rather, we are explaining why a very interesting episode of natural law reasoning in the 1930s fell flat. Not only in America, but even more so in Europe, there prevailed a popular urge to remove whatever was deemed an impediment to strong legislative and executive action in addressing the crises of the decade. In any event, with the retirement in 1938 of Justice George Sutherland this era of judicially enforced natural rights came to a close.[17]

Interestingly, although Heinrich Rommen has relatively little to say about the Anglo-American traditions of natural law jurisprudence, he does mention the institution of judicial review.[18] Indeed, he refers approvingly to the project of juridically applied natural law. On this matter, two points need to be made. First, Rommen was not trying to insinuate himself into a debate over American constitutional law. He shows little or no awareness of the currents and riptides of debate over use of natural law by the Supreme Court. Rommen refers to the institution of judicial review in order to make the philosophical (rather than constitutional) point that the mere fact that a law is posited by the will of a lawmaker is neither the first nor the last word in what

---

Law" Background of American Constitutional Law (Ithaca: Cornell University Press, 1955), p. 89.

17. See Hadley Arkes, *The Return of George Sutherland: Restoring a Jurisprudence of Natural Rights* (Princeton: Princeton University Press, 1994).

18. Infra pp. 36–37, 220–21, 232–33.

constitutes a law. Wherever there is a Bill of Rights, he observes, there is a "strong presupposition" that the law is not out of harmony with natural law.[19] Second, we need to remember that in Europe—in Germany and Italy in particular—the problems of the Great Depression quickly led to centralized state authority that brutally trampled on individual rights in the name of the common good. Thus, for many Europeans like Rommen,[20] the discovery and defense of individual rights by the United States judiciary, especially in the face of a public emergency like the Depression, certainly appeared to be evidence of a tradition lost in Europe.

The renascence of natural law theory in the 1940s and 1950s owed little to this rather specialized issue of judicial review; if anything, it had to overcome an allergic reaction to that subject.[21] In any case, the recently transplanted Europeans were far more interested in philosophical, and in what might be called civilizational, issues. Consider, for example, the first round of publications produced by these thinkers: Rommen's *The Natural Law* was published in English translation in 1947; Leo Strauss's *National Right and History* in 1950; Simon's *Philosophy of Democratic Government*, and Maritain's *Man and the State* in 1951; and Voegelin's *New Science of Politics* in 1952. In these books the problem of the moral foundations of law and politics are treated speculatively, broadly, and, for lack of a better term, classically.

To some extent, the interests of these émigrés overlapped. They agreed, for example, that the origins of modern totalitarianism are to be found in the Enlightenment; they also agreed that the Romantic

19. Infra p. 232.

20. Jacques Maritain, for example, wrote, "I think that the American institution of the Supreme Court is one of the great political achievements of modern times, and one of the most significant tributes ever paid to wisdom and its right of preeminence in human affairs." *Reflections on America* (New York: Charles Scribner's Sons, 1958), p. 171. Maritain, who helped shape the UNESCO and UN statements on universal human rights, believed that the Fourteenth Amendment was a model for checking the mistaken notion of state sovereignty. Like Rommen, Maritain was vaguely aware of the Court's natural law jurisprudence in applying that Amendment; and, like Rommen, he was more interested in the problems drawn from the European experience than in U.S. constitutional law.

21. Of course, the problem of judicial review would reemerge later, but long after the renascence.

reaction worsened rather than corrected the Enlightenment's consequences. The contrast between the philosophy of the ancients and
moderns became a trademark of the Straussian school, but virtually all
of the émigré thinkers, including Rommen in *The Natural Law,* drew
some version of that distinction. Yet it would be a mistake to suppose
that their common interests and overlapping research programs
amounted to a common doctrine of natural law. Leo Strauss, Eric
Voegelin, and Catholics like Rommen, had distinctively different approaches to the subject.

Besides the obvious fact of their religion, the Catholic thinkers had
at least three things in common that distinguished them from the other
émigrés. First, Rommen, Simon, and Maritain shared a philosophical
vocabulary that was rooted in scholastic thought, specifically in the work
of Thomas Aquinas. Second, for the Catholic thinkers the philosophy of
natural law was a living tradition: that is to say, it was not only a
concept to be expounded according to the philosophy of the schools,
it was a tradition formed by centuries of application to a wide array of
intellectual and institutional problems. Third, the Catholic thinkers
were more confident in building and deploying a system of natural law.
Not only Heinrich Rommen, but also such well-known Thomists as
Jacques Maritain and the American Jesuit John Courtney Murray
wanted to rescue the concept of natural rights from what they deemed
the dead-ends and errors of modern philosophy—a project that was a
contradiction in terms to many, if not most, of the writings and students
of Leo Strauss.

At midcentury, then, these Catholic thinkers were confident that
the crisis of the Second World War provided an opportune moment
for reconsidering democratic institutions in light of traditional natural law theory. Because this Scholastic tradition informs almost every
page of Rommen's *The Natural Law,* it will be helpful briefly to
examine it.

The word *scholasticism* derives from the dialectical method of the
medieval schools, in which the dicta of authorities (*auctoritates*) in
matters of theology, law, and philosophy were submitted to a very
complex and open-ended form of systematization. Beginning with the

compilation and classification of authoritative dicta, the data were to be interrogated, distinguished, and disputed. The scholastic method was in part the legacy of the legal revolution of the twelfth century, when the Roman Catholic Church, having secured its legal autonomy from the Carolingians, consolidated its independence by systematizing ecclesiastical customs and legal rulings. In about 1140, for example, Gratian, a Camaldolese monk from Bologna, produced the *Concordantia discordantium canonum* (Concordance of Discordant Canons). Comprising some four thousand different texts and authoritative dicta, the so-called *Decretum Gratiani* formed the first part of what eventually became the *Corpis iuris canonici* (the Code of Canon law). Gratian's work was a conduit for legal, philosophical, and theological opinions about natural law as well as for many other legal subjects. His method of reconciling, or harmonizing, diverse opinions became a model for the golden age of scholasticism in the schools of the thirteenth century.

About fifteen years later (circa 1155), Peter Lombard adopted a similar method in treating theological opinions in *Sententiarum libri quatuor*, and as a young student in Paris a generation later, Thomas Aquinas studied and wrote a commentary on the four books of the "Sentences of Lombard." Thomas's unfinished *Summa theologiae*, which he composed off and on for more than a decade in Paris and Italy during the mid-thirteenth century, is widely regarded as the most masterful expression of medieval scholasticism. This is because Thomas set out not only to harmonize nearly a millennium of theological opinions but also to treat the "new" learning of the recently recovered pagan philosophers, especially Aristotle.

Though he was well aware of the emerging legal systems of both civil and canon law, Thomas was not professionally trained in the laws. He was, instead, a Dominican theologian. In all his writings there is but one discussion of law for its own sake; this is found in the *prima-secundae* (I–II) of the *Summa theologiae*, questions 90 through 108. Most of this so-called "Treatise on Law" examines human and divine positive law as well as the *lex nova*, or "New Law," of the Gospel. It is perhaps paradoxical that while Thomas's treatment of natural law is by far the most influential and certainly the most quoted discussion of the subject in the history of philosophy, Thomas himself had relatively little to say about natural law. Whereas his *Summa theologiae* consists of more than five hundred discrete questions, only one is devoted exclusively to the *lex naturalis*.[22]

In this case, however, quantity is misleading; for in terms of the clarity of its analysis and exposition, the synthesis of materials (legal, theological, philosophical, political), and the deft application of natural law to disputed issues of human conduct (just war, theft, polygamy, etc.), Thomas's work in this area was a significant achievement. It is written serenely and in a manner that a modern reader might regard as understated, but it is all the same a tour de force. It outlived its immediate medieval context and the various "Thomisms" that have evolved in the intervening centuries.

Thomas's natural law theory had its greatest influence long after the Middle Ages. During the period of late scholasticism (roughly, the sixteenth and seventeenth centuries) Dominican and Jesuit theologians resurrected Thomas in order to respond both to the Reformation and to a series of international political crises. These crises were brought about by new and potent expressions of royal absolutism on the part of Protestant and Catholic sovereigns and by moral and political conflicts ignited by their colonial policies in the New World. In a period of civil wars and domestic disturbance, theories of royal absolutism were geared to enhance executive power. It is the recurrent story of natural law theory that it crops up precisely when the political order removes barriers to legislative and executive will.

Such is what happened during the Baroque era, where these issues were debated in the seminaries and in the courts of the Hapsburgs. Two centuries before the American Revolution, and nearly three centuries before the American Civil War, issues of political self-determination and slavery were debated in terms framed by Thomistic natural law theory. For example, the Dominican theologian Francisco Vitoria argued successfully for the natural rights of native peoples in the Indies and developed exacting criteria for the use of war by nations. His lectures, called the *Relectiones* (1527–40), influenced Hugo Grotius and

---

22. *Summa theologiae* I–II, q. 94 (hereafter abbreviated *S.t.*). At II–II, q. 57.2, there is one article devoted to *ius naturale*.

the emerging modern jurisprudence of international law. Another Spanish Dominican, Bartolomé De Las Casas, whose *Historia de las Indias* (1561) was translated into several languages, worked and wrote tirelessly for the natural rights of Indians to political liberty and property. Consequently, the transition from medieval doctrines of natural law to modern conceptions of natural rights was achieved in no small part by Spanish scholastics.[23]

The best known of the late scholastics was the Spaniard Francisco Suárez (1548–1617), whose *De Legibus ac Deo Legislatore* (1612) was the most ambitious effort in the modern period to construct a Thomistic legal theory. Noteworthy for our purposes is that Rommen's first book, *Die Staatslehre des Franz Suarez* (1927), was on Suárez, and there are repeated references to the Spanish Jesuit in *The Natural Law*. It was Suárez who vigorously defended the legality of natural law, which he applied to problems of political consent, just war, and right of revolution against unjust political authority. His emphasis upon the divine ground of natural law, and his critical application of it against the exaggerated imperial power of temporal sovereigns suggests that Suárez is more deserving of the title "father of modern natural law" than merely to be known as a "late" interpreter of Aquinas. Indeed, Suárezian natural law exerted considerable influence on both Catholic and Protestant legal and political theorists. That during the Second World War the Carnegie Endowment for International Peace published a Latin-English edition of Suárez's *De Legibus* is but one measure of his continuing influence.

More immediately, Rommen and his fellow Catholic thinkers were the products of a new wave of scholasticism that can be traced to Pope Leo XIII's encyclical *Aeterni Patris* (1878). Leo called for a return to the primary sources of scholastic philosophy, especially to Thomas Aquinas. Whereas "late scholasticism" was bred primarily in Roman and Spanish seminaries, the "neo-Thomism" prompted by the Leonine reform was led by lay scholars, many of whom taught in secular universities.

---

23. This chapter of intellectual history is covered by Brian Tierney, "Aristotle and the American Indians—Again," *Christianesimo Nella Storia* 12 (Spring 1991): 295–322.

Neo-Thomism was marked by two main traits. The first was scholarly attention to original texts, which in turn led to fresh interpretations of the premodern natural law traditions. The second, and somewhat opposite tendency, was a lively interest in making the old traditions relevant to contemporary political and legal problems. Indeed, it was the combination of the two that made neo-Thomism the most creative period of scholasticism, which flourished in the absence of anything resembling the medieval schools.

Papal encyclical letters became another significant transmitter of the scholastic tradition by setting forth in brief form the principles that ought to apply to controverted issues of social, political, and economic policy. Rommen was imprisoned by the Nazis precisely because of his efforts in behalf of just such encyclical teachings. Pope Leo XIII himself issued more than eighty such encyclicals that addressed social issues such as the rights of workers and church-states relations, as well as more philosophical questions such as the origin of political authority. As Europe moved through the crises of the First World War, the Depression, the rise of Fascism, and the Second World War and its aftermath, the encyclicals became an increasingly important source of Catholic thinking on political matters.

Two points need to be made about the social encyclicals. The first is that these encyclicals produced an extensive body of applied natural law on issues both great and small, from the problem of socialism and rights of private property to the morality of dueling. The second point is the more important one for understanding Rommen's work. The encyclicals provided a model for integrating two philosophical perspectives that had not been successfully unified in scholastic natural law doctrines. On one hand, the encyclicals were "conservative" on the intellectual grounding of natural law and quite traditional on particular matters of moral conduct; on the other hand, they were operationally "liberal" on many of the great political questions of modernity. For example, they favored the principle of subsidiarity against the practically unlimited powers of modern states; they supported the people's right to select the particular form of government; they upheld the rights of individuals to organize into labor unions, to hold property, and to enjoy religious liberties.

Rommen, Maritain, Simon, and John Courtney Murray certainly shared the conviction that a traditional metaphysics of natural law could be expounded without its having to adopt an antimodernist stand on political institutions. As Rommen put the question in *The State in Catholic Thought*, the perennial philosophy must eschew the romantic reaction against modernity, a reaction that led many Catholic apologists of the nineteenth century to want to "restore the lost thrones and support restored ones."[24] On that view, natural law would degenerate into an ideology that aspires to identify contingent social and political forms with first things in the metaphysical order. Perhaps the greatest achievement of Rommen and the other European neo-Thomists of his era was to decouple the traditional doctrine of natural law from the nineteenth-century conservative reaction against the constitutional democracies born in the age of revolution.[25] This freed such American Thomists as Mortimer Adler and John Courtney Murray to be, at once, metaphysical conservatives and partisans of constitutional democracy.

Having surveyed the historical background and foreground of Rommen's *The Natural Law*, let us turn to his philosophy. Rommen divides *The Natural Law* into two parts, historical and systematic. At the outset, Rommen poses his central question: "How can laws bind the conscience of an individual? Wherein lies, properly speaking, the ethical foundation of the coercive power of the state's legal and moral order?"[26] Whatever else law accomplishes—teaching civic values, inducing harmony, preserving social order, rendering justice, punishing the recalcitrant—everyone will admit that law is a peremptory command: it does not merely give advice or counsel but takes something off the menu of options for private judgment and choice. Etymologically, the word *law* (*lex*) is derived from the verb "to bind" (*ligare*). The perennial question

24. *SCT*, p. 9.

25. See, for example, *SCT*, p. 113, for Rommen's critical remarks about the reactionary French political movement Action Française, which attracted the young Jacques Maritain, who broke with the movement after it was condemned by Rome in 1926. Both in France and in Spain, Catholic thinkers had to come to grips with the possibility that antimodernist political movements were only superficially traditional.

26. Infra p. 4.

is *how* law binds a multitude of free agents who are capable of forming their own judgments and making their own decisions.

Answers to the question of how law binds free agents gravitate toward one of two poles, which Rommen characterizes as *lex-ratio* versus *lex-voluntas*.[27] In the first part of the book he investigates the intellectual history of the question; in the second part, he investigates the philosophical issues. Here, it will suffice to give a brief summary of Rommen's position.

For Rommen, natural law thinking has always thrived in the *lex-ratio* tradition. According to this tradition, law binds by way of rational obligation. To use the older scholastic terminology, law is neither force (*vis coactiva*) nor mere advice (*lex indicans*) but is rational direction (*vis directiva*). The *lex-ratio* position contends that the intellect's grasp of what ought to be done comes first; the force executing that judgment comes second, after the directive of reason. Interestingly, Thomas Aquinas insisted that command is principally a work of reason. He believed that without the measure of action grasped and communicated by the intellect executive force is blind and arbitrary.[28] For example, when we say that force must be justified by law, we recognize at least implicitly that law and force are not the same thing. So, it is one thing to say that force without law is unjustified, but it is quite another thing to suppose that law is force. Thus, for the intellectualist tradition, law and liberty are not necessarily in opposition, because they are grounded in the same source, namely the intellect's measuring of action.[29] The *lex-ratio* tradition holds that only on the ground of the primacy of reason can we make sense of law as obligation rather than as a literal binding in the fashion of force.[30]

27. Infra p. 36.

28. *S.t.* I–II, q. 17.1.

29. Thomas Jefferson called law, very simply, "written reason." Thomas Jefferson, *The Writings*, ed. Paul Leicester Ford (New York, 1898), 9:480, 18:1 ("The Batture at New Orleans"), 15:207.

30. Infra p. 169–72. Here, Rommen discusses the famous *definitio legis* of Thomas Aquinas: "law is naught else but a work of reason, made and promulgated by a competent authority for the common good." *S.t.* I–II, q. 90. Thomas did not include the coercive aspect of law in the definition, for he held that although coercion is an act of law (q. 92.2), it is not of the essence of law. This stands in marked contrast to the equally famous definition of law given by the English positivist, John Austin, who said in *The*

The *lex-voluntas* tradition, however, holds that law binds human liberty because of the superior power or will of the legal authority. That authority may have proper credentials to exert such force (the governed perhaps have *willed* for him to do so). Moreover, the sovereign may take care to express his commands in proper syntactical form. Nevertheless, the law remains a species of force. It may be a human artifact that proves quite useful and even necessary for social life, but it is force none the less. Thus, the *lex-voluntas* tradition insists that the will comes first, and reason, which guides the application of the command, comes second. On this view, law and liberty stand in opposition, for the free motion of an individual can be counteracted or redirected only by the will of another. Hence, the coercive function of law is not secondary, but primary.

Rommen traces the idea of law as *force majeur* to debates in the Medieval schools—debates that initially concerned issues of theology and metaphysics rather than jurisprudence.[31] In deference both to divine omnipotence and to supernatural charity—traditionally understood to be perfections of the volitional power—Franciscan theologians (e.g. Ockham and Scotus) depicted God's governance principally in terms of the will. The doctrine of voluntarism holds that the will legislates and reason executes. Some scholastic theorists in this school held that by a pure posit of the will God can change the terms of justice, even to the point of abrogating the Decalogue and the natural moral law. Accordingly, reason cannot count as a reason, as it were, against a

---

Province of Jurisprudence Determined (1832. Reprint, New York: Noonday Press, 1954) that law is the command of a sovereign, backed by sanctions, and habitually obeyed. The Austinian definition also contains four elements: (1) the *command* expresses "a wish that I shall do or forbear from some act, and if you will visit me with an evil in case I comply not with your wish"; (2) the *sanction* is the "evil" or "pain," either threatened or imposed; (3) the *sovereign* is defined, first, as one who has "might," which is to say "the power of affecting otherwise with evil or pain, and of forcing them through fear of that evil, to fashion their conduct to one's wishes," and, second, as one who is not so affected by any other agent; (4) whose wishes, when stated in imperative form, produce a predictable result, namely, *habitual obedience,* at least by "the bulk of a given society." Provided that certain syntactical and sociological conditions obtain (that words can express imperatives, and that a chain of power terminates at a determinate superior), law is the unilateral projection of force.

31. Infra p. 51–58.

unilateral projection of will on the part of the sovereign, beginning with the divine sovereign. Rommen believes that modern secular varieties of world-view positivism are the legacy of this theological debate.

He likewise calls attention to the philosophical doctrine of nominalism, also advanced by Franciscan theologians in the medieval schools. Nominalists held that the human intellect is capable of grasping only singulars; universals are but vocal utterances or names imposed upon an aggregate of singulars. Thus, nominalists could assign to the human intellect only the work of logically and analytically organizing names, which, at bottom, are arbitrary, possessing no extramental foundation. This philosophy could not but influence jurisprudence. Debates over what is to be deemed "good," "bad," "just," and "unjust" could be resolved on nominalist premises in one of two ways: either by looking in a dictionary or by imposing a solution by dint of force. Again, for Rommen, this medieval debate provided the historical background for the disrepair of the legal profession as he knew it. Law was to be conceived as a unilateral projection of will on the part of the sovereign, and lawyers became technicians of the dicta.

In Rommen's view, despite claims of giving preeminence to reason in public affairs, the Enlightenment generally followed the *lex-voluntas* philosophy. Concerning Locke, for example, Rommen writes, "Locke substitutes for the traditional idea of the natural law as an order of human affairs, as a moral reflex of the metaphysical order of the universe revealed to human reason in the creation as God's will, the conception of natural law as a rather nominalistic symbol for a catalog or bundle of individual rights that stem from individual self-interest."[32] Legal and distributive justice are reduced to the model of contract, in the fashion of commutative justice; the will of the contractors creates not only the determinate form of political institutions but the political common good itself. So, in answer to the question of how law binds the conscience to act in accord with the common good, Locke emphasizes the principle of consent, which itself is motivated chiefly by interest in preserving life and property. Though the Enlightenment natural law theories began (in Grotius) and ended (in Kant) with efforts to preserve the principle

32. Infra p. 79.

of *lex-ratio,* Rommen interprets the era as a cumulative erosion of the philosophical grounds for maintaining the authority of reason with respect to the will, the priority of the natural order of sociability and common good with respect to contracts, and generally the notion of a moral law not reducible to the lower "laws" of psychophysiological forces. Thus, for Rommen, the Enlightenment delivered into the hands of its successors a natural law tradition much weakened and ill-prepared to resist the full-fledged positivisms of the nineteenth and twentieth centuries.

Of all the versions of law as *force majeur* the one that triumphed in Germany developed in the soil of nineteenth-century romanticisms and vitalisms, which viewed the state as an expression of a nonrational *Volksgeist* or *la tradition.* Rommen was convinced that the Fascist idea of the state as an organic expression of a collective racial or ethnic will was the legacy not just of Rousseau but of medieval Franciscan mysticism and supernaturalism.[33] But, however its mythology differed from the positivisms of the English-speaking world, and however its notions of collective vitalism and will differed from the individualist doctrines of appetite across the English Channel, European Fascism took the side of *lex-voluntas.*

The classical definition of justice is giving to each what is his due, *ius suum cuique tribuere.*[34] Rommen points out that in commutative justice the *ius* is what is owed to another person; in distributive justice the *ius* is what the community owes to the individuals; and in legal justice the *ius* is what individuals owe to the polity. In any case, there can be no act of giving, and hence no command to perform the act, unless there is first a *ius.* Until or unless someone can rightfully claim "this is owed to me [him, or them]," there is literally no issue of justice. So, the most rudimentary form of natural law thinking arises in connection with the question of whether the *ius* is the mere artifice of positive law. Does this life, property, dignity, and status belong to me (him or them) exclusively by virtue of a contract or decree of the state or, for that matter, by the assertion of an individual?[35]

33. *SCT,* p. 19.
34. Infra p. 182–83.
35. Infra p. 204–9.

Both natural lawyers and positivists agree that some terms and relations of justice arise by the artifice of legal contracts and positive decrees.
There is no natural law requiring motorists to drive on the right side
of the road (legal justice), or for money lent to be repaid at a certain
rate of interest (commutative justice), or for providing college education
benefits to veterans (distributive justice). Undoubtedly, in each of these
examples the issue of what is "mine and thine," and of who owes what
to whom, is determined by customs, contracts, or statutes. In this
respect, Rommen calls attention to what every lawyer knows: namely,
that much of the law consists of norms that are quite arbitrary—
arbitrary, that is, not in the pejorative sense of being irrational or merely
willful, but rather in the sense that the material norm is not in itself
an issue of morality. "Many police ordinances (e.g., traffic regulations),
which serve merely a subordinate purpose of means to an end, exhibit
no materially moral content. The same is true of the technical rules
governing legal procedure or the organization of law courts. These
norms bear such a technical, formal, and utilitarian character that the
qualifications of moral or immoral cannot be applied to them."[36] Because
these laws have no material moral content in themselves, they can bind
conduct only because there exists a prior scheme of obligation. One
might presume that the traffic ordinance is related to an antecedent
obligation of legal justice to act in accord with the common good; so,
no one naturally or even morally owes the community the act of stopping
at a red light until that ordinance is seen in the context of a more
fundamental obligation.

And this brings us back to the deeper and more interesting question:
Are laws, all the way down, as it were, merely a human posit, none
having material moral content until conjoined with a declaration of
the will? Whether that will be the little will of an individual, the
communal will of custom, or the sovereign will of the state makes no
difference to the central philosophical question. The train of causality
in law will have to begin and end in an act of force. The terms of
justice must be arbitrarily constructed and laid as a template over a
social world that bears no objective terms of relations of justice. Indeed,

36. Infra p. 188.

if law is but a posit of the will, then the law can make it "right" to give death to an innocent person intentionally, or to make the perpetrator of violence the innocent person; to exact penalties with no finding of guilt or fault; to treat adults as children, persons as chattel; and to declare property ownership by individuals a crime. To be sure, most positivists would declaim the aforementioned acts. They might claim that if the law tries to reverse everyone's ordinary expectations of justice, disorder would quickly ensue. Further, the positivist might agree that there are some limits—of a physical, psychological, or even social nature—that influence the making of positive law and set parameters for any efficient posit of the will.

For the natural law tradition, what stands prior to the declaration of the will is not a set of contingent facts that a lawgiver would be prudent to bear in mind; rather, positive law presupposes obligations that arise independent of any decree or application of force by a human legislator. The social and legal world does not consist of mere facts organized and moved around by acts of force, but of principles of obligation, discovered by experience and reason. As Rommen points out, natural law is opposed to positivism, not to the positive law.[37] The art of positive law is a creative extension of the order of justice discovered by the intellect. The positive law neither creates all obligations from scratch nor deduces every new term of obligation from the natural law. Thus Rommen insists that the positive law cannot be well understood either by positivism or by rationalism. The former, he explains, requires human law to arbitrarily construct all norms of justice; the latter leaves to human law no creativity or novelty.[38] Rommen writes:

> The natural law calls, then, for the positive law. This explains why the natural law, though it is the enduring basis and norm of the positive law, progressively withdraws, as it were, behind the curtain of the positive law as the latter achieves a continually greater perfection. This is also why the natural law reappears whenever the positive law is transformed into objective injustice

37. Infra p. 221–22.
38. Infra p. 190–91.

through the evolution and play and vital forces and the functional changes of communities.[39]

Here, our brief review of the philosophical question makes the problem look deceptively simple. In *The Natural Law* Rommen is at pains to show that although the question is relatively simple the vindication of a jurisprudence of natural law is quite complicated. This is because the vindication depends upon an array of principles about the human person, the relation between intellect and will, and the nature of society. In a relatively healthy culture, these principles are given expression through social, political, and legal institutions as well as through the judgments of common sense. When these institutions are challenged, however, it becomes necessary once again to inquire into first things. It is fitting, then, to conclude this introduction just where we began. *The Natural Law* is not the work of an academician but is the effort of a German lawyer to understand the moral and social bases of the positive law and to exert philosophical intelligence in the face of *Adolf Légalité*. The problem of the German legal profession in the 1930s rendered the book timely, but the philosophical inquiry leads the reader to the perennial questions.

RUSSELL HITTINGER
University of Tulsa

39. Infra p. 230–31.

Translator's Preface

The present volume is a translation of *Die ewige Wiederkehr des Natur-rechts* (Leipzig: Verlag Jakob Hegner, 1936). The English version, how-ever, amounts to a revised and enlarged edition of the original work. The author has, at my suggestion, added many new sections; and he has further made, or consented to, several alterations in the text itself. Thus the worth and importance of an already valuable study of the history and philosophical foundations of the idea and doctrine of natural law have been considerably enhanced, especially for readers of the English-speaking world.

The studies and activities of the author peculiarly fitted him to interest himself in the striking phenomenon of the perpetual recurrence of the natural-law idea. Having completed his studies and obtained degrees in political economy as well as in civil and canon law at the universities of Muenster and Bonn, he dedicated his talents and abilities to the cause of Catholic social action in Germany during the last fateful years of the Weimar Republic. From 1929 to 1933 he was head of the Social Action Department, Central Office of the *Volks-Verein* at M.-Gladbach. More or less simultaneously, too, he served as chairman, vice-chairman, director, and executive vice-president of various other national and local German Catholic organizations and institutes with educational, social, and economic aims. In one of these he was closely associated with such well-known German Catholic students of society as Oswald von Nell-Breuning, S.J., G. Gundlach, S.J., P. Tischleder, Goetz Briefs, Franz Mueller, and the late Theodore Brauer.

With the advent to power of Hitler and his Nazi party, Dr. Rommen, who had distinguished himself in the struggle against the Weltanschau-ung and concrete aims of growing Nazism, was closely watched, carefully investigated, and finally arrested. His thorough knowledge of law, however, besides the care he had taken to destroy evidence which might prove incriminating in Nazi eyes, contributed at length, after a month of confinement, to procuring his release. With his former sphere of activity now closed to him, he lived henceforth under continual police surveillance. For some years he worked as legal advisor of a Berlin corporation. It was during this period of stress and personal insecurity that, in his leisure time, he wrote and published the German original of the present volume, intended as a protest against the widespread abuse of the idea of natural law in contemporary legal and political philosophy generally, but in particular in those circles most influenced by the Nazi Weltanschauung. It is to this circumstance that the author attributes what he modestly refers to as shortcomings of the work.

In 1938 Dr. Rommen at last secured permission to go to England. Having then obtained a teaching position in a Connecticut college, he brought his family to the United States in the same year. Since that time he has been engaged in teaching, in lecturing, and in writing. An American citizen, he now holds the position of professor of political science in the College of St. Thomas, St. Paul, Minnesota.

Dr. Rommen is the author of numerous scholarly and semipopular books, articles for periodicals, and articles for encyclopedias in the field of legal and political philosophy. In 1945 appeared his *The State in Catholic Thought; a Treatise in Political Philosophy* (St. Louis: B. Herder Book Co.).

Except in works destined for restricted scholarly circles, the use of footnotes has been declining in recent years. When scholars write for the general public, or even for the educated portion of the public, they are accustomed to omit all scholarly apparatus. Their reputation is the presumed guaranty of their undocumented statements and of the authenticity of what quotations they do make. Thus the German original of the present translation is entirely devoid of footnotes. However, the provenance of the scattered quotations is almost always indicated by the respective author's name in parentheses, and the relatively few specific references to passages in such works (especially in the case of St. Thomas Aquinas) are similarly inserted in the text.

Nevertheless, it seemed best, in adapting the volume to the Anglo-Saxon cultural milieu, to take liberal advantage of the handy device of the footnote. Wherever it has been practically possible, all citations and references have been identified and given in full for those who may wish to check them. But a few quotations, which could not be readily located, have been retained on the author's responsibility. Moreover, in view of the importance of many aspects of the problem of natural law in history and philosophy, I have considered it desirable, and indeed eminently worth while, to add on my own responsibility a considerable number of footnotes of a bibliographical, illustrative, explanatory, and critical nature. It is hoped that the reader will find them stimulating and helpful rather than distasteful and impeding; at all events, they can be skipped or ignored at will. It would not, of course, have been difficult to multiply such footnotes, particularly on the bibliographical side; but to overload the book with footnotes would undoubtedly have been to defeat the purpose of the author.

Accordingly, apart from perhaps a dozen bibliographical indications furnished by the author himself and a small number of precise references to passages in the works of St. Thomas and in Roman law, the translator must be held responsible for all footnotes, bibliographical and other.

An extensive treatment of moral problems from the standpoint of the natural law or rational ethics often leaves the impression that ethics, as a branch of philosophy, is quite sufficient to lead man to perfection and happiness, individual and social. From such a viewpoint the supernatural order, with its elevation of man, divine revelation, and divine grace, all too often takes on the appearance of something artificial or unnatural, something unnecessary and superfluous. Mature reflection, however, will show that such an impression is quite unwarranted. Neither as a science nor as an art is ethics, or the doctrine of the natural moral law in its concrete applications, able of itself to lead man as he actually is to his individual and social goal.

In the first place, past and present human experience forces us to agree with theologians who hold that in the present condition of mankind divine revelation is morally necessary in order that the natural moral law itself may be known by the masses of men with sufficient ease, certainty, and fullness. It is true that by the light of unaided reason men can know with certainty the more general and more fundamental principles of right and wrong in their simplest applications; but for the more remote conclusions of the natural moral law and for more complicated cases of human conduct they stand practically in need of some help over and above natural reason; and such assistance is afforded by divine revelation. In this sense revelation is morally necessary for the sure and complete knowledge of the natural law. In addition to divine revelation itself, an authentic and authoritative interpreter of both divine revelation and the natural moral law, the Church, is likewise morally necessary to safeguard and inculcate moral truths and values, to apply with sureness explicit and implicit moral principles to concrete, complex, and changing circumstances of human life and activity, and to settle moral difficulties and doubts that harass even the most learned. This is true especially in domains where human interests and passions of great driving power continually urge the acceptance of solutions that are specious but disastrous. It is indeed undeniable that the great development, refinement, and certainty of rational ethics in Christian circles owe very much to the extrinsic aids afforded by divine revelation and Christ's Church. Surely, as St. Ambrose, I think, so well expressed it, *Non in dialectica voluit Deus salvum facere populum suum.*

But there is much more to the matter than this. Knowledge of what our duty is is one thing; but, as daily personal experience teaches every one of us, the actual doing of our duty is quite another thing. As the practical science which, in the light of the primary moral principle and of human nature adequately considered, tells men what acts are good and what are evil, ethics has its great drawbacks. What, then, shall we say of ethics as the art which seeks to teach mankind an easy and efficacious way of doing good and avoiding evil? Experience seems to teach clearly that it is far easier to discover and propagate moral truth than to generate and generalize moral action. If divine help is morally necessary for mankind's adequate and sure knowledge of the natural moral law, divine assistance is even more necessary for its due observance. Indeed, the Church teaches that without special aid or grace from God a person cannot observe the entire natural moral law for any great length of time.

In the second place, it is a fundamental article of the Christian faith that man has from the very beginning been gratuitously elevated by God to an order of existence which totally exceeds the strict requirements and capacities of his nature. This supernatural order, with the supernatural goal to which man is destined, calls for a supernatural principle of knowledge—revelation of both speculative and practical truths—and a supernatural principle of activity in man, divine grace in its various aspects and with its various effects. Hence no system of natural ethics, however perfect might be man's knowledge and observance of it, can meet all the needs of his *de facto* supernatural elevation and orientation. As a consequence, divine revelation and divine grace, besides being morally necessary for the knowledge and observance of the natural law, are absolutely necessary for the knowledge and observance of the supernatural obligations incumbent upon man by virtue of his actual destination to a supernatural end.

But this supernatural order is neither artificial nor unnatural. Grace does not destroy nature; it presupposes, perfects, and elevates it. The supernatural order perfects and elevates the natural order in such a way that the latter is, as it were, integrated into the former. Yet human nature, unchanged in principle, retains its full value as a source of knowledge of the direction in which man's individual and social development, perfection, and happiness lie. In fact, the Church and its theologians have always viewed human nature, man's natural end and inclinations, man's natural faculties and their objects, the natural law—in a word, the natural order—as indispensable sources for determining the proper lines of human conduct which, with the aid of divine grace and with supernatural equipment, man must follow in his quest of his supernatural goal. We can and must distinguish, but without separating, the natural from the supernatural order. Rational ethics, founded on the natural moral law, preserves, therefore, its independence and value like any other branch of philosophy. In this way it performs the valuable function of serving as a basis of understanding and agreement between Catholics and all those who fail or refuse, for one reason or another, to recognize consciously their actual and inescapable incorporation into the supernatural order and their call to actual, full, and living membership in the authentic Church of Christ.

In the arduous task of preparing this translation for the English-speaking world, my requests for assistance met with a heartening response. The author himself, with unfailing kindness and patience,

rendered invaluable help by clearing up numerous points which sometimes perplex the translator of a German work. Several other scholars
also contributed valuable suggestions in regard to certain thorny and
involved questions with which I have dealt: Rev. Dr. Francis J. Connell,
C.SS.R., of the Catholic University of America; Rev. Dr. Francis B.
Donnelly of the Seminary of the Immaculate Conception, Huntington,
New York; Rev. Dr. John J. Galvin, S.S., of St. Edward's Seminary,
Kenmore, Washington. But I owe most to the courteous generosity of
several of my confreres and colleagues. Rev. Leo P. Hansen, O.S.B.,
prepared the first rough draft of the present translation before he left
to serve as chaplain in our armed forces. Rev. Meinrad J. Gaul, O.S.B.,
and Rev. Luke O'Donnell, O.S.B., gave unstintingly of their time and
special knowledge throughout the preparation of the manuscript. As
on a former occasion, however, it is to Rev. Matthew W. Britt, O.S.B.,
that I am most profoundly indebted. Expertly and meticulously he
labored over the entire manuscript and strove mightily to impart a
degree of readability to the translation. In many other ways, too, his
patience, knowledge, interest, and encouragement made it possible to
bring to a conclusion a task which, it is now easy to feel and see, should
have been left to another.

THOMAS R. HANLEY, O.S.B.,
St. Martin's College,
Lacey, Washington

PART ONE

History of the Idea of Natural Law

CHAPTER I

The Legacy of Greece and Rome

The doctrine of the natural law is as old as philosophy. Just as wonder,[1] according to Aristotle, lies at the beginning of philosophy, so, too, is it found at the beginning of the doctrine of natural law.

In the early periods of all peoples the mores and laws, undifferentiated from the norms of religion, were looked upon as being exclusively of divine origin. The order according to which a people lives is a divinely instituted order, a holy order. This is true of the ancient Greeks, among whom all law was stamped with the seal of the divine. It likewise holds good for the early Germans: their law bore in the primitive period a distinctly sacred character. Nor is it any less true of the Roman people, whose legal genius enabled its law twice to become a world law.[2] For

1. "It is owing to their wonder that men both now begin and at first began to philosophize; they wondered originally at the obvious difficulties, then advanced little by little and stated difficulties about the greater matters, e.g., about the phenomena of the moon and those of the sun and of the stars, and about the genesis of the universe. And a man who is puzzled and wonders thinks himself ignorant (whence even the lover of myth is in a sense a lover of Wisdom, for the myth is composed of wonders); therefore since they philosophized in order to escape from ignorance, evidently they were pursuing science in order to know, and not for any utilitarian end" (*Metaphysica*, A. 2, 982b; trans. W. D. Ross).

2. That is, in the third and fourth centuries of the Christian era, after all the free inhabitants of the Roman Empire had been made citizens (212), and in the Middle Ages through its incorporation in the canon law of the Church, its systematic study in the universities, and its subsequent reception in Western Europe. Cf. Roscoe Pound, "The Church in Legal History," in *Jubilee Law Lectures, 1889–1939*. School of Law,

among the Romans, too, law in the earliest times was divine law. Moreover, even the later period, when the Romans had already hit upon the distinction between strictly sacred law (*fas*) and profane law (*ius*), still afforded clear evidence of the sacred origin of Roman law: the pontifices remained the dispensers and custodians of the law until Roman legal reason emancipated itself from this secret law of the priests.

This theological cast of all primitive law has two characteristics. Such law is essentially unchangeable through human ordinances, and it has everywhere the same force within the same cultural environment.

The idea of a natural law can emerge only when men come to perceive that not all law is unalterable and unchanging divine law. It can emerge only when critical reason, looking back over history, notes the profound changes that have occurred in the realm of law and mores and becomes aware of the diversity of the legal and moral institutions of its own people in the course of its history; and when, furthermore, gazing beyond the confines of its own city-state or tribe, it notices the dissimilarity of the institutions of neighboring peoples. When, therefore, human reason wonderingly verifies this diversity, it first arrives at the distinction between divine and human law. But it soon has to grapple with the natural law, with the question of the moral basis of human laws. This is at the same time the problem of why laws are binding. How can laws bind the conscience of an individual? Wherein lies, properly speaking, the ethical foundation of the coercive power of the state's legal and moral order? Closely connected with these problems is the question of the best laws or best state, a matter which from the time of Plato has engaged the attention of nearly all exponents of the great systems of natural law. Before long, however, a related idea made its appearance. This was the view that the tribal deities are not the ultimate form of the religious background of reality. For if an eternal, immutable law obliges men to obey particular laws, behind the popular

---

The Catholic University of America (Washington, D.C., 1939), p. 25, quoting Rudolph von Jhering. Of considerable value, especially for the historical portion of the present volume, is Jerome Hall, *Readings in Jurisprudence* (Indianapolis: Bobbs-Merrill Co., 1938).

images of tribal deities exists an eternal, all-wise Lawgiver who has the power to bind and to loose.[3]

It is quite understandable, then, that the philosophical conception of the natural law should have made its first appearance in the area of Western culture among the ancient Greeks. This dynamic people was endowed with a penetrating critical intelligence, with an early maturing consciousness of the individual mind, and with great power of political organization. Indeed, Western political philosophy likewise originated in this gifted people.

It is a remarkable fact that at the very beginning of the Greek philosophy of law (or rather of the laws), and therewith of the natural law, a distinction came to light which has survived down to the present time, a distinction between two conceptions of the natural law. One is the idea of a revolutionary and individualistic natural law essentially bound up with the basic doctrine of the state of nature as well as with the concept of the state as a social unit which rests upon a free contract, is arbitrary and artificial, is determined by utility, and is not metaphysically necessary. The other is the idea of a natural law grounded in metaphysics that does not exist in a mythical state of nature before the "laws," but lives and ought to live in them—a natural law which one would fain, though somewhat ineptly, style conservative. It is further significant that the notion of God as supreme Lawgiver is intimately connected with the latter conception. Both of these tendencies are already plainly visible in the first Sophists and in Heraclitus, the great forerunner of Plato.

Heraclitus of Ephesus (*cir.* 536–470 B.C.) is famous for his thesis that "all things flow; nothing abides." But this ceaseless changing of things led him directly to the idea of an eternal norm and harmony, which exists unchangeable amid the continual variation of phenomena. A fundamental law, a divine common *logos,* a universal reason holds sway: not chance, lawlessness, or irrational change. Natural occurrences are ruled by a reason that establishes order. Man's nature as well as his

3. See, in general, Otto Karrer, *Religions of Mankind,* trans. by E. I. Watkin (New York: Sheed and Ward, 1936), chaps. 1 and 2.

ethical goal consists, then, in the subordination or conformity of individ-ual and social life to the general law of the universe. This is the primordial norm of moral being and conduct. "Wisdom is the foremost virtue, and wisdom consists in speaking the truth, and in lending an ear to nature and acting according to her. Wisdom is common to all. . . . They who would speak with intelligence must hold fast to the (wisdom that is) common to all, as a city holds fast to its law, and even more strongly. For all human laws are fed by one divine law."[4] The laws of men are but attempts to realize this divine law. Wherefore, declares this conservative aristocrat, the people ought not to resist the laws, which to him are the embodiment of the divine law. On the contrary, "the people ought to fight in defense of the law as they do of their city wall."[5] Thus in the diversity of human laws (not beyond them) there flashed upon Heraclitus the idea of an eternal law of nature that corres-ponds to man's reason as sharing in the eternal *logos*. The variety of human laws does not exclude the idea of the natural law. For through the contingency and diversity of human laws rational thought perceives the truth of the eternal law, whereas sense perception—the eye and the ear—notices only what is different and unlike. With Heraclitus, the "Obscure Philosopher," the thinker who speaks in obscure symbols, the idea of the natural law for the first time emerged as a natural, unchangeable law from which all human laws draw their force.

Heraclitus' doctrine had a practical aim. It was intended to stress the value of the laws and their binding force against the fickleness of the uncritical masses. Prone to novelties of all kinds and woefully lacking in powers of discrimination, the masses were subject to capricious fluctuations of opinion. They thus fell easy prey to the demagogy of the Sophists.

It is no easy matter to judge the Sophists fairly. For one thing their teachings have come down to us in a very fragmentary form and are known to us chiefly from the dialogues of Plato, their great adversary. Moreover, as popular orators with a leaning toward demagogy, they were fond of oversimplified slogans and paradoxical statements. This

4. Fragments 112–14, in Charles M. Bakewell, *Source Book in Ancient Philosophy* (New York: Charles Scribner's Sons, 1907), p. 34.

5. Fragment 44; *ibid.*, p. 31.

earned for them, among posterity, the sinister reputation of philosophical ropedancers, rationalistic revolutionaries, and contemners of the law. For this reputation Plato has been particularly responsible. But this judgment is, to say the least, far too harsh. That the Sophists had of necessity to appear to the Greeks as revolutionary rationalists is explained, on the one hand, by their reckless criticism of contemporary social institutions and their cynical skepticism in political matters, and, on the other, by the high esteem in which their opponents held the laws and the polis, or city-state.

Their laws were the pride of the citizens of the Greek polis, and the Sophists were mostly foreigners. Heraclitus had looked upon the laws as equal in worth to the walls of the city. The philosophers spoke of the *nomoi*, or laws, with the greatest respect: the peoples who had no polis were to them barbarians. Hence it happened, too, that Socrates, despite his distinction between what is naturally right and legally right, pronounced the laws of Athens to be "right" without qualification. The citizens, consequently, were under obligation to obey them, even as he also obeyed them to the bitter end. For Plato likewise the laws of Athens were for the most part something inviolable. He regarded the social order founded upon them as good, even if capable of improvement; never did he term it bad. Therefore to these aristocrats in political outlook as well as in thought, the social criticism of the Sophists necessarily passed not only for an attack upon the foundations of a particular order of a particular polis, but also for a malicious assault upon the right order of the polis itself.

Moreover, in point of fact the Sophists had much in common with the revolutionary natural-law ideas of the eighteenth-century Enlightenment, especially with Rousseau's doctrine and its reckless criticism of existing society. In the case of the conservative natural law (if one wishes to speak of a political tendency) the distinction between natural and positive law served to justify and improve the existing positive law. It was, however, the tendency, an avowedly political tendency, of the natural-law concept of the Sophists to point out, by contrasting the current positive law with what is right by nature, not merely the accidental need for reform of the laws but the substantial wrongness of the laws. To the Sophists the laws were not venerable because of tradition or by reason of having stood the actual test of life in the city-state: they were artificial constructs and served the interests of the powerful (Thrasymachus). Thus the laws possessed no inherent value, for only what is right by nature can have such value, and to this the Sophists were continually appealing. They did not deny, therefore, the form of the natural law and of what is moral by nature. They merely brought out the sharp contrast between the prevailing order of the city-state and the natural law as they preached it, and they ridiculed Socrates who looked upon the laws of Athens as purely and simply "just." Callicles, who was the first to advance the thesis that might makes right, wished thereby to give expression to a fact which he was criticizing. This was that the ruling classes, while they declared their laws, i.e., those which worked to their advantage, to be naturally just, were misusing the idea of truly natural justice, and were desirous only of subjecting the people to their class interests.

By contrasting, in the light of their social criticism, what is naturally right with what is legally right, the Sophists attained at this early date to the notion of the rights of man and to the idea of mankind. The unwritten laws, said Hippias, are eternal and unalterable: they spring from a higher source than the decrees of men. To Hippias' way of thinking, all men are by nature relatives and fellow citizens, even if they are not such in the eyes of the law. Therewith the distinction between Greeks and barbarians, fundamental for Greek cultural consciousness, vanished into thin air. "God made all men free; nature has made no man a slave" (Alcidamas). The whole ethical and legal foundation was thereby taken away from slavery, which was in turn the very basis of the Greek social and economic system. Nevertheless Plato held fast to the institution of slavery, and Aristotle was ever striving to justify it by means of his theory that certain men are slaves by nature.

Three ideas, heavily charged with social explosives for the world of Greek culture, were thus put forward by the Sophists as part and parcel of the natural law. These ideas were thenceforth to be subjected to a ceaseless reprocessing in the history of the mind. Time and again they were to serve revolutionary thinkers as molds and vessels into which these could pour their revolutionary emotions, their schemes for reform, and their political aims. The first idea was that the existing laws serve class interests and are artificial constructions. Only what is naturally moral and naturally right can be properly called moral and right. Next came the idea of the natural-law freedom and equality of all human beings and, as a consequence, the idea of the rights of man as well as the idea of mankind, the *civitas maxima,* or world community, which is superior to the city-state. According to the third idea, the state, or polis, is nonessential: it owes its origin to a human decision, i.e., to a free contract, not to a necessity of some kind. The political organization of man must therefore have been preceded by a state of nature (portrayed optimistically or pessimistically), in which the pure natural law was in force. According to the optimistic view of the state of nature, this law can in its essential contents be neither altered not abrogated by the state; in the pessimistic view, which leads to positivism, it is merged in the will of the state. But after the lofty flight of speculation had been exposed to the needed self-criticism, the successors of the Sophists fell quickly into skepticism and into a sheer positivism when the underlying optimistic outlook ran afoul of the facts. This was, for instance, the case with the Epicureans, who were the first legal positivists.

The Sophists' criticism of the positive laws, together with the rapidly growing prominence of the notion of utility, led Epicurus, whose sensistic epistemology left no room for metaphysics, to doubt that anything can be objectively and naturally right. Utility and pleasure became for him the sole principles of ethics and law. But since the resultant subjectivism must endanger the social order and with it the peaceful enjoyment of pleasure, he inferred from the principle of utility that justice as such is a chimera, that it rather exists only in agreements which have been entered into for the prevention of mutual injuries. Justice thus consists entirely in positive laws. Before men entered into agreements and before there were laws founded upon such agreements, men had lived in a haphazard manner, like wild beasts, lawlessly. The state of nature, upon which the Sophists had placed an optimistic construction but which they had not particularly stressed, was thus interpreted in a pessimistic sense in Epicurean circles. From this, however, sprang also the respect of the Epicureans for the existing laws as well as their emphasis upon the value of the legal notions and customary law of individual peoples. The parallelism between the Sophist and

Epicurean doctrine on the one hand and, on the other, the natural-law schools of modern times is quite unmistakable. Rousseau, Hobbes, Pufendorf, Thomasius, and the adherents of historical schools of law, who variously combine the elements of individual systems, merely repeat and develop these ancient ideas.

The starting point of the Sophists was a criticism of the *nomoi* of the Athenian democracy. In their role and guise of popular philosophers and in their political and skeptical snobbery they frequently defended the opposite theories. As if the revolutionary criticism of the *nomoi* in behalf of slaves and non-citizens, considered barbarians, and the conservative utilitarianism of Epicurus were not sufficiently unsettling, Callicles, if we are to trust tradition, stood forth as champion of the doctrine of the right of the stronger, i.e., that might makes right. A pure materialist in his philosophy, Callicles reached the conclusion that law, such as obtained in the Athenian democracy, was in reality injustice. For, he contended, the many who are weak have united to fetter with the bands of law the few who are strong. But nature teaches, as a glance at the animal kingdom and at warring states reveals, that the stronger naturally overcomes the weaker. Natural law, then, is the force of the stronger. For this snobbish leader of the oligarchic faction such was the way one could and should get at the Athenian democracy. But other Sophists, among them Hippias, put forward the demagogic formulas of human rights and of the freedom and equality of all to achieve the selfsame purpose—the overthrow of the bourgeois democracy.[6]

The metaphysical natural law of Plato as well as the more realistic one of Aristotle formed the high-water mark of moral and natural-law philosophy in Greek civilization. Stoicism, on the other hand, in a remarkable eclectic synthesis of single principles drawn from many philosophers, furnished in its system of natural law the terminology or word vessels into which the Church Fathers were able to pour the first conceptions of the Christian natural law and to impart them to the world of their time.

6. On these ideas of the Sophists, see the excellent discussion of George H. Sabine, *A History of Political Theory* (New York: Henry Holt and Co., 1937), pp. 25–34.

The danger of skepticism, to which the extreme rationalism of the Sophists lay exposed, was first clearly perceived by Socrates. The Sophists' juggling of ideas and their paradoxes threatened to dissolve the notion of goodness and morality, just as their extremist social criticism and their libertarian ideology, directed in the name of the natural law against law and custom, called into question the value of the *nomoi*. Socrates did not merely teach the essence of goodness and justice by his inductive, question-and-answer method. Through the thesis that virtue consists in knowledge, he also showed that there exists a knowable objective world of such values as goodness, beauty, and justice, and that no one does evil for evil's sake but because it somehow, culpably or through ignorance, appears to him as good. Wherefore knowledge means the contemplation of the idea of justice, and so on. The daimonion, conscience and its voice, he regarded as a reflection and testimony of these ultimate values and of the divinely instituted order of the world. Herein lies the significance of Socrates for the idea of the natural law. It does not lie in his frequently stressed fidelity to the law, although, to counteract the criticism of the Sophists, he placed so much emphasis upon the value of the laws that, out of respect for the law's function of safeguarding right, he went so far as to condemn absolutely any disobedience to a particular unjust law.[7]

The great masters of Greece, Plato and Aristotle, also directed their

7. On the other hand, Socrates' older contemporary, the dramatist Sophocles (496–406 B.C.), has the heroine of the tragedy *Antigone* declare that her conscience is altogether clear even though she had deliberately overstepped a law of King Creon by burying her brother against the royal orders. She defends herself by appealing to a law higher than any ordinance made by man (ll. 450–60):

> "Because it was not Zeus who ordered it,
> Nor Justice, dweller with the Nether Gods,
> Gave such a law to man; nor did I deem
> Your ordinance of so much binding force,
> As that a mortal man could overbear
> The unchangeable unwritten code of Heaven;
> This is not of today and yesterday,
> But lives forever, having origin
> Whence no man knows: whose sanctions I were loath
> In Heaven's sight to provoke, fearing the will
> Of any man." (George Young's translation.)

The validity of this particular use of the higher-law doctrine is beside the point.

attacks at the Sophists and their destructive criticism. Plato and Aristotle were chiefly, though not in the same degree, concerned with goodness and with its realization in the state. Their interest, however, did not center in the individual. It is quite common, rather, to speak of both as leaning toward state socialism or totalitarianism. For them, then, in accordance with the idea of order, the first and fundamental aim of justice is not freedom for its own sake, but order. Freedom is aimed at only so far as it realizes order. For this reason the law occupied the foreground of their thought. They were at great pains to discover and to establish the ethical basis of the laws; not like the Sophists, however, in the interest of freedom from the laws. The state and its order as the sphere of morality, as the realization of all virtue, engaged their attention. This explains their preoccupation with the best form of state or government, in which the individual, whom the Sophists made so much of, is swallowed up. If we should think of the natural law in terms of its long accepted identification with socio-philosophical individualism, there would really be little room for the idea of the natural law in Plato or even in Aristotle.

A deeper penetration into the thought of Plato and Aristotle will show, however, that they too distinguish between what is naturally just and what is legally just. Nor is this distinction merely a borrowed formula: it is an integral part of their doctrinal structure. Yet in the case of both we can observe a certain aversion to the "naturally just," which is accounted for by the Sophists' abuse of this distinction, an abuse which Plato severely censured.

The disciples of Socrates arrived at the notion of something naturally just by quite another route than the one the Sophists had taken. They arrived at it by way of the doctrine of ideas and through teleological thinking. Following in the footsteps of Heraclitus, Plato acknowledges the world of the senses and the world of ideas that become manifest in intellectual contemplation. For speculative reason, sense phenomena are the bridge of memory to the ideas, which dwell and live on in their supermundane, heavenly abode. The things of this world are or exist only so far as they participate in the being of the eternal ideas, or so far as man in his creative capacity of craftsman, artist, and especially lawmaker copies these ideas. Here teleological thinking enters the scene.

In the concept which gropes after and apprehends the essence or the idea of the thing there is contained at the same time also its end, the completion or perfection of the idea of the thing. Inversely, too, the mind lays hold of the essence of a thing by finding the ideal concept which corresponds exactly to the literal meaning. Hence we speak of the true physician, the true judge, the true lawmaker, the true law. These two starting points of Platonic speculation lead then to such conclusions as that the judge ought to be a true judge, i.e., he ought to complete in himself the idea of judge. The ideal concept becomes a norm. So declares the Athenian in Plato's *Laws:* "When there has been a contest for power, those who gain the upper hand so entirely monopolize the government as to refuse all share to the defeated party and their descendants. . . . Now, according to our view, such governments are not polities at all, nor are laws right which are passed for the good of particular classes and not for the good of the whole state. States which have such laws are not polities but parties, and their notions of justice are simply unmeaning."[8] The law should be a true law: one that benefits the common weal. Therein its idea achieves its completion. Thus Plato contrasts the true and proper law with the positive law, and he makes the former the measure and criterion of justice for the latter.

This true law, this true right, abides in the realm of the ideas and remains forever the same. On the other hand, the positive laws change, and they may claim legal force only because and so far as they partake of the idea of law. Indeed they are but a reflection of true law. The lawmaker must look up into the realm of the ideas, where dwells the real essence of the immutable, eternally valid law. However, philosophers and philosopher-kings, freed through disciplined thinking from the blinding illusions of the senses, can alone do this. Moreover, this world of ideas, whereof the world of sense appears only as an imperfect copy, is *kosmos,* or order; it is not *akosmia,* or disorder. But this order of the ideas is the pattern for the fashioning of moral and legal conduct in the present world. The being of the ideas is oughtness for man who shapes things in accordance with contemplative knowledge, whether

---

8. *Laws*, IV, 715 (Jowett's translation).

he forms himself or a community unto goodness. Underlying all this, of course, is the conception of a human nature with impaired powers of contemplation. Only the man of disciplined mind, not the great mass of men, can see intellectually. This doctrine is the opposite of the optimism of the Sophists. If Plato, then, scarcely ever makes use of the Sophists' antithesis of *physis* and *nomos,* he by no means identifies the natural law, which he recognizes, with the positive law.

The difference between Plato and the Sophists lies elsewhere. The Sophists started from the freedom of the individual, who had to be liberated from traditional religious and politico-legal bonds. For the polis, the state, is not something eternal, nor is its law. It is mankind that is eternal: the *civitas maxima* of free and equal men. In the eyes of Plato, however, the polis and its law were the indispensable means for realizing the idea of humanity, which reaches completion in citizenship, in the ethical ideal of the citizen, of the law-abiding and just man. The state is the great pedagogue of mankind. Its function is to bring men to morality and justice, to happiness in and through the moral virtues. Hence Plato's thought revolves continually around the idea of the best state or government. But this is also why he recognizes a natural law as ideal law, as a norm for the lawmaker and the citizen, as a measure for the positive laws. His metaphysics and the ethical system which he built thereon made a natural law possible and furnished the foundation.

Aristotle passed for centuries as the "father of natural law." St. Thomas, in that section of his *Summa theologica* which deals with law, repeatedly appeals to him as the Philosopher par excellence. Aristotle, however, as should now be clear, was not the father of the natural law. Nevertheless his theory of knowledge and his metaphysics have provided ethics, and consequently the doctrine of natural law, with so excellent a foundation that the honorific title, "father of natural law," is readily understandable.

Plato had totally separated the world of sense perception from the world of pure ideas, the objects of scientific, necessary, and true knowledge (*universalia ante rem*). Aristotle transferred the idea as the form which determines the formless matter into the individual (*universalia in re*). This "becomes" through the union of the form (or the essence or the true whatness) with the matter (or the potency or the possibility) and thus gives actuality to the individual. The archetype for Aristotle was human artistic activity: the architect who constructs a house according to the plan in his mind; the sculptor who molds a statue in accordance with his artistic conception; even organic nature which causes the plant to grow from the actualizing essential form that exists in the seed in an incorporeal manner. Aristotle wished to comprehend motion, development, becoming. To him, therefore, the essence, and the perfect expression of it in the individual, is also the *telos,* or end. The form is thus the efficient and the final cause at one and the same time. Applied to the domain of ethics, however, this means that pure being or the pure essential form is likewise the goal of becoming for the man who is to be fashioned by education into a good citizen. From the essential being results an oughtness for the individual man. In this way, from the content of the primary norm, "strive after the good," arises the norm, "realize what is humanly good," as it appears in the essential form of man. The supreme norm of morality is accordingly this: Realize your essential form, your nature. The natural is the ethical, and the essence is unchangeable.

But a criterion of actions is thereby established. Some actions correspond to nature, and hence are naturally good; others are repugnant to nature, and hence are naturally bad. This settled, Aristotle advances to the distinction between what is naturally just and what is legally just. Both are objects of justice. Justice, however, taken in the narrower sense (for in the wider sense the virtuous man is the just man purely and simply) and distinguished from morality, is directed to the other, to the fellow man, whether as equal (commutative justice) or as fellow member of the comprehensive polis-community (distributive and, in the behavior of the member with regard to the whole, legal justice). It finds expression in the natural law and in the positive law. The latter originates in the will of the lawmaker or in an act of an assembly; the natural law has its source in the essence of the just, in nature. That which is naturally right is therefore unalterable. It has everywhere the same force, quite apart from any positive law that may embody it. Statute or positive law varies with every people and at different times.

Yet the natural law does not dwell in a region beyond the positive law. The natural law has to be realized in the positive law since the latter is the application of the universal idea of justice to the motley manifold of life. The immutable idea of right dwells in the changing positive law. All positive law is the more or less successful attempt to realize the natural law. For this reason the natural law, however imperfect may be its realization in the positive law, always retains its binding force. Natural law, i.e., the idea and purpose of law as such, has to be realized in every legal system. The natural law is thus the meaning of the positive law, its purpose and its ethically grounded norm.

Recognition of the fact that no system of positive law is altogether perfect brought Aristotle to the principle of equity. The law is a general norm, but the actual matters which it has to regulate issue from the diversity of practical life. Of necessity the positive law exhibits imperfections; it does not fit all cases. Equity thereupon requires that the individual case get its right, i.e., that the imperfection of the formal law be overcome by means of material justice, through the content of the natural law. Thus Aristotle already viewed the judge's function of filling up gaps in the law as an attempt to apply the natural law—if indeed the positive law is rightly to bear the name of law at all. The gaps are consequently the gateways through which the natural law continually comes into play. In such cases the judge has to decide in accordance with the norm which the true lawgiver would himself apply if he were present; the true lawgiver of course is always assumed to will what is just. This is a celebrated formula which in these very words or in the form, "which he [the judge] would lay down as lawmaker," still found its way into the great codifications of civil law undertaken in the nineteenth and twentieth centuries (e.g., the Austrian and Swiss Civil Codes).

Concerning the content of the natural law Aristotle had as little to say as Plato. This was in sharp contrast to the Sophists, who because of their political and socio-critical bias had admitted many reform proposals and demands into their natural law. The silence of Plato and Aristotle finds its explanation in their idea of the natural law: they set out from the conservative conviction that the positive law wishes to realize the natural law. Added to this was their strong belief in the excellence of the existing laws of the polis as well as in the conformity of such laws to the natural law. The city-state, its general welfare, and its happiness occupied so prominent a place in the ethical thinking of Plato and Aristotle—for whom indeed the idea of man achieves ultimate perfection in the good citizen—that they looked upon the existing laws as something holy. In contrast to the individualistic attack launched by the Sophists against them, the natural law of Plato and Aristotle served precisely to justify the existing laws and not merely as a basis for criticizing them, although the function of criticism was regarded as included in the idea of natural law. Furthermore, for Aristotle as for Plato the polis or city-state was the great pedagogue, against which, strictly speaking, no natural, subjective right of the citizen could be admitted. They acknowledged no goal of man that transcends the ideal polis. They remained state socialists. Their doctrine of natural law was from the political standpoint conservative, but it was based on metaphysics. With the effective discovery, through Christianity, of human personality and with the recognition of God's intellect and will as the source of the natural moral law, rational thought would thenceforth be in a position to work its way through to the true natural law.

In the public squares of Athens and on the steps of its public buildings the wordy Sophists had once taught their rationalistic philosophy, their revolutionary natural-law doctrine. In the same places Socrates, the "lover of wisdom," and Plato and Aristotle, following him, had risen up against the skepticism that was already making its appearance among the Sophists, a skepticism evoked by the doctrine of man as the measure of all things[9] and by the resultant subjectivism in epistemology and ethics. This trio of thinkers had anchored anew in philosophy the natural law which at the hands of the Sophists had been threatening to decline into a mere rationalization of political interests.

With the disappearance of these intellectual giants from the scene, however, the Skeptics, the positivists of their day, began at once to hold forth in the same halls and gardens of the Academy at Athens.

9. Cf. Werner Jaeger, *Humanism and Theology* (The Aquinas Lecture, 1943. Milwaukee: Marquette University Press, 1943), pp. 38–40, 50 f.

The senses, they taught, do not convey true knowledge but only illusion; even reason does not guarantee the truth and certitude of knowledge; certainly, then, truth cannot arise from the illusions of both the senses and reason. All laws, whether of art, speech, morality, or right, are arbitrary. They have their origin in mere agreement, and they vary with the change of the free will which establishes them. As no assertion is of more value than its opposite, so, too, no law is worth any more than its opposite. Likewise, since we cannot perceive the essence or nature of things and of man, a natural law is impossible.

Skepticism attained its highest point in the teaching of Carneades (*cir.* 215–125 B.C.), who for a long time was scholarch at Athens. About 155 B.C., in Rome, he directed his attacks against the natural-law doctrine of the Stoics, a contest which he had made the principal mission of his life. There he won fame through his pro-and-con method of demonstration, whereby he strove to heap ridicule upon the notion of justice. One of his most celebrated arguments was drawn from the borderline case known as "the plank of Carneades." At a time of shipwreck two persons swim to a plank and grasp it simultaneously. But the plank can hold up and save only one of the two. In the light of this case what is right, and who has the right to the plank? Both and neither, he answered, in such a case of dire necessity and self-preservation. (Seventeen centuries later Suarez furnished the correct solution: the order of justice here terminates, and the order of charity governs the case.) Positivism in ethics and law reached its climax with Carneades, again in connection with the repudiation of objective knowledge of reality and essences and with the denial of metaphysics.

Stoicism prepared the way for the Christian natural law. It was founded in Greece as a school of philosophy by Zeno, who lived from about 340 to 265 B.C. It came to its full flowering in Rome in the imperial age. The great figures of Seneca and the emancipated slave Epictetus as well as the appealing personality of Emperor Marcus Aurelius there adorned the Stoic school. Cicero, however, was its great popularizer, and the wealth of Stoic thought was handed down to the medieval world mainly in his writings. Stoicism, moreover, greatly influenced the various schools of Roman jurisprudence. The passages of Roman law which touch the natural law have their source mostly in Stoic philosophical literature.

Stoicism thus reached its height at a time when the society of the ancient world was definitively splitting into two classes. On the one side stood the plebeian proletariat, kept tractable by largesses of food and other articles and by shows; on the other side stood the new aristocracy and bourgeoisie, largely given over to unrestrained pleasure-seeking and vice. Over both classes, deified and sometimes crazed Caesars eventually established a despotic rule. This environment conditioned the eclecticism of the Stoa, that circle of the few from all ranks and provinces of the world empire who placed the idea of a virtuous life and of attaining happiness of mind through the true, the good, and the beautiful above base sensuality, pursuit of wealth, and pride of life. The Stoics were individualists but, unlike the Sophists, they were not militantly opposed to the polis; indeed, the city-state no longer existed, only the world empire. Therefore they extolled, besides the individual, the social impulses and feelings. They drew upon and assimilated the intellectual goods of Heraclitus, Socrates, Plato, and Aristotle.

The core of Stoic teaching is ethics with its Socratic and, in final analysis, general Greek stamp of intellectualism, according to which correct knowledge is the basis of ethics, and the unity of knowledge and conduct forms the ideal of the sage. This last and most striking representative of the spirit of the declining civilization of antiquity comes closest to the grander representative of Christianity, the saint.

The sage is the man who carries his happiness within himself, who in inner self-sufficiency remains undisturbed by external events. Knowledge and conduct are not dependent on the irregular influences of the world: the sage is calm, unmoved by passion. It is owing to the passions and their excesses that clearness of perception and judgment becomes impossible. For this reason man does not attain to a clear knowledge and judgment of what is truly worth striving for. This consists essentially in conformableness to the rational nature of the sage. Virtue consists in the positive determination of conduct through will power in accordance with rational insight into man's essential nature. Virtue is right reason. Nature and reason are one. Right reason and the universal law of nature, which holds undisputed sway throughout the universe, are also one. Obedience to the eternal world law in a life lived according to reason: such, embraced with religious fervor, is the ethical principle of Stoicism. It thus means to live in harmony with oneself, to live in accordance with one's rational nature; for the latter manifests the world law.

Law, too, has its basis in nature. Man has an inborn notion of right and wrong, and law in its very essence rests not upon the arbitrary will of a ruler or upon the decree of a multitude, but upon nature, i.e., upon innate ideas (*non scripta sed nata lex*).[10] Cicero (106–43 B.C.) was the interpreter and transmitter of the Stoic doctrine of natural law. The *lex nata*, the law within us, he regards as the foundation of law in general. It is not to be gathered, as a general concept by way of abstraction, from the law of the Twelve Tables or from the praetor's edict—that is, from the positive law—but *ex intima philosophia*. Since it is identical with right reason, it is universally valid, unchangeable and incapable of being abrogated; for its author is the divine reason itself—taken, of course, in a pantheistic, impersonal sense. It is also called eternal law. Cicero could thus write: "If the principles of Justice were founded on the decrees of peoples, the edicts of princes, or the decisions of judges, then Justice would sanction robbery and adultery and forgery of wills, in case these acts were approved by the votes or decrees of the populace. But if so great a power belongs to the decisions and decrees of fools that the laws of Nature can be changed by their votes, then why do they not ordain that what is bad and baneful shall be considered good and salutary? Or, if a law can make Justice out of Injustice, can it not also make good out of bad? But in fact we can perceive the difference between good laws and bad by referring them to no other standard than Nature: indeed, it is not merely Justice and

10. This phrase is used by Cicero in his speech *For T. A. Milo*, apropos of the right of self-defense: "This, therefore, is a law, O judges, not written, but born with us, which we have not learnt, or received by tradition, or read, but which we have taken and sucked in and imbibed from nature herself; a law which we were not taught, but to which we were made, which we were not trained in, but which is ingrained in us, namely, that if our life be in danger from plots or from open violence or from the weapons of robbers or enemies, every means of securing our safety is honourable" (Yonge's translation). Cicero's conclusion, it is worth observing, is too broad: not every means of self-preservation is morally allowable.

Injustice which are distinguished by Nature, but also and without exception things which are honourable and dishonourable. For since an intelligence common to us all makes things known to us and formulates them in our minds, honourable actions are ascribed by us to virtue, and dishonourable actions to vice; and only a madman would conclude that these judgments are matters of opinion, and not fixed by Nature."[11] Time and again the gifted rhetorician contrasts in this manner the law of nature, as the measure and inner source of validity, with the positive law, which to him is a shadow and reflected image of the true law.[12]

Epictetus (*cir.* A.D. 60–110) likewise called attention to the diversity of the laws that prevail at various times and among different peoples. He taught that the test of whether or not a law accords with nature consists in its agreement or non-agreement with reason. The laws that upheld slavery he called laws of the dead, an abysmal crime. Seneca (d. A.D. 65), in the teeth of the prevailing institution of slavery, gladiatorial combats, and shows featuring the throwing of human beings to beasts, voiced this magnificent sentiment apropos of human dignity: *homo sacra res homini.*[13] What were originally Sophist doctrines were gaining fresh currency: the dignity of the human being and the natural-law basis of freedom and equality. Slaves, too, are men, blood relations and brethren. Like freemen, they are God's own children, members of a great commu-

---

11. *Laws,* I, xvi, translated by C. W. Keyes, in the Loeb Classical Library. Cf. also *ibid.,* I, x, xv, xvii f.

12. The following is another celebrated passage of Cicero on the same subject: "True law is right reason in agreement with nature; it is of universal application, unchanging and everlasting; it summons to duty by its commands, and averts from wrongdoing by its prohibitions. And it does not lay its commands or prohibitions upon good men in vain, though neither have any effect on the wicked. It is a sin to try to alter this law, nor is it allowable to attempt to repeal any part of it, and it is impossible to abolish it entirely. We cannot be freed from its obligations by senate or people, and we need not look outside ourselves for an expounder or interpreter of it. And there will not be different laws at Rome and at Athens, or different laws now and in the future, but one eternal and unchangeable law will be valid for all nations and all times, and there will be one master and ruler, that is, God, over us all, for he is the author of this law, its promulgator, and its enforcing judge. Whoever is disobedient is fleeing from himself and denying his human nature, and by reason of this very fact he will suffer the worst penalties, even if he escapes what is commonly considered punishment" (*The Republic,* III, xxii, trans. by C. W. Keyes, in the Loeb Classical Library).

13. *Epistulae morales ad Lucilium,* XCV, 33.

nity. The city-state has thus lost its power, and with it has disappeared the differentiation of mankind into Greeks and barbarians, into freemen and slaves. "All that you behold, that which comprises both god and man, is one—we are the parts of one great body. Nature produced us related to one another since she created us from the same source and to the same end. She engendered in us mutual affection, and made us prone to friendships. She established fairness and justice."[14] A magnificent statement of the *civitas maxima*, the great society or world state, and of its fundamental law, the natural law! As Marcus Aurelius expressed it: "My city and country, so far as I am Antoninus, is Rome, but so far as I am a man, it is the world."[15]

These Stoic views are singularly impressive in an environment that was replete with despotic brutality and contempt for man, with excesses and misuse of power, with a many-sided suppression of freedom. It is of far greater consequence, however, that they penetrated into Roman law, led to a recognition of the individual in private law, and elevated to the dignity of natural law the more liberal principles of the *ius gentium* which had developed out of the law of foreigners. Above all, they brought to the original tribalism and formalism of Roman law a universalism which fitted it "to survive, as a world law, the life of the nation in which it had originated" (Puchta). Among the later Stoics, too, we find the doctrine of a state of nature, a happy condition of mankind in which all the Stoic ideals of right and freedom had been realized and where the pure natural law had consequently been in force.[16] The *status civilis*, on the other hand, with slavery organized and protected by the positive law, was looked upon as a state of affairs in which the natural law, though continuing in force, no longer holds sole sway.

In Stoicism, then, the mind of the ancient world had come to embrace whatever views Heraclitus, Plato, Aristotle, and the moderate Sophists

14. *Ibid.*, XCV, 52, trans. by R. M. Gummere, in the Loeb Classical Library. The pantheistic cast of Stoic thought is here unmistakable.

15. *Meditations*, VI, 44.

16. Cf. R. W. Carlyle and A. J. Carlyle, *A History of Mediaeval Political Theory in the West* (6 vols., Edinburgh and London: William Blackwood & Sons, 1903–36), I, pp. 23 ff.

had held regarding the natural law—all that they had taught touching the *lex aeterna, recta ratio, lex naturalis, ius naturale,* as well as concerning the connections of these with positive law and their evaluating force in relation to it. It thus preserved the "seeds of the Logos," and it found the literary forms or word vessels into which the Christian spirit was to pour its own ideas, which eventually matured into a new, yet related, doctrine of natural law.

Under the influence of Stoic philosophy the doctrine of the natural law passed into Roman law. The great jurists of the golden age of Roman law were for the most part also philosophers. Through the medium of eclectic Stoicism they were acquainted with Aristotle's teaching on justice and with Zeno's work *On the Laws;* especially, however, they were familiar with the writings of Cicero, the popular philosopher of Stoicism. Besides, the forensic orators were interested in philosophy in their pleadings at the bar. Among these Cicero held first place, but there were also Q. Mucius Scaevola, Calpurnius, and Rutilius, as Cicero himself informs us. This philosophical bent is likewise evidenced by the frequency with which the jurists cite the philosophers. Gaius, for example, quotes Aristotle and Xenophon; Ulpian and Celsus quote Cicero; Paulus mentions *Graeci* in general. The peculiar function of the jurists, "responding," i.e., imparting legal information and counsel to the judges and litigants alike,[17] involved for the jurists this deeper kind of intellectual labor. Thus Stoic philosophy may with considerable justice be called the mother of Roman jurisprudence. The latter, to keep up the metaphor, sucked in the doctrine of the *ius naturale* with its mother's milk.

Down to the time of Cicero neither science nor the natural-law doctrine had exercised any practical influence on Roman law. Then, however, theory broke in along a broad front. For Gaius, Paulus, and Marcian the *ius naturae* is a norm which from the very beginning lies forever imbedded in the nature of things; since it also reveals itself in

17. On "responding" and on its later development, the *ius respondendi,* see, e.g., W. W. Buckland, *The Main Institutions of Roman Private Law* (Cambridge: Cambridge University Press, 1931), pp. 14 f.; James Hadley, *Introduction to Roman Law* (reprint, New Haven: Yale University Press, 1931), pp. 61–69.

things, it can be discovered in them. The Stoic idea of an eternal law of the order of the universe was present to their minds. This law emanates from the logos, which in turn is itself the law of things. The logos, moreover, expresses itself conceptually in the nature of things, and it destines them for harmony with the universe. Hence wherever two beings, whether man and thing or two men, find themselves related to each other, a rule covering what is naturally and essentially conformable to this relationship is present in the law of the logos—and is at the same time expressed a priori in the very nature of the correlates. A law rules as an ordering force in the *natura rerum,* in the world of both irrational and rational creatures.

This became of practical importance as a norm for positive legislation and for the deciding of cases for which the positive law contained no norm. But the natural law especially became the magic formula whereby the jurists in their *responsa* replaced the ancient law, which had by then become inadequate, with new law introduced under the concepts of *lex naturae* and *aequitas.* This they accomplished by means of the edict of the magistrates who were under their influence as well as through the imperial constitutions. In addition, the new law had in its favor the splendor of inherent truth or reason, the charm of simple conformity with nature, and the grandeur of transcending peoples and ages. But to the jurists *aequitas* was the echo of the *lex naturae,* the command of an inner voice through which speaks the *ratio* of the *natura rerum* immanent in things. *Aequitas* is the legal conscience which speaks even when a positive norm is at hand, for it is the "meaning" of the positive law. Adjudication, or applying the law, is not a logical and automatic process of subsuming under a general norm: it is interpretation in the light of *aequitas.*

As material contents of the law of nature the jurists designated such things as the rules touching kinship (marriage—family), good faith, adjustment or weighing of interests (*suum cuique*), the real meaning of the actual will of the legal subject as opposed to the formalism of the law governing expression of will. To these may be added the original freedom and equality of all men, and the right of self-defense (*vim vi repellere*).

Furthermore, the jurists, e.g., Paulus, Ulpian, and Marcian, regarded the *ius civile* as possessing special force. Yet even according to them the *ius naturae* must prevail in case of conflict: what the *ius naturae* forbids, the *ius civile* may not allow; nor may the *ius civile* repeal such prohibition (compare the scholastic teaching: the negative precepts of the natural law are forever immutable). To be sure, this question occasioned no real trouble, since the *responsa* of the jurists possessed, so to speak, legislative force. Thus their doctrine of the *ius naturae* forthwith gained a footing, along with the finding and the judgment, in the *responsa*. It also took on positive form in the *lex casus*, in accordance with which the magistrates were thereafter to proceed in similar cases. In like manner, too, the royal judge in Anglo-Saxon lands, bearing the law, i.e., the natural law, "in the shrine of his breast," in the very act of handing down a decision conferred positive character upon the natural law in the rule of the case.

The Roman world empire, with its toleration of the legal institutions of subject peoples, placed in the hands of the jurists still another important source of knowledge. This was the unwritten *ius gentium*, which arose out of actual practice and was substantially "found" by the jurists and magistrates. The *ius naturale*, derived from metaphysical and ethical reflection, appeared identical with the universal element in the legal systems of individual peoples. As the idea of law thus issued from ethical speculation as a teleological apriorism for the positive law, so it emerged as concept of law in the positive law through abstract treatment of the legal systems of particular peoples. This led to the *ius gentium*. Consequently the results which philosophical thinking arrived at by way of deduction from *logos, ratio,* and *rerum natura* turned out to be identical with the idea of law in the systems of positive law. These in turn are products of the universal, law-creating *societas humana* and of reason that governs in it.

The equating of *ius naturae* and *ius gentium* that is met with even in Gaius has here its origin. Ulpian, on the contrary, defined *ius naturale* as "that which nature teaches to all animals" (*quod natura omnia animalia docuit*); but this is the *ordo rerum*. The *ius gentium* thereupon becomes that part of the *ius naturale* which has force for mankind.[18] This, however, is a product of the will of universal reason, not of the will of some particular historical lawgiver.

The Roman jurists still lacked a clear distinction between law and morality. Even the norm "worship must be paid to God" pertained to law, and so did "live honorably." To the jurists, indeed, jurisprudence was "a knowledge of things divine and human, the science of what is just and unjust."[19]

But the greatest intellectual gain stemmed directly from Stoic ethics. The Greeks, except for a few revolutionary Sophists, had regarded the citizens of the polis as the sole subjects of law. For the Roman jurists, on the other hand, it was not merely the Roman citizen who was in the true sense a subject of law, but every member of human society (the *civitas maxima* of the Stoics). Therefore they held that man as such is possessed of natural rights, which he continues to retain even in a state of slavery. Slavery was thereby, in contrast to Aristotle's doctrine, a positive-law institution which could and should be displaced in keeping with being and oughtness.

Even after the revival of imperial sovereignty in the later Roman Empire (under Justinian, A.D. 527–65), the natural law remained the first, supreme, and true legal norm: the basic law of human relations, the model and ideal set before the eyes of the lawmaker for realization. But it was no longer such for the judge, who was henceforth dependent upon the law, or for the citizen. For these the positive law alone had force. Nevertheless the idea of *ius naturae* had so strong a hold that, in contrast with modern absolutism, as, for instance, in the doctrine of Hobbes, the lawmaker remained subject to the natural law not merely as an empty form, but as a system of content-laden norms.

It remains an eloquent proof of the eternal truth of the doctrine of natural law that Roman law, the finest legal system yet developed in the West,[20] enveloped the natural law in its deepest thinking and taught it in its noblest terms.

---

18. Cf. *Digest,* I, i, 1–4; Carlyle and Carlyle, *op. cit.,* I, 34–44.

19. *Digest,* I, i, 10.

20. Anglo-Saxons will be disposed to demur. But this is not the place to attempt to weigh the claims of the English system of common law, in which the natural law

Like Stoic philosophy, Roman law also passed on this idea to the new Christian era and to the age of scholastic philosophy, which as true *philosophia perennis*[21] has remained the permanent home of the natural law. Scholastic philosophy has been the place of sanctuary for the natural law when arid positivism has driven the latter out of secular

---

has also played an important role, to equal or superior excellence. In a general way, cf. W. W. Buckland and A. D. McNair, *Roman Law and Common Law. A Comparison in Outline* (Cambridge: The University Press, 1936).

21. *Philosophia perennis* (a term seemingly coined by Steuchus in 1540, used by Leibnitz, and popularized by the Neo-Scholastic movement) denotes a body of basic philosophical truths that is perennial, enduring, abiding, permanent, eternal–a philosophy that "is as old and as new as philosophical speculation itself." It is one whose "validity and truth content is not confined to any particular age or civilization but is absolute and enduring" (K. F. Reinhardt, *A Realistic Philosophy* [Milwaukee: Bruce Publishing Co., 1944], p. 17; cf. also pp. 18 ff.). In other words, *philosophia perennis* is the accumulated fund of sure philosophical truths: "the eternal store of primordial philosophical truths which remains in spite of all evolutions and changes" (*Philosophia Perennis. Abhandlungen zu ihrer Vergangenheit und Gegenwart*, herausgegeben von Fritz-Joachim von Rintelen [2 vols., Regensburg: Josef Habbel, 1930], I, ix); "a stock of fundamental truths which survive the change of time and prevail over and above the difference of systems" (Franz Sawicki, "Die Geschichtsphilosophie als Philosophia Perennis," *ibid.*, I, 513). It is in the main identified with the philosophy of Aristotle as purified, synthesized, developed, deepened, and enriched through the genius of St. Thomas Aquinas. Its leading traits are aptly summarized by Jacques Maritain: The "philosophy of Aristotle and St. Thomas is in fact what a modern philosopher has termed *the natural philosophy of the human mind*, for it develops and brings to perfection what is most deeply and genuinely natural in our intellect alike in its elementary apprehensions and in its native tendency towards truth.

"It is also the *evidential* philosophy, based on the double evidence of the data perceived by our senses and our intellectual apprehension of first principles—the philosophy of *being*, entirely supported by and modelled upon what is, and scrupulously respecting every demand of reality—the philosophy of the *intellect*, which it trusts as the faculty which attains truth, and forms by a discipline which is an incomparable mental purification. And for this very reason it proves itself the *universal* philosophy in the sense that it does not reflect a nationality, class, group, temperament, or race, the ambition or melancholy of an individual or any practical need, but is the expression and product of reason, which is everywhere the same; and in this sense also, that it is capable of leading the finest intellects to the most sublime knowledge and the most difficult of attainment, yet without once betraying those vital convictions, instinctively acquired by every sane mind, which compose the domain, wide as humanity of common sense. It can therefore claim to be abiding and permanent (*philosophia perennis*) in the sense that before Aristotle and St. Thomas had given it scientific formulation as a systematic philosophy, it existed from the dawn of humanity in germ and in the pre-

jurisprudence. Yet it has always come back into jurisprudence whenever the human mind, weary of the unsatisfying hunt for mere facts, has again turned to metaphysics, queen of the sciences.[22]

Everyone is at least familiar with the distinction between legal norm and moral law, even though he does not completely separate them. It must surely have come as something of a surprise, then, that in antiquity such a distinction, let alone a separation, was altogether wanting. Aristotle in his treatise on ethics says that justice, which in this context he takes in the narrower sense, is directed "to another," and, as essentially concerning the social order, governs the relations of man with his fellow man. But he speaks still more frequently of justice as the general virtue which embraces all others, makes man virtuous, and guides him to the highest goal. He likewise asserts, on this point following Socrates, that the just man is obedient to the laws, i.e., to the written laws and to the unwritten mores. Among these he includes the relations of man to himself, e.g., the curbing of the passions, as well as the ceremonial law and reverence for the divine.

This view rests substantially upon the fact that the sole and exclusive moral fulfillment of the idea of man was held to lie in citizenship. Whence, too, the acceptance of slavery. The slave, it was maintained, is by nature unfitted for citizenship; he is incapable, in the Aristotelian sense, of being educated to virtue. The virtuous life is the goal of man.

---

philosophic state, as an instinct of the understanding and a natural knowledge of the first principles of reason and ever since its foundation as a system has remained firm and progressive, a powerful and living tradition, while all other philosophies have been born and have died in turn. And, finally, it stands out as being, beyond comparison with any other, one; one because it alone bestows harmony and unity on human knowledge—both metaphysical and scientific—and one because in itself it realizes a maximum of consistency in a maximum of complexity, and neglect of the least of its principles involves the most unexpected consequences, distorting our understanding of reality in innumerable directions" (*An Introduction to Philosophy*, trans. by E. I. Watkin [New York: Sheed & Ward], pp. 99–101).

22. See, in general, Etienne Gilson, *The Unity of Philosophical Experience* (New York: Charles Scribner's Sons, 1937), pp. 298–320. Metaphysics is but "the knowledge gathered by a naturally transcendent reason in its search for the first principles, or first causes, of what is given in sensible experience. . . . As metaphysics aims at transcending all particular knowledge, no particular science is competent either to solve metaphysical problems, or to judge their metaphysical solutions" (*ibid.*, pp. 308–10).

But he can achieve this goal only as citizen of the polis and in obedience to its laws. All education and training in virtue consequently become politics, and the latter is ethics. The ancients knew only a politico-legal morality. The city-state, in their view, is the ultimate and absolutely supreme pedagogue, the fulfillment of the moral being of man.

The notion of human personality was in its deepest meaning hidden from the ancients, as was also the eternal, superterrestrial goal of the immortal soul. Moreover, they had but a faint idea of a personal God as the supreme lawgiver distinct from the world; nor did they know anything of a Church as the medium of salvation. For them the polis and its divine worship remained the ultimate. Wherever the idea of human rights forced its way through (among the moderate Sophists and in Stoicism), its effect was revolutionary: either it dissolved the city-state or it encouraged dreams of the great society (*civitas maxima*) of mankind, which of course merely raised the question of its own meaning. Thus the ancients failed to arrive at the distinction between natural law and natural moral law.

Nevertheless, the main problems connected with the idea of natural law existed already in antiquity. The positivism of the Skeptics, of Epicurus, and of Carneades stood in opposition to the natural law in its two recurring forms: the metaphysical one in Plato and Aristotle, and the individualistic one in the earlier Sophists. Furthermore, the continually recurring definitions of law, which have stirred up and divided philosophico-legal thinking down to the present day, had already been formulated: law is will, law is reason; law is truth, law is authority. The doctrine of an original state of nature, of fundamental importance for individualism but of merely persuasive value for other thinkers, appeared already among the Sophists. It appeared also among the Stoics for a similar reason but with another object in view, namely, to provide the basis for a distinction between a primary and a secondary natural law. This distinction, valuable to the Church Fathers in connection with their doctrine of original sin, served the Scholastics to differentiate the self-evident principles of the natural law from the conclusions obtained through reasoning the content of the natural law is more exactly determined—as well as to solve more or less successfully certain thorny theological problems.

CHAPTER II

The Natural Law in the Age of Scholasticism

A new philosophy and a new world order did not follow at once upon the entrance of the Christian faith into the ancient world, into a socio-cultural complex that was in process of dissolution and was addicted to somber mystical beliefs and practices. Indeed, precisely because of the advancing disintegration, or rather decomposition, of ancient society and culture, a considerable number of early Christians were eschatologically minded; that is, they were unduly concerned with the supposed imminence of the last things, the end of the world and the second coming of the Lord. At all events and for a variety of reasons, the transforming power of Christian doctrine could at first accomplish little.

Christianity, however, contains three ideas of decisive importance for the present problem: the idea of the supermundane, transcendent, personal God as Lawgiver in the absolute sense, the idea of Christian personality, whose eternal goal transcends the state, the law, and the mores of the polis; and the idea of the Church as the institution charged with the salvation of mankind standing alongside and, in matters of faith and morals, above the will of the state. Such ideas had in the long run to affect the whole problem of natural law: not, indeed, in order to revolutionize it, but to explore it more thoroughly, to strengthen its foundations, and to complete it materially.[1]

The history of the natural-law idea shows that Christianity took it over at a very early date. Paul, the Apostle of the Gentiles, declares that the natural law is inscribed in the hearts of the heathen, who do not have the Law (of Sinai), and is made known to them through their conscience. It is valid both for pagans and for Jews because it is grounded in nature, in the essence of man. (Cf. Rom. 2:12–16).

The Fathers of the Early Church made use of the Stoic natural law, finding in its principles "seeds of the Word," to proclaim the Christian doctrine of the personal Creator-God as the Author of the eternal law as well as of the natural moral law which is promulgated in the voice of conscience and in reason. Thus, for instance, we read in St. John Chrysostom (d. 407): "We use not only Scripture but also reason in arguing against the pagans. What is their argument? They say they have no law of conscience, and that there is no law implanted by God in nature. My answer is to question them about their laws concerning marriage, homicide, wills, injuries to others, enacted by their legislators. Perhaps the living have learned from their fathers, and their fathers from their fathers and so on. But go back to the first legislator! From whom did he learn? Was it not by his own conscience and conviction?

---

1. It is thus correct to speak of a Christian natural law, but solely in the sense in which we use the term Christian philosophy. A Christian philosophy, to adopt the balanced view of Etienne Gilson, is one "which, although keeping the two orders [of reason and the supernatural] formally distinct, nevertheless considers the Christian revelation as an indispensable auxiliary to reason" (*The Spirit of Mediaeval Philosophy*, trans. by A. H. C. Downes [New York: Charles Scribner's Sons, 1936], p. 37). See also his *Christianity and Philosophy*, trans. by Ralph MacDonald, C.S.B. (New York–London: Sheed and Ward, 1939), p. 101. As Johannes Messner has pointed out, "when we speak of a 'Christian' natural law, this does not mean that the natural law knowable by us through reason alone is replaced or amplified by one derived from supernatural revelation, but that our knowledge of its existence, its essence and its content is confirmed and clarified through the guidance of reason by faith. . . . For the Catholic the designation 'Christian' natural law further includes the conviction that the Church, in virtue of its divine mission, is the unfaltering guardian and infallible expounder of the same" (*Die Soziale Frage* [5th ed., Innsbruck-Vienna: Verlagsanstalt Tyrolia, 1938], p. 492).

Nor can it be said that they heard Moses and the prophets, for Gentiles could not hear them. It is evident that they derived their laws from the law which God ingrafted in man from the beginning."[2]

The Fathers also took over the Stoic distinction of a primary and a secondary natural law, which they interpreted in a theological sense. They regarded the former as applying to the state of unimpaired nature or innocence, while they assigned the latter, with the coercive authority of the law, with bondage and slavery, to the theological condition of fallen nature. Nature, somehow wounded indeed but not destroyed, is therefore still able fully to recognize the first principles of morality and law. But the conclusions from the first principles, which were also plainly intelligible in the state of unimpaired nature, are now attainable only by means of deductive reasoning, since the practical reason is also weakened. Accordingly law takes on a harsh, compulsory character, and the state bears a sword. But the state as such was not regarded by the Fathers as some sort of consequence of sin. An age ignorant of tradition has been able to take such a view of the state only on the basis of patristic texts torn from their context and because of a want of understanding of the mental outlook of the Fathers.

The Fathers did not attempt to construct a system of ethics and jurisprudence. Their speculative thinking was wholly taken up with elucidating the truths of faith, which were in danger of being swamped in the upsurge of pseudomystical doctrines characteristic of the numerous mystery cults of declining antiquity. In addition, their heavy pastoral duties in the period of persecutions, organization, and evangelization left them little leisure for thorough theoretical treatment of questions of moral and legal philosophy.

St. Augustine (d. 430), it is true, forms an exception, and a very brilliant one. In his extremely fertile mind the ideas of ancient philoso-

2. *Ad pop. Ant.*, XII, 4 (Migne, *PG*, Vol. CXXXII), quoted by Stanley Bertke, *The Possibility of Invincible Ignorance of the Natural Law.* The Catholic University of America Studies in Sacred Theology, No. 58 (Washington, D.C.: Catholic University of America Press, 1941), p. 8, where also (pp. 5–11) the views of the other Church Fathers on the natural law are conveniently presented in summary fashion. Bertke's study is a real contribution to the whole problem of the natural law.

phy came once again to life and were worked into the new Christian mentality. His talents and the struggles against the Pelagian and Manichaean heresies, as well as the shattering experience of the breakdown of the Roman Empire, of the earthly city, brought ethico-legal problems home to the great bishop of Hippo.

For Augustine the substantial ideas, which Plato had conceived of as dwelling in a heavenly abode, became thoughts of God. The impersonal world reason of the Stoics became the personal, all-wise and all-powerful God. The purely deistic *Nous* of Aristotle became the Creator-God who transcends the world, but who continually sustains it through His omnipotence, directs it through His providence, and governs it according to His eternal law. This eternal law was for Augustine identical with the supreme reason and eternal truth, with the reason of God Himself, according to whose laws the inner life and external activity of God proceed and are governed. God's reason is order, and His law rules this ontological order, the order of being, of essences and values. But since this norm is identical with the immutable, immanent nature of God, it does not stand above Him; it is connatural to Him, and it is as unchangeable as He. No power, no chance event, not even the complete collapse of all things can alter it. No obscure, occult fate is any longer enthroned, as in ancient thought, above the personal God.

Through this law God, so far as He produces external effects, directs, guides, and sustains the universe. God, supreme reason, unchangeable being and omnipotent will: this is oneness in its highest form. But the natural moral law and its component part, the *ius naturale,* is precisely this divine law with reference to man, so far as the latter participates in the divine law. The eternal law dwells as blind necessity in irrational nature. As oughtness, as norm of free moral activity, it is inscribed in the heart of man, a rational and free being. It appears in the moral, rational nature of man; it is written into the rational soul. There is no soul, however corrupt it may be, in whose conscience God does not speak, if only it is still capable of rational thought. There are human actions, consequently, which are in themselves good or bad. Bad acts are not qualified as such by force of law, but because they are such in themselves: because they constitute a disturbance of the natural order. Thereupon, because they are such, the lawmaker prohibits them under threat of punishment, which thereby obtains its moral justification. Not the will of the earthly lawgiver, but variance with natural reason is the ground of the intrinsic immorality of determinate actions.

The doctrine of natural law was transmitted to the golden age of Scholasticism not only in the works of the Church Fathers but also through the study of Roman law and through the development of canon law. The classical authors of the *Corpus iuris civilis,* as has been seen, stood in close contact with natural-law thinking. It is not merely in passing that we meet with the natural law in their writings: the natural law is there pronounced valid, unconditionally binding law. Considerably greater, however, was the influence of canon law in the form of Gratian's *Decretum* (*cir.* 1148), especially since during the first period of the flowering of Scholasticism the study of Roman law by theologians was frowned upon and even, for a time, prohibited. Gratian distinguished between *ius naturale* and the mores. The *ius naturale,* which is contained in the Law (i.e., the Decalogue) and the Gospel, is of divine origin. It resides in human nature, it is alike in all men, and it has force independently of human statute. Natural rights and duties may indeed have to be more closely defined by positive law, but they stand as a norm and rule above the positive laws. To Gratian the latter were, like customary law or mores, liable to change according to time, place, and people. In short, Gratian merely set forth what tradition had handed down.

As the great philosophical movement of the Middle Ages, Scholasticism,[3] approached its peak, the natural-law doctrine attained its most masterly expression. It was carried to speculative heights which have never been surpassed in the centuries that followed. Since then the

---

3. Scholasticism, which follows the main lines of Aristotle's thought, in part "advocates a natural dualism of God and creature, mind and matter, thought and thing, as against monism and pantheism; it defends a moderate realism, as against ultrarealism, nominalism, and conceptualism, in the problem of the universals; it is spiritualistic and not materialistic, experimental and not aprioristic, objectivistic and not subjectivistic; in sense-perception it is presentational and not agnostic or representational or idealistic; concerning intellectual knowledge it defends a moderate rationalism, as against sensism, positivism, and innatism; it is common-sense knowledge critically examined and philosophically vindicated" (Celestine N. Bittle, O. M. Cap., *Reality and the Mind* [Milwaukee: Bruce Publishing Co., 1936], p. 146).

doctrine of natural law has never wholly perished. Even though it might be neglected in the official academic philosophy which has been dominant in the chairs of the secular universities, and even though at the close of the nineteenth century and at the opening of the twentieth century jurisprudence might pronounce it dead, the natural-law doctrine has ever found a home and tender care among the adherents of the *philosophia perennis.* These have preserved it even throughout the decades in which legal positivism held fullest sway. Moreover, they carried it over, as Christian natural law, into an environment that is once again more favorable to the idea of natural law. For World War I and its consequences, to say nothing of World War II and its effects (which promise to be still more fateful), have brought men to recognize more and more openly the questionableness of a philosophy without metaphysics, of an epistemology without certainty of truth, of a jurisprudence without an idea of right.

The history of the natural-law idea exhibits a uniform doctrinal development from the first Scholastics down to the able leaders of the scholastic revival of recent times. Its two culminating points were the synthesis of St. Thomas Aquinas and, following the heaviest assault made inside Scholasticism by the Occamists on the idea of natural law, the work of Vittoria, Bellarmine, Suarez, Vasquez, and De Soto (to mention only the most distinguished of the Late Scholastics). And the period after World War I again produced more understanding and esteem for a uniform doctrinal development that has been substantially independent of fashionable philosophies and of a jurisprudence with special sociological or political ties.

Scholasticism has dealt exhaustively with the problem of natural law. Not one of its exponents has failed to treat of the natural law, either in general in connection with the discussion of the virtues or in particular under such headings as *De legibus* or *De iure et iustitia.* And with the *lex naturalis* they handled, though not always with the aid of special distinctions, the *ius naturale* and *ius gentium* in the sense of the traditional formulas of Roman law. This holds true from Alexander of Hales to Thomas Aquinas, and thence down to the great masters of Late Scholasticism. It further holds good for the theologians and philosophers of the *philosophia perennis,* whether they were contemporaries of Pufendorf and Thomasius or of Savigny, down to the increasingly esteemed representatives of the scholastic revival which set in at the close of the nineteenth century.

In following the doctrinal development it is worthy of note that the antithesis of *lex-ratio* and *lex-voluntas,* applying here in the setting of theological speculation and in general to the *lex naturalis* inclusive of the natural law in the stricter sense, coincided structurally with the doctrines of the respective thinkers concerning God. But it is also noteworthy that later, when the natural-law doctrine had been severed from its theological moorings and hence secularized, the same thought patterns repeated themselves. Now, however, they were detached from the medieval form of *Summa* and applied solely to law in the narrower sense. The result has been that natural law is the consequence of the doctrines of the priority of the intellect over the will (law is reason) in both God and man, of the knowability of the essences of things and their essential order, their metaphysical being and the ordered hierarchy of values. Positivism, on the other hand, is the consequence of the doctrine of the primacy of the will with respect to the intellect in both theology and human psychology. Besides, *voluntas* here means more than mere will: it denotes passion, irrational appetite, and so on. Positivism signifies the renouncing of all efforts to know the essences of things (nominalism), the repudiation of the metaphysics of hierarchized being and value. Accordingly it is also found in the same conceptual pattern in the thinking of the nineteenth and twentieth centuries, even though it is concealed under different names.

Relativism in ethics, legal positivism, the theory of will in public and international law, nominalism and agnosticism in epistemology and metaphysics form down to the present a united front with the mysticism of a biological positivism appearing in natural-law dress. On the other side stands the conviction of unalterable principles of morality and law, of the idea of right as object of a philosophy of right, of the natural law, of the possibility of knowing the nature of things, of objective values and an ultimate unity of being and oughtness as well as the possibility of a true theodicy, or natural theology. And this antithesis continues on, in an ever more acute form, into the domain of constitutional theory and practice. The powerful position, in Anglo-

Saxon countries, of the judiciary which understands and interprets (functions of the intellect) in contrast to the enactment of law through the will of the legislature rests ultimately upon the philosophical view that law is reason, not will. This means that right is discernible in the nature of the case or lies in the legal institution regulated by law, not in the will of the legislator: not, that is to say, in the wording of the law representing such a will or command. Such formulas as those found in the administration of justice in Anglo-Saxon countries (especially in the United States), where formal natural-law thinking has never disappeared among judges, are continually recurring even today.[4]

It was not with St. Anselm of Canterbury (1033–1109), often called the first of the Schoolmen, that Scholasticism began to concern itself more seriously with the natural law, but rather with the first great author of a *Summa*, Alexander of Hales (d. 1245). Deeper interest in it thus arose first and foremost from the philosophical preoccupation with laying a solid foundation for ethics, for law and the social forms of family and state, for a doctrine of society and the state. This interest was considerably heightened, however, in connection with the exegesis of certain passages in the Old Testament.

That is, the thesis of the immutability of the *lex naturalis* and *ius naturale* presupposes the intrinsic immorality and unlawfulness of certain actions, and it consequently excludes any dispensation from the norms of the *lex naturalis*. But such a position seemed to conflict with some Old Testament stories, whose moral tone and authority made it necessary to conclude that a dispensation is nevertheless possible. Such cases are, for instance, Yahweh's command to Abraham to offer up his son Isaac in sacrifice (Gen. 22:2); the polygamy of the patriarchs; God's instruction to the prophet Osee: "Go, take thee a wife of fornications" (Osee 1:2; cf. also *ibid.*, 3:1); the injunction laid upon the Jews or permission accorded them at the time of the Exodus to take away with them vessels of silver and gold as well as raiment lent to them by the

---

4. Cf. Charles Grove Haines, *The Revival of Natural Law Concepts* (Cambridge: Harvard University Press, 1930), pp. 104–234; Benjamin Fletcher Wright, Jr., *American Interpretations of Natural Law* (Cambridge: Harvard University Press, 1931), especially pp. 292–306.

Egyptians (Exod. 3:21 f.; 11:2 f.; 12:35 f.); divorce openly allowed to husbands in the Mosaic legislation (Deut. 24:1–4); the reply of the angel Raphael to Tobias' question about his identity: "I am Azarias the son of the great Ananias" (Tob. 5:18), which seems materially and formally to amount to a lie. All these cases called for a thorough discussion, from the theological and exegetical angles, of the question of the immutability, i.e., the essential nature, of the *lex naturalis*. But at the same time they were a warning not to be too doctrinaire in determining the content of the natural law.

Alexander of Hales, falling back upon St. Augustine's teaching, hit upon a beautiful figure: the eternal law is the seal, and the natural moral law is its impression in the rational nature of man, which in turn is an image of God. Now, the laws of thought, as unchangeable norms of thinking, must govern speculative reason, the understanding, if the latter is to serve the purpose of its nature, the perception of truth; and such laws are immediately evident and certain. In the same way there exist for willing and acting in the domain of the practical reason supreme moral principles which are equally evident and sure. Thus every deed and action is moral only when it is performed in accordance with these principles. Moreover, this immanent natural moral law can never be destroyed. Yet the further conclusions from the supreme principles may well become obscured in individuals through the working of the passions and through a turning away from God, the Author of the natural law. To explain this possibility Alexander borrows a figure from Plato: the sun ever remains the same, yet darkness ensues when clouds pass before the sun or when, during a solar eclipse, the moon prevents the sun's light from reaching the earth.

Although he held fast to the immutability of the first principles, Alexander of Hales at first sought to explain the changeableness of the further conclusions, observable in the Old Testament as well as elsewhere, by adopting the Stoic distinction, transmitted in the writings of the Church Fathers, of a primary natural law anterior to original sin and of a secondary one subsequent to original sin. The *status naturae integrae*, the theological state of nature preceding original sin, would in itself, as St. Augustine had already taught, have produced life in society, marriage, the family, and the political community. (This state of nature accordingly differs considerably from the individualistic state of nature, which indeed was directly opposed to the *status civilis*.) But had this state of nature been realized, community of goods, equal personal freedom, and a legal order unaccompanied by the use of force would have prevailed. Only in the state of fallen nature, after original sin, did private property, restrictions upon liberty, the coercive power of the state, and personal inequality arise. But the natural law underwent thereby no alteration; for even now the basic norm, men must live peacefully with one another, remains in force. Hence only the application of this norm has changed, not the norm itself. The secondary natural law, the second table of the Decalogue (i.e., the last seven of the Ten Commandments), is a consequence of original sin.[5]

But this theory had to be completely abandoned. For this type of argument was unable to furnish what it was intended to provide, namely, an ethico-philosophical explanation of the actions apparently contrary to the natural moral law recorded in the Old Testament. And so Alexander of Hales had recourse, as did St. Albert the Great and other contemporaries, to the doctrine of the primacy of the will in God as well as to God's sovereign dominion that transcends all laws. These thinkers perceived clearly enough that in this way everything again became uncertain, but they were unable to prevent this outcome. For an adequate solution of the problem the genius of a Thomas Aquinas was needed.

St. Thomas (1225–74) starts from the likeness of human nature to the divine nature. Understanding and free will are the most essential marks that distinguish man from every other earthly creature. It is precisely through them that man is in a special degree the image and likeness of God. Man's intellect and free will constitute the closest image of God in the material universe, His creation. St. Thomas, indeed, is fond of setting out from the notion of analogy of being: namely, that all created being, though of an altogether different kind

---

5. It may be observed that the common assignment of the first three of the Mosaic Commandments to the first tablet of stone, and of the last seven Commandments to the second tablet, is merely conventional. We simply do not know how the Ten Commandments were distributed on the two stone tablets, as the Bible itself gives no information on the matter. Cf. Louis Hartman, C.SS.R., "The Enumeration of the Ten Commandments," *Catholic Biblical Quarterly*, VII (1945), 105, note 1.

from the divine Being, is an image of the latter and a participation in it—from merely inanimate being of inorganic nature up to man, whom God created after His own image.

Here teleology, the doctrine of ends or final causes, enters the scene.[6] The essences of things, which are exemplifications of the ideas conceived by the divine intellect, constitute at the same time the end or goal of the things themselves. The perfection or fulfillment of the things is their essence: formal cause and end are one (*causa finalis* is ultimately identical with *causa formalis*). Accordingly in the essential nature of the created world, as it came forth in conformity with the will of the Creator, are imbedded also the norms of its being. In the essential nature is likewise founded essential oughtness, the eternal law, which is God's wisdom so far as it directs and governs the world as first cause of all acts of rational creatures and of all movements of irrational beings. The eternal law, then, is the governance of the world through God's will in accordance with His wisdom. This law is thus the order of this world. Creatures fulfill this law in conformity with their nature as it has been fashioned by God: from the lifeless and inorganic realm of creation, through the living but dumb creatures, to the rational and free beings.

The eternal law, therefore, comprises several elements. First, it includes what today we call the laws of the natural sciences: the laws of movement taken generally, in accordance with which the stars in the heavens and the stones upon earth are moved from without. Secondly, it embraces what in living creatures, plants and animals, we term the laws of their evolution and growth, the laws of reaction to external influences or stimuli, instinct, and the like, which, however, involve movement from within, after the manner of an entelechy.[7] Thirdly, it

6. For an excellent discussion of the all-important and universal metaphysical principle of finality, "every agent acts for an end," see R. Garrigou-Lagrange, O.P., *God: His Existence and His Nature,* trans. by Bede Rose, O.S.B. (2 vols., St. Louis: B. Herder Book Co., 1934–36), I, 199–204; also K. F. Reinhardt, *A Realistic Philosophy,* pp. 87–89.

7. "In Aristotle's vitalistic holism," entelechy "is the substantial form or soul which unites with primary matter to constitute the unitary substance of the organic body; it is primarily an entitative principle" (Celestine N. Bittle, O.F.M. Cap., *The Whole Man* [Milwaukee: Bruce Publishing Co., 1945], p. 632). For a comparison of the Aristotelian notion of entelechy with that of Hans Driesch, cf. *ibid.,* p. 473.

contains the laws by virtue of which man, as a rational and free being, knows and wills, hence the laws of theoretical and practical reason. Since man is *quodammodo omnia*—herein consists his likeness to God, who is *eminenter omnia*—he is wholly subject to the eternal law in his material, sentient, and rational being, but ever in keeping with his essence. Oughtness, not blind compulsion and necessity, characterizes the way man obeys the law. Hence for man, as a free rational being, the eternal law becomes the natural moral law. Man must (i.e., ought to) thus both will and achieve the perfecting or fulfillment of the potentialities of his being which God has put into his nature, as he perceives them in virtue of his reason and becomes conscious of them.

Furthermore, this natural moral law is alone law in the proper sense: a norm which ought to be obeyed, not one that must be blindly obeyed. Our modern laws of nature are law only in a metaphorical sense. Law, indeed, is a norm and measure for acts which rational creatures alone are capable of. Its basic norm may be simply stated: Act in conformity with your rational nature. For rational nature, known through self-consciousness or reflex thinking, constitutes the ontological criterion of man's oughtness. Through its free realization he becomes a man, a free rational being. God's wisdom and knowledge as well as His will stand revealed in the essential idea of man.

St. Thomas reaches the same conclusion from still another consideration, from the metaphysical notion of goodness.[8] Reason is the first

8. See, in general, Gustaf J. Gustafson, S.S., *The Theory of Natural Appetency in the Philosophy of St. Thomas*. The Catholic University of America Philosophical Series, Vol. LXXIV (Washington, D.C.: Catholic University of America Press, 1944), especially pp. 84–90. Among the numerous recent analyses and expositions of St. Thomas' doctrine of the natural moral law, may be mentioned: Walter Farrell, O.P., *The Natural Moral Law According to St. Thomas and Suarez* (Ditchling, England: St. Dominic's Press, 1930); *A Companion to the Summa* (4 vols., New York: Sheed and Ward, 1938–42), II, 365–89; Hans Meyer, *The Philosophy of St. Thomas Aquinas*, trans. by Frederic Eckhoff (St. Louis: B. Herder Book Co., 1944), pp. 455–73; Karl Kreilkamp, *The Metaphysical Foundations of Thomistic Jurisprudence*. The Catholic University of America Philosophical Studies, Vol. LIII (Washington, D.C.: Catholic University of America Press, 1939), pp. 39–73; Stanley Bertke, *op. cit.*, pp. 1–45. For an undoubtedly well-intentioned but pathetic attempt to outline, weigh, and criticize the moral philosophy of a St. Thomas (as well as to devise a positivistic methodology which will advance ethics from the alchemy stage to the high plane of science and thus accelerate the urgently needed moral progress of mankind), see Louise Saxe Eby, *The Quest for Moral Law* (New York: Columbia University Press, 1944).

and proximate rule for judging the moral quality of an action, which
is moral precisely because it is inherently conformable to reason and
nature, or immoral because it is at variance therewith. By what does
reason gauge, however, whether an action or object is suited to the
essential nature? St. Thomas gives the following explanation. Every
agent, supposing that he is actually in possession of reason and freedom
of will, acts for an end or purpose. The moving principle, the end, is
thereby perceived and willed as something good. But a thing is an end
only so far as it is a good, whose acquisition makes it worth one's while
to act. Goodness induces one to act. Goodness is, in final analysis, that
which is in itself worth desiring and striving for. As cognition is directed
to being, so the will is directed to goodness. And just as the intellect
knows the thing so far as it has being, so the will lays hold of the
thing, perceived as desirable or worth striving after, as good. All being
is good. A being is a good so far as it appears suited to the essential
nature. Now the supreme principles of speculative reason (the principle
of contradiction, and so on, the immediately evident, axiomatic laws
of thought) guide the intellect in its thinking. In the same way St.
Thomas recognizes a supreme principle, a law, for the practical reason,
for the will: good is to be done. The very same being which the
theoretical reason knows as being and in which it apprehends truth,
the agreement of knowledge with being, appears to the will and the
practical reason as a good. That which is, also ought to be. Being,
truth, and goodness are convertible. The law is truth; it wills what is
good; and it presupposes knowledge of being.[9]

9. "Now as *being* is the first thing that falls under the apprehension absolutely, so
good is the first thing that falls under the apprehension of the practical reason, which
is directed to action (since every agent acts for an end, which has the nature of good).
Consequently, the first principle in the practical reason is one founded on the nature
of good, viz., that *good is that which all things seek after*. Hence this is the first precept
of law, that *good is to be done and promoted, and evil is to be avoided*. All other precepts
of the natural law are based upon this; so that all the things which the practical reason
naturally apprehends as man's good belong to the precepts of the natural law under
the form of things to be done or avoided" (*Summa theologica*, Ia IIae, q.94, a.2).
Wherever possible, all English quotations from St. Thomas are taken from Anton C.
Pegis, *Basic Writings of Saint Thomas Aquinas* (2 vols., New York: Random House,
1945). "For St. Thomas truth and goodness are one; there is a science of truth which
is a science of the good; there is accordingly a truth of conduct which carries with it

Good is to be done: such is the supreme commandment of the natural moral law. The highest and basic norm of the natural law in the narrow sense, then, may be stated thus: Justice is to be done. Yet this principle is altogether general. It needs still to be determined to what extent the object striven for by means of a concrete action is a true good. This is done more or less with the aid of a syllogism (which, of course, is not worked out in every case by concrete reasoning): Good is to be done; this action is good, it strives after a good; it is therefore to be performed. Good is that which corresponds to the essential nature. The being of a thing also reveals its purpose in the order of creation, and in its perfect fulfillment it is likewise the end or goal of its growth and development. The essential nature is thus the measure. What corresponds to it is good; what is contrary to it is bad. The measure of goodness, consequently, is the essential idea of a thing and the proportionateness thereto of actions and of other things. That is, "Good is to be done" means the same as "Realize your essential nature." Moreover, since this essential nature issued from God's creative will and wisdom in both its existence and its quiddity, the principle continues: "You thereby realize the will of God, which is truly manifested to you in the knowledge of your essential nature." The same being is truth to the theoretical reason, and goodness to the practical reason.[10]

---

its own stringent obligations. There is, of course, a distinction between knowledge and action but there is only one intellect which is both speculative and practical. We might then define the object of St. Thomas' moral science as 'what conduct ought to be in virtue of what man really is, the right ordering of life to life's true goal.' The viewpoint is completely realistic" (Gustaf J. Gustafson, S.S., *op. cit.*, p. 100).

10. But it is man's natural tendencies or inclinations which disclose to his reason and will in what direction the perfection of his essential nature lies and, therefore, more precisely what is to be done as good, and what is to be avoided as evil. "Since, however, good has the nature of an end, and evil, the nature of the contrary, hence it is that all those things to which man has a natural inclination are naturally apprehended by reason as being good, and consequently as objects of pursuit, and their contraries as evil, and objects of avoidance. Therefore, the order of the precepts of the natural law is according to the order of natural inclinations. For there is in man, first of all, an inclination to good in accordance with the nature which he has in common with all substances, inasmuch, namely, as every substance seeks the preservation of its own being, according to its nature; and by reason of this inclination, whatever is a means of preserving human life, and of warding off its obstacles, belongs to the natural law. Secondly, there is in man an inclination to things that pertain to him more specially,

The train of thought thereupon widens. It follows that there are some actions which, because they correspond to the essential nature and its end, are in themselves good, moral, just; and that there are others which, because they are at variance therewith, are in themselves bad, immoral, unjust.[11] At any rate, this is true on the assumption that both in God and in man the intellect, not the will, holds the primacy. For a natural moral law as an immutable basic norm, and the essential

according to that nature which he has in common with other animals; and in virtue of this inclination, those things are said to belong to the natural law *which nature has taught to all animals,* such as sexual intercourse, the education of offspring and so forth. Thirdly, there is in man an inclination to good according to the nature of his reason, which nature is proper to him. Thus man has a natural inclination to know the truth about God, and to live in society; and in this respect, whatever pertains to this inclination belongs to the natural law: e.g., to shun ignorance, to avoid offending those among whom one has to live, and other such things regarding the above inclination" (*Summa theologica,* Ia IIae, q.94, a.2). "It is at this point that the theory of natural appetency enters the field of ethics. To know what man must do, one must first of all know what man is, know his nature, his needs, his possibilities and his limitations. In more technical language, this is to know his natural appetites, which, as orientations of that nature, point out his goal and the means which are at his disposal for its attainment" (Gustaf J. Gustafson, S.S., *op. cit.,* p. 101).

11. The "first necessary and natural dictate of practical reason is: Do good, avoid evil. The 'good' here is that which is according to natural inclinations, the 'evil' that which is against those inclinations; for the whole purpose of man's natural inclinations, as natural, is to indicate what nature needs for its perfection.

". . . In the practical order, which deals with actions, the first principle is founded on the object of appetite, the root of desire and action—on 'good'—and is: 'good is to be done, evil is to be avoided.' In other words, the goal or end, the object of desire, is at the root of all action, is indeed the sole explanation of intelligent action; this first principle demands that man act for his end.

"But what is good? That is easy. Good is what is in accordance with the natural inclinations of man. The natural inclinations guide the practical reason to good; then the practical reason guides the appetites of man and their inclinations to the attainment of that good. Nor is this a vicious circle. The inclinations of man's appetite are his guide to truth relative to the end or goal; for the means by which that end is to be attained, reason takes the lead and points out the path. This is only to say again that law does not establish an end, or point it out, but rather, as an act of the virtue of prudence, guides our steps to that end" (Walter Farrell, O.P., *A Companion to the Summa,* II, 380 f.). Michael Cronin likewise observes that "the natural law is wider in its scope than the ends of the appetites. It extends also to the means necessary for attaining those ends. For, if we *must* attain the end, then we must also adopt the means" (*The Science of Ethics* [2 vols., 2nd rev. ed., New York: Benziger Brothers, 1929–30], I, 644).

nature as a valid measure of what is moral and just, are possible only when this essence is itself unalterable. This presupposes, however, that the essential nature owes its idea, its quiddity, and its existence to the unchangeable essence of God Himself, of which they are reflections. "If, too, human nature is the immediate measure of moral goodness, it can be the norm of unalterable moral judgments only insofar as it itself embodies the idea of man as this rests from all eternity in the divine mind. But the ideas of things in the divine mind are, in their content, nothing else than the images through which God knows His own essence as imitable. This is true also of the idea of man."[12]

The divine essence and, in one and the same act, the divine knowledge thereof and the creative will of God, likewise thereby informed in one and the same act, are (or rather, is) the basis for the essential nature and its immutability. "That God of necessity enacts and cannot alter that law which we call the natural law comes merely from the fact that His will cannot do away with His most perfect essence, that God cannot be at variance with Himself and cannot, as the Apostle says, deny Himself" (Kleutgen). This is the fundamental reason for rejecting moral and legal positivism. The will is not the law; on the contrary, it can only be right law when it is guided even in God by reason and intellect. "But to say that justice depends upon mere will is to say that the divine will does not proceed according to the order of wisdom, which is blasphemy."[13]

Good is to be done, evil is to be avoided: this basic norm of the natural moral law has thus the character of an axiom. The real question, however, is that of its application to the concrete case. As another expression for the first rule of the *lex naturalis,* as general principles known to all, St. Thomas mentions love of God and of one's neighbor. Man knows other principles only through deductive reason, yet not with altogether unerring certitude. For, in contrast with the speculative

12. Viktor Cathrein, S.J., *Moralphilosophie* (2 vols., 4th ed., Freiburg im Breisgau: Herdersche Verlagshandlung, 1904), I, 185 f. All this, too, should enable one to appreciate the profound statement of St. Thomas: "We do not wrong God unless we wrong our own good" (*Summa contra Gentiles,* Bk. III, chap. 122).

13. St. Thomas, *De veritate,* q.23, a.6.

reason, the knowledge of the practical reason is more severely menaced in its clarity by the passions, by sinful inclinations. These conclusions from principles are for St. Thomas, as he explains in a searching inquiry into the problem, identical with the Decalogue, or Ten Commandments. The Decalogue contains the most essential conclusions for the simple reason that its precepts do not result from an arbitrary arrangement made by God, but from the fundamental distinction of good and evil. The first table of the Decalogue (first three Commandments) embraces the moral norms that relate to the worship of God; these required a special promulgation, in the view of St. Thomas, because they are not so evident as the laws found in the second table. The latter (the last seven Commandments), which are derived from the mutual relations among men and from the essence and goal of human nature, are, on the other hand, known more readily and with greater evidence. Human society in all its groupings ought to be built up in accordance with justice.

The Decalogue (second table) presents the norms that follow from the essential relationships which in their turn are given in the essential nature of man as a rational, free, and social being. These precepts, as norms with a material content, protect the family and parental authority (Fourth Commandment), human life (Fifth Commandment), the person in the capital sense of husband and wife (Sixth Commandment), property (Seventh Commandment), and honor (Eighth Commandment); lastly they forbid (Ninth and Tenth Commandments) inordinate, illicit longing for those goods which are especially exposed to covetousness and, moreover, whose wrongful appropriation does not arouse that natural abhorrence which infractions of the Fourth, Fifth, and Eighth Commandments do.[14] St. Thomas regards it as self-evident that the further deductions from these conclusions do not possess the same evidence, since they necessarily lose, in favor of particular prescriptions, the universal character required for evidence. Furthermore, they are not so unmistakably recognizable that errors about them

14. The problem of the correct numbering of the Ten Commandments is well handled by Louis Hartman, C.SS.R., article cited, *Catholic Biblical Quarterly*, VII (1945), 105–8.

may not arise in the minds of individuals as well as among groups.[15] Moreover, they do not share in the prerogative of immutability enjoyed by the *principia communissima* as well as by the conclusions which make up the contents of the Decalogue.

For instance, from the nature of the legal institution, from the agreement with reason and from the right of property, which in the general sense is protected by the Seventh Commandment, it follows that goods held in trust should be restored to their owner. Nevertheless, as St. Thomas points out, such goods may be withheld from their owner in case they are to be used for treasonable purposes.[16] Here the further conclusion does not hold good, although the universal norm of acting according to reason, the *suum cuique,* continues absolutely to govern the case. Some "matters cannot be the subject of judgment without much consideration of the various circumstances. Not all are able to do this carefully, but only those who are wise."[17] "In the very application of the universal principle to some particular case a mistake can occur through an inadequate or false deduction, or by reason of some false assumption";[18] and in the matter of its secondary precepts, "the natural law can be blotted out from the human heart, either by evil persuasions . . . or by vicious customs and corrupt habits."[19] Therein, moreover, practical reason differs significantly from theoretical reason, which is less subject to such disturbing influences.

This does not, then, mean merely that there is in St. Thomas no trace whatever of the extravagances of the rationalistic natural law current in the seventeenth and eighteenth centuries, since according to him only the Decalogue belongs to the contents of the natural law. It further means that the *lex naturalis* or *ius naturale* does not render positive laws superfluous, but actually calls for them. St. Thomas gives

---

15. Cf. Jacques Maritain, *The Rights of Man and Natural Law,* trans. by Doris C. Anson (New York: Charles Scribner's Sons, 1943), pp. 62–64.

16. *Summa theologica,* Ia IIae, q.94, a.4.

17. *Ibid.,* q.100, a.1.

18. *De veritate,* q.16, a.2 ad 1.

19. *Summa theologica,* Ia IIae, q.94, a.6. Cf. *ibid.,* q.77, a.2; q.94, a.5; Maritain, *loc. cit.*

scarcely any attention to the doctrine of a state of nature, because he has no need of the latter for establishing the natural law. Now, the farther removed the conclusions are from the *principia communissima*, the more numerous and varied become the possible decisions. Hence a positive law must determine, must decide with greater exactness for concrete cases, what the correct application and conclusion are. There is all the more need of such determination because human nature, deprived and hence wounded somehow (though not destroyed or depraved) by original sin,[20] must be—and in conformity with its inner goal also ought to be—constrained to good and restrained from evil. Self-education or addiction to goodness does not pertain to man as such. Consequently men stand in need of a clearly prescribed and adequately sanctioned system of norms, which emanate from an authority and power that in their inmost reality serve justice, and in the individual serve to perfect the essential nature of man. They are therefore ethical. St. Thomas is no romantic optimist like Rousseau.

Furthermore, it is precisely the object of the positive law to render the citizen virtuous. It is not merely a question of maintaining order,

---

20. It is well to point out that, in developed Catholic teaching, original sin is not something positive but the privation of those supernatural (especially sanctifying grace with its allied virtues) and preternatural gifts which God had gratuitously bestowed upon the human race in the person of its head, Adam. Yet it is an habitual sin of human nature itself which consists in a privative aversion toward God as man's *supernatural* end and whose voluntariness springs from the actual will of Adam in his capacity as the natural head of the human race. Cf. J. M. Hervé, *Manuale theologiae dogmaticae* (4 vols., 17th ed., Paris: Berche et Pagis, 1935), II, nos. 429–43. Moreover, it is the far more common teaching among Catholic theologians that the natural powers of man have not been intrinsically weakened by original sin: fallen man no more differs from man in the (hypothetical) purely natural state than one who has been despoiled of his clothing differs from him who has been going about in the nude; but it is quite commonly held also that the natural powers of fallen man have been extrinsically weakened. Such traditional formulas as *vulneratus in naturalibus* and *natura vulnerata* must seemingly be understood, consequently, of nature taken historically, not philosophically (cf. *ibid.*, II, nos. 444–48). In short, the difficulty which man in the present order experiences in doing good "comes rather from the obstacles to virtue that man encounters than from any intrinsic diminution of his natural powers." Francis J. Connell, C.SS.R., in *The American Ecclesiastical Review*, CXIII (1945), 70. See also John A. Ryan, *Original Sin and Human Misery* (pamphlet, New York: Paulist Press, 1942), particularly pp. 39–42, 52–55.

or external peace; the law should rather act as a medium of popular education to transform those who live under common legal institutions into perfect citizens. For this very reason positive norms, determinate coercive measures, and a more exact definition of the circumstances in which the general principle shall be applied, are imperative. Thus the definition of what theft consists in is given with the lawfulness of private property. But the punishment which should follow theft, if arbitrariness is to be avoided, requires, with respect to the procedural verification of the theft as well as to the sentence and its execution, exact legal provisions which vary with times, cultures, and individual peoples.

Here, in connection with the positive law which is therefore always "something pertaining to reason," St. Thomas arrives at the nature of law. It has to do essentially with community life. On the other hand, it is distinguished from and contrasted with social ethics through its being directed to external order. The law wills that man conduct himself in such and such a manner; it concerns the external forum (*vis directiva*). It is the norm to be enforced: compulsion (*vis coactiva*) is proper to law, not to morality.

From this inner connection of every positive law with the *lex naturalis* St. Thomas rightly concludes that the positive law may not conflict with the natural law. So far as it is in conflict with the latter, i.e., with the unchangeable norms, it is not law at all and cannot bind in conscience. For the force and significance of the law consist precisely in the obligation in conscience. Yet it may at times be right to obey even an unjust positive law (one that is not against the natural law: e.g., a law that imposes an unjust tax burden), because the higher natural-law norm enjoins in individual cases the sacrifice of a particular good to a more general good. For instance, the general goods of security under law and the external order of peace constitute a higher value than does the individual right to just treatment in the levying of taxes. It is consequently not the unjust law that binds, but the higher norm of peace and of maintenance of the community.

In this fashion, then, all law, down to and inclusive of its positive individualization, is connected by means of the natural moral law with the eternal law and lives on the latter. Thus *rectitudo practica*, reasonableness or the relation to human nature still is, and ought to be, the essential element even in the positive law. For St. Thomas the law is somehow reason, not mere arbitrary will.[21] The natural law remains the measure of the positive law. But this position is intimately connected with the doctrine of the immutability of the natural law and the enduring essential nature of man, as well as with the primacy of the intellect over the will in both God and man.

But can God, by His absolute power, dispense from the precepts of the Decalogue? St. Thomas unqualifiedly answers that the Ten Commandments admit of no dispensation whatever. "Precepts admit of dispensation when there occurs a particular case in which, if the letter of the law be observed, the intention of the lawgiver is frustrated. Now the intention of every lawgiver is directed first and chiefly to the common good; secondly, to the order of justice and virtue, whereby the common good is preserved and attained. If, therefore, there be any precepts which contain the very preservation of the common good, or the very order of justice and virtue, such precepts contain the intention of the lawgiver, and therefore are indispensable. . . .

"Now the precepts of the Decalogue contain the very intention of the lawgiver, who is God. For the precepts of the first table, which direct us to God, contain the very order to the common and final good, which is God; while the precepts of the second table contain the order of justice to be observed among men, namely, that nothing undue be done to anyone, and that each one be given his due; for it is in this sense that we are to take the precepts of the Decalogue. Consequently the precepts of the Decalogue admit of no dispensation whatever."[22]

21. Hence St. Thomas is easily able to bring custom into harmony with law: "Therefore by actions also, especially if they be repeated, so as to make a custom, law can be changed and set forth; furthermore, something can be established which obtains the force of law, in so far as, by repeated external actions, the inward movement of the will and the conceptions of the reason are most revealingly declared. For when a thing is done again and again, it seems to proceed from a deliberate judgment of reason. Accordingly custom has the force of a law, abolishes law, and is the interpreter of law" (*Summa theologica*, Ia IIae, q.97, a.3).

22. *Ibid.*, q.100, a.8. For "God cannot dispense a man so that it be lawful for him not to direct himself to God, or not to be subject to His justice, even in those matters in which men are directed to one another" (*ibid.*, ad 2). Walter Farrell, O.P., aptly indicates the metaphysical basis of this position of St. Thomas: "These precepts do not depend on the will of God; they are not extrinsically but intrinsically valid, for

But what of the Old Testament passages that appear to involve divine dispensations from the natural law? In reply, St. Thomas notes the sovereign dominion of God over men and over concrete human actions and institutions: "The precepts of the Decalogue, as to the notion of justice which they contain, are unchangeable; but as to any determination by application to individual actions—for instance, that this or that be murder, theft, or adultery, or not—in this point they admit of change; sometimes by divine authority alone, namely, in such matters as are exclusively of divine institution, as marriage and the like; sometimes also by human authority, namely, in such matters as are subject to human jurisdiction; for in this respect men stand in the place of God, though not in all respects."[23]

With Duns Scotus (d. *cir.* 1308), and with the principle of the primacy of the will over the intellect so much emphasized by him, there began inside moral philosophy a train of thought which in later centuries would recur in secularized form in the domain of legal philosophy. The principle that law is will would be referred in legal positivism, as well as in the theory of will in jurisprudence, to the earthly lawmaker (self-obligation).

For Duns Scotus morality depends on the will of God. A thing is good not because it corresponds to the nature of God or, analogically, to the nature of man, but because God so wills. Hence the *lex naturalis* could be other than it is even materially or as to content, because it has no intrinsic connection with God's essence, which is self-conscious in His intellect. For Scotus, therefore, the laws of the second table of

---

the Natural Moral Law, like all law, is essentially the work of reason not of will; in this case it is the divine reason which cannot be changed" (*The Natural Moral Law According to St. Thomas and Suarez*, p. 120).

23. *Ibid.*, ad 3. Cf. also *ibid.*, q.94, a.5 ad 2. In other words, St. Thomas supposes that in such cases of apparent dispensation God did not act as Lawmaker, but as Lord and Master, with sovereign dominion over human life and property. But see the cautious and sobering remarks of Jacques Leclercq, *Les droits et devoirs individuels*, Part I, "Vie, disposition de soi" (Namur: Maison d'Édition Ad. Wesmael-Charlier, 1937), pp. 53 f., on this now common solution. Of course, whether or not the traditional exegesis of all such Old Testament episodes and passages is correct is another question. For instance, there is neither any need nor any sound reason for holding that Yahweh ordered Osee to commit fornication or adultery. Cf. A. Van Hoonacker, *Les douze Petits Prophètes* (Paris: J. Gabalda & Cie., 1908), pp. 13 ff.

the Decalogue were no longer unalterable. The crux of theology, namely, the problem of the apparent dispensations from the natural law mentioned in the Old Testament and thus seemingly granted by God (the command to sacrifice Isaac, Raphael's apparent lie, Osee's alleged adultery, the polygamy of the patriarchs, and so on), was now readily solved.[24] Yet St. Thomas, too, had been able to solve such cases. Now, however, an evolution set in which, in the doctrine of William of Occam (d. *cir.* 1349) on the natural moral law, would lead to pure moral positivism, indeed to nihilism.

The will is the nobler faculty; the intellect is but the ministering torch-bearer of the will, which is the master. Between God's essence and that of man there exists, apart from the fact of creation, no inherent connection, no analogy of being. Hence, too, there exists no unchangeable moral order grounded in the nature of things, in the ordered universe of being and value. As all being is founded on the mere absolute will of God without participation in His essence, so all oughtness or obligation rests solely on the same absolute will. Oughtness is without foundation in reality, just as the universals are merely vocal utterances (*flatus vocis*) and not mental images of the necessary being of the ideas in God. In this way Occam arrived at a heightened supernaturalism, but only to deprive almost completely the natural order of its value.

For Occam the natural moral law is positive law, divine will. An action is not good because of its suitableness to the essential nature of man, wherein God's archetypal idea of man is represented according to being and oughtness, but because God so wills. God's will could also have willed and decreed the precise opposite, which would then possess the same binding force as that which is now valid—which, indeed, has validity only as long as God's absolute will so determines. Law is will, pure will without any foundation in reality, without foundation in the essential nature of things. Thus, too, sin no longer contains any intrinsic element of immorality, or what is unjust, any inner element of injustice; it is an external offense against the will of God.

As a result, Occam, who sees only individual phenomena, not univer-

---

24. Cf. Walter Farrell, O.P., *The Natural Moral Law According to St. Thomas and Suarez,* pp. 122–30.

sals, the concepts of essences, can likewise admit no teleological orientation toward God is inherent in all creation and especially in man; or at least he cannot grant that it can be known. The unity of being, truth, and goodness does not exist for him. Moral goodness consists in mere external agreement with God's absolute will, which, subject only to His arbitrary decree, can always change. To such an extent were God's omnipotence and free will extolled that much subtle speculation was devoted to the question of whether God can, through His absolute power, will hatred of Himself; a question which Occam and many of his disciples answered in the affirmative. Man sins, therefore, because and only so far as a positive law, by which he is bound, stands over him. God, on the other hand, cannot sin because no law stands above Him, not because it is repugnant to His holiness. Hence there exists no unchangeable *lex naturalis,* no natural law that inwardly governs the positive law. Positive law and natural law, which indeed is also positive law, stand likewise in no inner relation to each other. The identity of this thought structure with *The Prince* of Machiavelli, with the *Leviathan* of Hobbes, and with the theory of will of modern positivism (the will of the absolute sovereign is law, because no higher norm stands above him) is here quite obvious.[25]

The dispute over whether the intellect of the will is the nobler faculty had, in the moral positivism of Occam's school, split the scholastic doctrine of natural law to its very core. The scholastic revival of the age of the Protestant Revolt, however, successfully understood the speculative rehabilitation of the *lex naturalis* and *ius naturale* on an ontological basis, just as it also went back to St. Thomas in its theology.

The philosophy of law received special and thoroughgoing treatment at the hands of the Late Scholastics. The outstanding figures in this field were, to mention but a few of the many important scholars, the Spaniards Vittoria (d. 1546), Suarez (1548–1617) and Vasquez (d. 1604), and the Italian St. Robert Bellarmine (1542–1621).

The reasons for this more intensive preoccupation with the problems

25. On the positions of Scotus and Occam in this far-reaching controversy, see Anton-Hermann Chroust, "Hugo Grotius and the Scholastic Natural Law Tradition," *The New Scholasticism,* XVII (1943), pp. 101–12.

of the natural moral law and philosophy of law were many. To begin with the doctrinal ones, Occamism had wrought havoc in theology as well as in metaphysics and ethics. Reason had been rendered barren. The so-called Reformers had drawn the ultimate conclusions from Occamism with respect to theology. Contemptuous of reason, they had arrived at a pregnant voluntarism in theology as well as at the doctrine of *natura deleta,* of nature as destroyed by original sin. Thereby the traditional natural law became speculatively impossible.[26] The spirit of the Renaissance, too, had made use of Occam's separation of faith and knowledge to emancipate secular thought or worldly wisdom, and to place it in opposition to sacred learning. Pomponazzi (1462–1530), after the manner of the Averroists, had spoken of a twofold truth: what is true in philosophy may be false in theology, and vice versa. Law as such was separated in a positivist fashion from the eternal law when the natural moral law had been made into a positive act of God's absolute will. Machiavelli (1469–1527) had secularized this view and had drawn the consequences for politics. The absolute power of God in

---

26. The true relationship between the natural order (the realm of natural laws and of the natural moral law) and the supernatural order (the realm of divine grace) is clearly and concisely set forth by Oswald von Nell-Breuning, S.J.: "Elevation to supernature leaves human nature unchanged in principle. Therefore, human nature retains its full value as a source of knowledge for social order. All principles for the structural plan of human society are impressed upon human nature by God, and remain so; therefore, they can be recognized in and deduced from this human nature with certainty. This is also true of man exalted by grace or abased by sin. Just as grace elevates man above his mere nature as a being without taking away anything from his human nature, so sin has not changed the condition of human nature into something else. True enough, there is no longer a purely natural order since God has introduced a supernatural order and has destined man for a supernatural goal; in fact, there never existed a man in the purely natural order. (Thus the sinner can miss the supernatural goal, but he cannot nullify his destiny for this goal.) The natural order is consummated by the supernatural order in such a way that it remains fully unchanged. That is why the natural order, although we can separate it from the actually given supernatural order only by abstract thinking, is not merely a fancy, but a living reality whose misappreciation, denial, or debasement at the same time not only misappreciates, denies, and debases supernature, but actually deprives it of its foundation, thus making it untenable" (*Reorganization of Social Economy. The Social Encyclical Developed and Explained,* trans. by Bernard W. Dempsey, S.J. [Milwaukee: Bruce Publishing Co., 1936–37], p. 17, note).

Occam's doctrine became at the hands of Thomas Hobbes the absolute sovereignty of the king.

But there were also practical reasons. Not only in idea, but also in actual fact the *orbis christianus* had ceased to be "the world." The Spanish and Portuguese discoveries had brought to light the East Indies and America, and the *gentes* dwelling there. This event raised new and great problems for the *ius gentium*. The first and extremely important treatise on international law, the work of Francis de Vittoria, bears the title, *De bello et de Indis*. Besides, the enormous expansion of trade in the early period of modern capitalism raised new moral problems for the Late Scholastics, as did also the process of political transformation from feudal society to a world of states ruled by absolute sovereigns. Thus it came about that nearly every scholar of the time composed treatises entitled *De legibus* and *De iure et iustitia*.

The task of the Late Scholastics was, then, as Petavius so well pointed out, to work out further, to develop fully and completely, what the thinkers of the golden age of Scholasticism, in particular St. Thomas Aquinas, had taught implicitly and in outline. They saw and carried out this task in the case of the natural-law doctrine, too. The decline of the doctrine of natural law set in only after them. So competent a scholar as Joseph Kohler has held that "if, then, a natural law is to be fashioned today, it must be attached to these Spaniards of the age of Spain's greatness, not to Hugo Grotius."

In their theology and psychology these thinkers of Late Scholasticism restored to honor the Thomistic doctrine of the divine essence as source of the entire moral order and, with it, that of the primacy of the intellect over the will. The natural law is grounded in essence and reason, not in mere absolute will, in God's absolute power. God's omnipotence is subordinated, humanly speaking of course, to the decrees of His wisdom. Like these, therefore, the essences of things are also unchangeable. *Potentia ordinata* is that power in virtue of which God has created, among all possible worlds and orders of being, precisely the present one. Absolute power, on the other hand, is the power through which He can do everything that is not in itself contradictory. Hence God cannot cooperate in human sinning, and still less can He be its total cause. The Occamist question of whether God could will hatred of Himself involves an intrinsic impossibility.

In short, the intellect grasps the pure essence of a thing, its quiddity or whatness, and prescinds from actual existence. The will, on the contrary, can lay hold of a being only as something existing or to be brought into existence; it is directed to the particular, to the individual. Intellectual apprehension is more immaterial; it grasps essential being. The will in itself is blind, in contrast to the intellect which apprehends the object immediately. The will lays hold of the object only when the latter is presented by the intellect as a known and valuable good. On this depends the question of the possibility of an immutable natural law. Positivism in law and ethics corresponds to agnosticism in epistemology.

Like the idea of God, the idea of law was also purged of Occamist positivism. For the Late Scholastics the law belongs more to the reason than to the will. The will, it is true, moves all faculties to action. Yet it is blind: to arrange and direct are the work of reason. The will is related to the intellect as a queen is to a king. The will, the queen, manifests her desires to the king and moves him. But the intellect, the king, enacts the law (Bellarmine).

The *lex naturalis*, therefore, is not related to the will of God in a simple positivist manner. It is related to God's essence, to His reason, whence emanates the eternal law whereof in turn the natural law is, and ultimately every moral and positive law should be, a participation. The natural law has for its proximate principle the essential nature of man. It is a judgment of reason concerning the conformity of moral action and nature. But at the same time it shows that what is good ought also to be done. God, who fashioned the essential nature of man with reason and will, is simultaneously recognized as Lawgiver, too. To state it in another way, what the eternal law is in God actively, i.e., as will in accordance with His essence, that the natural law is in man passively: a law flowing from his essence and imbedded in it. The mere light of natural reason that indicates the agreement or disagreement of an action with man's essential nature (Vasquez) is insufficient by itself. There must in addition be the rational insight that an act in accord with reason and nature is also God's will (Suarez, Bellarmine).

This controversy had a still deeper significance. Suarez and Bellarmine wished to stress the inner oneness of natural law and eternal law. They wished to do this, moreover, by way of the recognition of God as the Lawgiver who wills that actions correspond to being, to essential nature. Vasquez, the Spanish Augustine, had regarded rational nature, irrespective of the positive will of God, as the primary ground of the obligation to obey the natural law. For him, consequently, since an act of the lawmaker's will belongs necessarily to the nature of law, the natural law is not properly law in the strict sense: it is not *lex praecipiens,* merely *lex indicans.* This view, a very uncommon one among the Late Scholastics,[27] assumed great importance in the rationalist doctrine of natural law. Arriaga and Grotius were already teaching, in order fully to bring out its immutability, that the natural law would have force even if there were no God.[28] Out of this there developed an autonomy of abstract human reason conditioned by the separation of the eternal law and the natural law, and also the ethico-legal rationalism of the individualistic natural law (a development which, by the way, Suarez had foretold in his controversy with Vasquez). This loosening was thus the signal for the outbreak of a fanatical rationalism in speculation, which was bent upon drawing all possible conclusions from this isolated and, later still, individualistically interpreted pure rational nature. Moreover, such fanaticism lacked all corrective of history as the domain of God's providential activity. To the rationalistic natural law corresponded Deism in theology.

The natural moral law is therefore a judgment of reason which presents actions as commanded or forbidden by the Author of reason, because the light of reason shows them to be in agreement or disagreement with man's essential nature; and at the same time reason judges that God wills that which accords with nature: essential being ought to be realized. In its essence and intellectual content the natural law

27. Cf. A.-H. Chroust, article cited, *The New Scholasticism,* XVII (1943), 114 f.
28. This important problem, together with its bearing on the nature of moral obligation, is discussed in Part II.

is absolutely dependent upon the divine intellect; in its real existence, upon the divine will.[29]

In this way, not only was the connection between the eternal law and the natural law maintained for later ages, but, for contemporaries, the true character of law was upheld against the so-called Reformers who belonged to the school of Occam. For the latter saw the natural law exclusively in the words of Scripture. Indeed, with their doctrine of *natura deleta* they could not even attain to a moral law that is naturally good. Gratian's formula, *ius naturae quod in Evangelio et lege* (Decalogue), which was now being misinterpreted, vanished. So, too, did Ulpian's formula, *quod natura omnia animalia docuit.* Only now was an elucidation of the *ius gentium* possible.

The Late Scholastics, like St. Thomas, included the Decalogue, regarded as belonging in its entirety to the *lex naturalis,* in the contents of the natural moral law. They distinguished in this connection the supreme principle, "Good is to be done, evil avoided," and equally evident though already less universal principles, which therefore embrace specific kinds of goodness. Such are the following: Give to everyone his due; Worship must be paid to God; Justice must be observed; Agreements must be kept. From these follow by way of deduction additional precepts, which concern individual goods and the institutions that protect them. Thus theft, lying, adultery, and perjury are always forbidden because they are intrinsically evil.

These teachers came to speak of the relationship of the natural law to the positive law mostly in connection with political science, and particularly in reference to the end of the state. Moreover, connected with this problem is the question of the nature of law in relation to morality.

Any positive law which offends against the natural moral law is not

29. On Suarez' doctrine of the natural law, see the widely divergent expositions and appraisals of Heinrich Rommen, *Die Staatslehre des Franz Suarez, S.J.* (M.-Gladbach: Volksvereins-Verlag, 1927), pp. 43–77, and Walter Farrell, O.P., *The Natural Moral Law According to St. Thomas and Suarez,* pp. 48–72, 147–55. For an excellent presentation of Bellarmine's doctrine in its historical setting, cf. Franz Xaver Arnold, *Die Staatslehre des Kardinals Bellarmin* (Munich: Max Hueber Verlag, 1934), pp. 13–75.

a law that is binding in a moral sense, i.e., in conscience. But only those laws are absolutely null and void that run counter to the prohibitive natural law. Therefore a law that would positively prescribe murder or perjury would not be a law at all, nor may one obey it. The case where a law is opposed to the affirmative natural law is different. The citizen must put up with encroachment on the part of a government that deals unjustly, e.g., in the matter of taxation, if through resistance the public order, already threatened by the very fact of the unjust law, would be still more gravely menaced. Only such authority as enacts laws which are in conflict with the prohibitive natural law ceases to be authority in the rightful sense and becomes tyranny. Mere power can impose no inner duty of obedience. But this truth has nothing to do with the fact that among the Indians, for instance, laws prevail which are contrary to natural law. For such laws are made by lawgivers and accepted by subjects or members of the community, not because these laws are immoral and bad, but because conscience, darkened through deficient rational insight and troubled by passions, is unable to recognize their inherent badness. Indeed, St. Thomas admitted such a possibility in the case of conclusions from the natural moral law.

Conversely, however, it follows from the fact of *natura vulnerata* as well as from the ethical character and goal of community life, and of the state in particular, that positive human laws are absolutely necessary for determining the further inferences from the first principles in the interest of a more exact and readily discernible establishment of order and for the setting up of institutions needed for community life. The natural-law prohibition of adultery implies at the same time an affirmation of marriage and of the general norms that are most needed for its functioning as an institution. "Thou shalt not steal" presupposes the institution of private property as pertaining to the natural law; but not, for example, the feudal property arrangements of the Middle Ages or the modern capitalist system. Since the natural law lays down general norms only, it is the function of the positive law to undertake the concrete, detailed regulation of real and personal property and to prescribe the formalities for conveyance of ownership.

The nature of law was likewise explored. As a rule, the Late Scholastics employed the terms *lex naturalis* and *ius naturale* as synonyms. But

Suarez and Bellarmine, for instance, made a distinction when they expressly declared that violation of the *lex naturalis* on the part of the Indians by no means constitutes grounds for a just war: hence Christian princes are not justified in subjugating these *gentes* by alleging their transgression of the *lex naturalis*. Only an offense against the *ius naturale* warrants such action. In this respect, indeed, states stand in the same relationship to one another as do persons, and the Indian states are true states in the sense of law. Law, therefore, stands out in the overall picture of the moral realm by reason of its social character, its reference to another (whether person or group). Justice is the virtue which has right (with which law in the technical sense is concerned) for its object. It is essentially directed to one's fellow man. As commutative justice it has to do with those who are upon an equal footing in the social complex; as legal justice it concerns the rights of authorities or superiors, which it commands subjects to respect; as distributive justice it obliges authorities, in their administrative activity, to give to everyone his right according to his function and merit in the ordered whole. Thus the norms that have to do with the life in common of men and groups (their social units, arrangements, and social functions) are the object of justice. They are thereby law.

These norms constitute natural law insofar as such regulations pertain, as immediately necessary, to the essential nature and essential fulfillment of man in the *vita oeconomica* (marriage, family, and occupational groups organizing themselves according to social functions in the service of the common good, for the peaceful ordering of the people) and in political life (state and international community). Since these regulations are necessary, their realization, improvement, and maintenance against lawbreakers are enforceable by the public authorities. Law wills that this be done without further ado, not merely because morality demands it. The *debitum iustum* (*ex iustitia*) thus differs from what is owed *ex pietate* or *ex gratitudine* precisely because gratitude is of its very nature unenforceable: if obtained by force, it ceases to be a moral action at all. Seneca in his day raised the question of why no suit can be brought against an ingrate. Owing to the failure of the ancients to work out this distinction, he did not find the right answer, namely, that gratitude, like *pietas,* is simply unenforceable. The son who has to be compelled by court action to support his impoverished, incapacitated father fulfills indeed a legal duty, and the state rests satisfied. No one will contend, however, that through this fulfillment by court order he has complied with the moral duty of *pietas*.

The great accomplishment of the Late Scholastics lay in the domain of the *ius gentium*. They cleared up, before Grotius, the ambiguous distinctions of Roman law that had crept in during the course of centuries. *Ius gentium* in the proper sense is not *ius naturale*, although the precepts of the latter are evidently valid for the ordering of the community of peoples. Thus differentiated, *ius gentium* is the quasi-positive law of the international community: it is founded upon custom as well as upon treaty agreements. The basic norm of this positive *ius gentium* is, besides the material principles of the natural law, especially the axiom, *pacta sunt servanda*. To positive international law belong the doctrines of war, truce and peace, international trade and commercial treaties, and, in addition, the law concerning envoys. But the requirements that a war must be just, and that the community of peoples must establish and foster friendly intercourse, pertain to the natural law.

From this *ius gentium* (most properly so called), they further distinguished international private law. The latter contains norms regarding legal institutions that are common to nearly all peoples, and hence are closely related to the natural law. Such are the general formal legal institutions touching purchases, leases, promissory notes, contracts, ownership, the family and inheritance. For, despite regulations that differ in detail, all these legal institutions have, among almost all peoples, many things in common over and above their natural-law foundation.

CHAPTER III

The Turning Point: Hugo Grotius

Among historians of philosophy the view prevailed for some time that René Descartes (1596–1650), a *deus ex machina* as it were, founded modern philosophy with its primary, indeed almost exclusive, concern with the thinking subject, with the study of individual consciousness and experience. But this view has long since been shown to be unwarranted. Descartes' philosophical system was no creation *ex nihilo*. The latest research has conclusively demonstrated Descartes' connection with Scholasticism. There existed before Descartes no "desolate waste of scholastic subtleties and sophistries." What did exist was a great philosophical system, and Descartes still stood in its stream, as the history of the various philosophical problems proves.

Quite as untenable is the view, long held, that the doctrine of natural law began with the Dutch scholar, Hugo Grotius (1583–1645), often hailed as the Father of Natural Law. For Grotius was still closely connected with the teachers of the preceding centuries. He stands out more through the first formal inclusion of natural law and positive law in international law than through any intellectual contribution of his own. He may be said to have marked the transition from the metaphysical to the rationalist natural law. The notion that the natural law would still have some validity, *etsiamsi daremus . . . non esse Deum, aut non curari ab eo negotia humana,*[1] played a certain role in his thinking. Yet

---

1. "What we have been saying would have a degree of validity even if we should concede that which cannot be conceded without the utmost wickedness, that there is no God, or that the affairs of men are of no concern to Him" (*De jure belli ac pacis libri tres,* Prolegomena, 11, trans. by Francis W. Kelsey and others for *The Classics of International Law,* edited by J. B. Scott, Oxford-London, 1925). According to A.-H.

Grotius did not profess the implied complete autonomy of human reason as the sole and not merely the proximate source of the natural law. He considered God to be the highest source of the natural law, and he likewise regarded Holy Scripture as a principle of knowledge on an equal footing with reason. Grotius still lived too much in and with tradition to be able to construe the natural law in a deistic manner.[2] He understood *recta ratio* in the same sense as did the great Spaniards. One may even say that, in a world which had forgotten the achievement of past ages, his celebrated definition of natural law represents an attempt to settle by compromise the controversy between Suarez and Vasquez, a controversy that bulked large in his day.[3]

The famous definition runs as follows: "The law of nature [*ius naturale*] is a dictate of right reason which points out that an act, according as it is or is not in conformity with rational [and social] nature, has in it a quality of moral baseness or moral necessity; and that, in consequence, such an act is either forbidden or enjoined by the author of nature, God."[4] Here, in fact, is Vasquez' doctrine of *lex indicans* combined with Suarez' intention to bring out the character of the *lex naturalis* as *lex*, which, in its coming into force or in its existence, is derived from the will of God. In addition, the significant adjective *socialis* occurs in the same way among the Late Scholastics for the purpose of distinguishing and contrasting *lex naturalis* and *ius naturale*. In Grotius' thought the *socialitas* of rational nature was not yet, as it was to be for Pufendorf, the sole source of natural law.

Chroust, "this famous passage from Grotius is but a rebuke of William of Occam's and Hobbes's voluntarism or 'positivism'—by that we mean something valid because of its being posited or willed by someone—and an indirect proof of Grotius's belief, quite in accordance with the Thomistic tradition, in the perseitas boni et iusti" ("Hugo Grotius and the Scholastic Natural Law Tradition," *The New Scholasticism*, XVII [1943], 126). Cf. also, *ibid.*, notes 88 and 89.

2. The thesis of Chroust is that "Hugo Grotius constitutes but a direct continuation of the great Natural Law tradition which stretches from St. Augustine to Suarez, and which culminated in St. Thomas" ("Hugo Grotius and the Scholastic Natural Law Tradition," *ibid.*, p. 125).

3. Chroust is of the same opinion (*ibid.*, pp. 129 f.).

4. *De jure belli ac pacis libri tres*, Bk. I, chap. 1. The important qualifying phrase *and social* is strangely missing both in Kelsey's English translation and in the Latin edition (1646) on which it is based.

Grotius followed the Scholastics even in his psychology. He placed the rectitude of voluntary action in a twofold conformity: that of the intellect with the thing or object, and that of the will with the intellect. Nevertheless his design of vindicating the absolutist doctrine of James I of England drove him back again to the primacy of the will. He accordingly defended the nominalist doctrine that essentially bad acts are evil, not because they are intrinsically at variance with God's essence, but because they are forbidden by God. Of course he looked upon the further question of why God in His freedom has so decreed as unanswerable by human reason.

The Late Scholastics had sought to determine the relationship between law and morality from the standpoint of the virtues: right is the specific object of justice as distinguished from the other cardinal virtues (prudence, temperance, fortitude). In its threefold form (commutative, distributive, and legal), justice regulates the social relations: first, of those possessed of equal rights; secondly, of public authorities to their subjects; and thirdly, of citizens to public authorities or to the state. In Grotius' system sociality plays a disproportionate part. Law is that which results from the *appetitus socialis*. Morality has little to do with sociality; it rather represents normative judgments concerning the worth or worthlessness of things.[5] Furthermore, like Suarez, Grotius did not regard the *debitum ex pietate* as a *debitum iustum,* since it is neither subject to an action at law nor enforceable. Again, as among the Greeks and Scholastics, the ancient conception of justice as virtue itself is found in his writings. Thus the *ius naturale* comprises the whole of natural ethics.

It was unfortunate for Grotius that he gave little or no heed to the circumstances which the Scholastics had always stressed: the circumstances and conditions which in the case of the affirmative precepts of the *ius naturae* determine the application of a norm that in itself is unchangeable. (Suarez says, for instance, that obedience to the state in time of war takes precedence over the natural-law duty of a son to care for his parents.) The Scholastics had held that only the first principle of the natural law is clearly evident, and that at most the immediate

5. But see A.-H. Chroust, *op cit.,* pp. 131–33.

conclusions (the Decalogue) share in such evidence, which, however, may yet be obscured by the passions. On this ground they had acknowledged the necessity of positive law, whose function, they contended, is to enlighten us on the good to be done and by penal sanctions to restrain us, dominated as we are by our passions, from the evil to be avoided. But Grotius was a rationalist. He believed it possible to derive by strict logic a suitable system of rational law having force that would be great enough to bind the will: a body of law with detailed prescriptions covering debts and property, the family institution and inheritance. The Scholastics, on the other hand, considered only the general institutions themselves of marriage, property, and contract as belonging to natural law, not the particular prescriptions about marriage and the family, possession and the form of private ownership, and the like.

Grotius' undying merit was his systematizing of international law, which he placed upon the solid foundations provided by natural law. Grotius, who paid homage to his predecessors, to Vittoria and Suarez among others, lived in an age of fierce wars. The *civitas christiana* was being rent asunder in its great civil war (Thirty Years' War, 1618–48), which, like all civil wars, was being fought with enormous cruelty and frequently outside the pale of legal norms. In the midst of all this, however, he put forward with great power and impressiveness, cogently and systematically, the idea of the rule of law even in wartime. He thereby revived the intellectual unity of the West, after its religious unity had been rent, by means of the great traditions of the very Christianity which had always honored reason. Thus he substituted intellectual solidarity based upon reason for solidarity based upon a now divided faith.

Yet it must be said that Grotius, precisely because of such rationalism, was not so happy in his treatment of the *ius gentium* as were the Late Scholastics. The clear separation between the natural-law contents and positive contents of the *ius gentium,* as occurs in Suarez' treatment, was, at the hands of Grotius, again partly lost. The path was thus cleared for Pufendorf's equation of *ius naturale* and *ius gentium.*

Grotius thus stood in the twilight between two great epochs. Still linked by many ties to the preceding age, he yet served to transmit to the natural-law theory of the modern period its distinguishing marks:

rationalism, sociality, and particular political aims. In all this he resembled Descartes, whose close connection with the epistemology and metaphysics of Late Scholasticism has been uncovered by recent research. Nature makes no leaps: this axiom is valid also in the history of thought. Historians of philosophy, unfortunately, sometimes mistake emphasis for novelty.

CHAPTER IV

The Natural Law in the Age of Individualism and Rationalism

The so-called age of natural law did not, properly speaking, commence with Hugo Grotius. It began rather with Pufendorf, who undertook to expound the doctrine of Grotius. The net result of the age was a disastrous setback, from the opening of the nineteenth century, for the natural-law idea among the modern philosophers and practitioners of law who were unacquainted with the older Christian tradition.

The new natural law differed in many respects from the traditional one. It represented a peculiar hypertrophy of the older conception. Numerous factors were responsible for this development, and they arose from the intellectual evolution and political circumstances of the period.

Humanism had declined, and with it had gone exaggerated esteem for antiquity in general and, in particular, for Roman law as *ratio scripta*. Roman law, in its degenerate form of *usus modernus* and with its many archaic-sounding formulas, could not satisfy this age of reason.

Deism in theology led to a high regard for the element of law in nature. It led also to an abhorrence of all sorcery, of belief in demons, of any supposed mystical influence of the transcendent Deity upon a world that moves in accordance with unalterable laws. A real enlightenment was declared necessary for a clear knowledge of the laws. Not faith, however, but reason was to provide such enlightenment. For the law lies in reason, and speculative reason is able to derive from itself, from contemplation of its own abstract nature, all laws, all morality, and all right in the form of axioms. Indeed this holds good even if there be no God, who thenceforth appears as merely the ultimate source of morality and law (apart from the continuation of tradition at the hands, for instance, of Leibnitz and the theologians). Whole systems of ethics and law were now worked out in minute detail by scholars who were carried away by a veritable passion for speculation. Such speculation also differed considerably from the prevailing inferior law which still recognized sorcery, belief in demons, and things of a mystical nature.

Furthermore, a jurisprudence adapted to the needs of the administrative machinery of the centralized absolute monarchy seemed, at least in the eyes of the rationalists, out of the question on the basis of the existing law. For this law was split up according to provinces and estates or social classes. Besides, its feudal forms had been rendered antiquated by the rise and growth of capitalism; it had also become rigid and unsuited to the time in the case of privileged guilds, not to mention the monstrosity of imperial law which no less a person than Pufendorf had so thoroughly ridiculed in a work, *De statu imperii,* that appeared under a pseudonym.

The thesis of the autonomy of human reason, as well as the view that the existing law constituted unwarranted fetters, was closely bound up with the nascent socio-philosophical individualism of the age. The clearest manifestation of this individualistic bent is found in the doctrine of the state of nature, which now became the starting point of natural-law speculation after having been in the Middle Ages but a condition of mankind with theological significance alone. (The difference may be schematized thus: the natural law as the idea of law in and above the necessary positive law—the natural law as law of the state of nature before and above the positive law.)

From the same source stemmed the peculiar methodological starting point of all these systems of natural law. Thinkers did not set out, as in the earlier period, from the essentially social nature of man in which the entire order of social institutions (marriage, family, state, international community) and the basic norms of these exist potentially in such a way that the essence is fulfilled only in the completion and hierarchical ordering of social forms through the various "imperfect" societies up to the "perfect" society. The point of departure was empirical nature discovered by means of abstraction, from whose psychological motive force, viewed as fundamental, the system of ethics and of natural law was deduced in a rationalistic manner. For Hobbes this was selfishness; for Pufendorf, sociableness as mere formal sociality; for Thomasius, happiness, i.e., "praiseworthy, pleasant, carefree life."

In this way a whole detailed system of natural law was in existence, or was considered to have been in force, before social life, with its essential forms and with the historically contingent particularities of such forms, had worked itself out in history, i.e., had evolved after the manner of an entelechy. This natural law was held to cover the civil law of contracts, the family, inheritance, and property; it was even made to include procedural law and especially constitutional law. Surrounded with the halo of naturalness and reasonableness, the various natural-law systems accordingly signified, in respect to existing conditions that cried out for reform, an ideal which the codifications of the close of the eighteenth century sought to realize, whether in a revolutionary (Rousseau) or conservative (Hobbes) or reformist manner (enlightened despotism). With all this was now readily combined the ancient Stoic glorification of the pre-political state of mankind, except where this condition was construed by Hobbes, as already indeed by Epicurus, as a war of all against all.

To these favorable factors of an ideal order corresponded practical ones that were no less favorable. The Enlightenment was first of all an affair of the ruling class, the nobility and the intellectuals of the age, clerics and men of science. The latter, however, were encouraged by the princes precisely because and so far as these recognized their function of governing as a duty. Enlightened despotism, to use the label current in resentful liberal circles, was a great patron of the natural law or, as it henceforth was usually and quite significantly styled, the law of reason. For this law placed in the hands of the princes the weapons with which to break down the class privileges of the nobility, and perhaps of the guilds and provincial estates as well, which hampered the uniform administration of the state. Furthermore the Enlightenment with its accent on education assigned to the state the task, through the agency of the police, of educating the citizen and of making the state wealthy in the mercantilist sense.

Thus this individualistic natural law was especially adapted to loosen the traditional, hardened social order and to furnish the princes with subjects, not, of course, as mere objects of arbitrary will, but as legal subjects with innate subjective rights. They were then, as objects of education, admirably suited to the higher idea of man that was proper to the Enlightenment. If, therefore, the individualistic root of this natural law was everywhere the same, this was in no way the case regarding the liberalist consequences which resulted from it when deeper thought was given to the matter. These consequences appeared in Rousseau's system and in the French Revolution, as well as in the natural-law doctrines of Locke and of early German liberalism: what was desired was a bourgeois natural law. They were wanting, however, both in Hobbes' doctrine and in the natural-law systems of Pufendorf and Thomasius.

Closely connected with this political consequence, whether of the police-state with its educational function or of the liberal state with its restricted function of guaranteeing individual liberty, was a further break with tradition on natural-law grounds. This newer natural law constituted the first attempt to construct a lay or secularist theory of ethics and politics. Hobbes' purpose in devising his doctrine of natural law was admittedly the destruction of independent ecclesiastical law. His aim was to subordinate the latter to, and incorporate it in, the natural law of the omnipotent and sole person of the state represented by the monarch. Enlightened despotism likewise held the view that the Church, though indeed of importance sociologically and practically, was but a division of the cultural and educational department of the absolute monarchy. The peculiar totalitarian character of the *ius naturae* of that period, identical as it was with moral philosophy, was the means adopted for forcing the Church into the service of the state.

Moreover, rationalism and the Enlightenment had rendered the old, mystical foundation, which had emerged from the semiobscurity of immediate divine origin, incapable of supporting the state and royal power. Now, however, the doctrine of a state of nature together with the various contract theories concerning the transition to the *status civilis* afforded a new basis, though an insecure and perilous one. The same intellectual device served Hobbes for laying the foundation of state absolutism; it served Pufendorf for laying the foundation of enlightened despotism, which denied the ancient, traditional right of the people to resist; and it served Rousseau for laying the foundation of the sole admissible omnipotence of the democratic state. The French revolutionaries also made use of it for reducing state functions to a minimum; for establishing the rights, acknowledged also on other grounds, of man and of the citizen; and for vindicating the right to resist the power of the state (Constitutions of 1792 and 1793). "The tamest and lamest theories, no less than the preaching of world betterment through the guillotine and the French wars of conquest, were carried out in the name of the law of reason. Natural law was an intellectual trend, not a uniformly expounded doctrine" (Pfaff and Hoffmann).

For social reformers, that is, for enlightened despots and for social revolutionaries like Rousseau, this magnified natural law based on individualism thus became the starting point. It was set down in constitutions as fundamental law. In the comprehensive codifications of the time it served to break down the organization of society by estates and to build up the modern bourgeois social order. As a special science, however, or as a general conviction, it thereupon vanished just as quickly. This outcome was caused either by the achievement of such eminently political aims of a natural law with reformist or revolutionary overtones; or by the fact that after the climactic orgy of 1793–96 the goddess Reason was deposed and History (Haller, De Maistre, Donoso Cortes) or rather Providence, working in history and discernible in its activity, was again enthroned.

What differentiated this newer natural law from the *ius naturale perenne* were not of course its political aims alone; these were merely more conspicuous. The essential distinguishing mark was the importance of the doctrine of the state of nature, which attained, as in Defoe's *Robinson Crusoe* (1719), such unexpected and widespread popularity. Thence stemmed the pregnant ideas of liberty and equality. And fully in keeping with it was also the comprehensive moral philosophy of deism, which concealed itself under the title of *ius naturale* and, after first disregarding the eternal law, finally culminated in the complete moral autonomy of reason (Kant).

The individualist starting point led also to a failure to recognize the necessary forms of social life. If the past had looked upon these as, so to speak, germinally contained in the idea of man, they could now, from the standpoint of the free individual, be regarded only as *status adventicii*, as superadded for various, nonessential reasons: sociality, utility, or mere external perfection. In view of the original freedom, they could no longer be acknowledged as intrinsically necessary; in their contents as well as in their existence they must be founded solely upon free association, upon the free contracts of individuals. For this type of natural law the contractual form is the basis not only for the coming into existence of concrete social forms, but also for their normative contents. The essence of social forms is not something objective; it is rather, like their existence, dependent upon the will of individuals. For the individualist doctrine there exists, as has already been stated, no categorical or a priori sociality of man as such, but only a pure sociability. In keeping with this view was a political theory that manifested itself in the two extremes of Hobbes' omnipotent monarchy and Rousseau's omnipotent democracy: the princely police-state with a maximum of functions and the constitutional state of 1789 and later with a minimum of functions. Individual rights belonging to the state of nature were viewed either as definitively surrendered in the political and governmental contract (Hobbes), or as inviolable and hence to be brought over intact into the *status civilis*.

These natural-law doctrines displayed little understanding of the graduated order of the forms of social life that resides in the nature of man as a social animal. They showed no appreciation for the family as a social institution with an essential end of its own (they dealt only with marriage and the parental relationship). They showed no concern for the occupational-group or corporative structure, hence for the multifarious social forms that in all domains of life lie between the state and the individual. They showed no regard for the well-known principle of subsidiarity, according to which the highest community, the state, should leave to other associations the functions and ends which these should and can fulfill. They knew, in effect, only the harsh antithesis of individual and state. They likewise lacked an understanding of the particular nature of the Church as a "perfect" society: it became either a department of the state or a spiritual free fellowship, not an institution.

These specific types of the newer natural law, so varied in their consequences, manifested themselves most clearly in Hobbes, with his pessimistic view of man; in Rousseau, who took an optimistic view of human nature; in Pufendorf and Thomasius, who lived in the shadow of enlightened despotism; and, finally, to say nothing of the numerous mixed forms, in Kant.

It was here that the definite break with tradition took place. From the time of Pufendorf fun began to be poked at the "fancies of the Scholastics." From here on, an anti-Aristotelian nominalism became, expressly or tacitly, the basis of philosophy. And it is permissible to believe that this disdain for tradition was later avenged when, in the nineteenth century, this natural-law thinking came in turn to be disparaged. Indeed, the same failure to understand tradition then led the nineteenth century to assume that, by refuting this natural-law doctrine of the seventeenth and eighteenth centuries, it had overthrown the natural law itself with its philosophical tradition of over two thousand years.

The entire theory of Thomas Hobbes (1588–1679) amounts at bottom to a denial of the natural law. The English thinker, who stands forth as a gloomy fellow-traveler of Epicurus, the cheerful ancient, pictured the state of nature as a savage, lawless condition of war of all against all, as chaos. Here we have another illustration of the relationship that exists between epistemology and moral philosophy. Hobbes, the nominalist of Occam's school, held that reason is utterly unable to know universals, i.e., ideas. Words denoting universal concepts are mere names. Reason finds itself obliged to devise and assign them arbitrarily, without any foundation in fact and reality, for the purpose of introducing order into the chaos of sense impressions. In moral philosophy, too, the passions hold first place. Man in the depths of his being is what the state of nature shows him to be: a wolf, wicked, devoted solely to self. In the state of nature, consequently, there exist only lawless individuals, in whom is found no natural tendency to live in society; and man's life is "solitary, poore, nasty, brutish, and short."[1] The war of all against all is the reverse side of the widely cherished and taught right of all to all things. In reality, no law of the *status naturalis* exists, as we find it in the dreams of Rousseau and in the fanciful deductions of Pufendorf and many of his disciples.

The same selfishness and the dictates of right reason, that is, the consideration of one's greater advantage and of peace, determine the individuals to enter by way of a covenant into the *status civilis* and to give up as many of their rights to everything as may make peace possible. But, that peace may be possible, all contracting parties must yield their rights to the Sovereign, the state personified, whether this be organized through the covenant in a monarchical manner or in a more or less democratic manner; either form is admissible, according to Hobbes.[2]

1. Thomas Hobbes, *Leviathan, or the Matter, Forme & Power of a Commonwealth, Ecclesiasticall and Civill,* ed. by A. R. Waller (Cambridge: The University Press, 1904), Part I, chap. 13.

2. Hobbes argues as follows: Whereas the agreement of irrational creatures is natural, "that of men, is by Covenant only, which is Artificiall: and therefore it is no wonder if there be somwhat else required (besides Covenant) to make their Agreement constant and lasting; which is a Common Power, to keep them in awe, and to direct their actions to the Common Benefit.

"The only way to erect such a Common Power, as may be able to define them from the invasion of Forraigners, and the injuries of one another, and thereby to secure them in such sort, as that by their owne industrie, and by the fruites of the Earth, they may nourish themselves and live contentedly; is, to conferre all their power and strength upon one Man, or upon one Assembly of men, that may reduce all their Wills, by plurality of voices, unto one Will: which is as much as to say, to appoint one Man, or Assembly of men, to beare their Person; and every one to owne, and acknowledge himselfe to be Author of whatsoever he that so beareth their Person, shall Act, or cause to be Acted, in those things which concerne the Common Peace and Safetie; and therein to submit their Wills, every one to his Will, and their Judgements, to his Judgment. This is more than Consent, or Concord; it is a reall Unitie of them all, in one and the same Person, made by Covenant of every man with every man, in such manner, as if every man should say to every man, *I Authorise and give up my Right of Governing my selfe, to this Man, or to this Assembly of men, on this condition, that thou give up thy Right to him, and Authorise all his Actions in like manner.* This done, the Multitude so united in one Person, is called a COMMON-WEALTH, in latine CIVITAS. This is the Generation of that great LEVIATHAN, or rather (to speake more reverently) of that *Mortall God,* to which wee owe under the *Immortall God,* our peace and defence. For by this Authoritie, given him by every particular man in the Common-Wealth, he hath the use of so much Power and Strength conferred on him,

Moreover, properly speaking, only this covenant, which springs from the basic natural-law norm of self-preservation, is natural law. For Hobbes, then, the natural law, despite all the formulas he adopts and cites from time to time, is wholly comprised in the axiom, "Agreements must be kept." Upon this fundamental principle is based the will of the omnipotent state, so that henceforward all law is but public authority; it is but the positive law of the state, inclusive of Church law. The political aim of the Hobbesian natural law, the ideological justification of absolute government (especially of the Stuart kings), becomes exceedingly plain here. Hobbes, whose individualism led him to insist that contract affords the sole possible basis of rights, derived from the principle that agreements must be kept even a son's duty to obey his father, and so on. The reckless rationalism of the man found expression both here and in his demand that in speculation one must start by viewing men as beings that have shot forth from the earth like mushrooms, as at once full-grown.[3] From his individualism sprang likewise his antagonism toward corporative organizations like the guilds and other self-governing economic and social groups. As sharers in the absolute power of the sovereign or limitations upon it, he considered such bodies directly opposed to the natural law: they are "like wormes in the entrayles of a naturall man."[4]

In the hands of Hobbes, therefore, the natural law became, paradoxically enough, a useless law, compressed into the single legal form of

---

that by terror thereof, he is inabled to forme the wills of them all, to Peace at home, and mutuall ayd against their enemies abroad. And in him consisteth the Essence of the Common-wealth; which (to define it,) is *One Person, of whose Acts a great Multitude, by mutuall Covenants one with another, have made themselves every one the Author, to the end he may use the strength and means of them all, as he shall think expedient, for their Peace and Common Defence.*

"And he that carryeth this Person, is called SOVERAIGNE, and said to have *Soveraigne Power;* and every one besides, his SUBJECT" (*Leviathan,* Part II, chap. 17).

3. Because of his clarity and pungency of style (not to mention his "scientific" materialism), George H. Sabine regards Hobbes as "probably the greatest writer on political philosophy that the English-speaking peoples have produced" (*A History of Political Theory,* p. 457). On Hobbes' political philosophy, cf. especially J. Vialatoux, *La cité de Hobbes. Théorie de l'état totalitaire* (Paris: J. Gabalda et Compagnie, 1935).

4. *Leviathan,* Part II, chap. 29.

the social and governmental contract of subjection. The natural law effectively comprises only the basic norm, "agreements must be kept," if one disregards the still more paradoxical natural law of the state of nature with its norm of selfishness. All else is pure will. Hobbes' doctrine is the theodicy of Occam secularized, and the extreme consequence of the proposition that law is will.

Thus Hobbes altered the meaning of the words "nature" and "natural," a process that characterizes the entire period of modern philosophy from the time of Descartes. "Nature" and "natural" become the opposite of *civitas*, "reason," and "order." In the philosophy of Hobbes and Baruch Spinoza (1632–77) human nature is at bottom governed by the passions and not by reason. The *status naturalis* is a condition without any obligation or duty. It is a state in which, as Spinoza repeatedly asserts, might is right. This natural state of man is ruled by two things: fear of the might of others and power to instill fear into others. Hobbes denied that man has a natural inclination toward mutual help and love, which St. Thomas speaks of so frequently. Hence law and the order of law cannot be derived from human nature; they become the work of the sovereign. What remains of the older conception of human nature as the source of natural law is the contention that the state originated in the fear of violent death and in the urge to render life and property secure. The state, together with its law which has its source in the absolute will of the sovereign, is the savior of man from the natural law of "might is right"; it affords security and protection by monopolizing all power; and it demands as a price strict obedience and subordination through identification of natural law with positive law.

The older idea of natural law as an ethical system with material contents thus loses all its functions: namely, to serve as a moral basis for positive law; to give men a standard and critical norm for the justice of positive law; to represent the eternal ideal for which the historical state, as lawgiver and protector of justice, ought to strive. As a consequence the state, unlimited because even the revealed divine law is authoritatively interpreted by it, becomes, in Hobbes' phrase, the "Mortall God." No appeal from this all-powerful being to natural law is possible, because the state is law in all its plenitude. In reading Hobbes we can feel the solemnity with which he invests the state, the sovereign power, a solemnity which earlier centuries reserved for God Almighty. What Hegel later says of the idea of the state, Hobbes, the nominalist denier of ideas, asserted of the individual historical state. The consequence of this change in the meaning of "nature" is thus clear. Since nature is bad, and since the *status naturalis* is a condition of "warre of every man against every man,"[5] the state becomes good, and its positive will becomes the supreme norm of justice, admitting of no appeal. The phrase "Mortall God" is to be taken literally, not as a mere figure of speech.

The philosophy of René Descartes underlay another shift in the meaning of human nature. From this shift sprang, as from its source, the individualist and starkly rationalist strains of the newer natural law. According to St. Thomas, it is, properly speaking, neither the intellect nor the senses that understand, but man through both; the natural law is a participation in the eternal law; and the moral law is objectively "given" in human nature and in the essential order of things. For Descartes, on the other hand, man is a *res cogitans,* a being that thinks. It has indeed been pointed out by Jacques Maritain that Descartes gives man the intellectual power of an angel, that his is an angelic epistemology. Descartes holds that man, from his innate ideas, from the ideas present in his consciousness, can construct the world along the lines of mathematical reasoning, the ideal of science. All that man needs to do is constructively to develop what is in human reason, that is, the innate ideas. The individual intellect or reason thus becomes self-sufficient. It does not need the educative cooperation of other minds. Thus the very spiritual root of sociability is denied. Through his "angelism," therefore, Descartes became the father of the individualist conception of human nature.[6]

But this is not all. The doctrine of the *res cogitans,* of self-sufficient human reason that has now become the nature of man, led to a passion

5. *Ibid.,* Part I, chap. 13.
6. Cf. Jacques Maritain, *Three Reformers. Luther-Descartes-Rousseau* (New York: Charles Scribner's Sons, 1929), pp. 54 ff.

for systematic constructions so typical of rationalism. According to St. Thomas, human reason was never the criterion of truth. The *ordo rerum*, of which man's nature is a part, is the measure of man's knowledge. Things themselves, as objective data, measure the human mind. But the angelic qualities of Descartes' *res cogitans*, as well as the view that all truth exists germinally in the mind, render the objective *ordo rerum* superfluous. Suarez' prediction of what would happen should human reason be made the source of the natural law now came true. Rationalism soon made human reason and its innate ideas the measure of what is. Human reason could now indulge in the uncontrolled construction of systems that has ever characterized the natural law of rationalism.

This process reached its climax in Kant. Human reason now becomes the sovereign architect of the order of knowledge; it becomes the measure of things. The objective basis of natural law, the *ordo rerum* and the eternal law, has vanished. What was termed natural law is a series of conclusions drawn from the categorical imperative and from the regulative ideas of practical reason, not from the objective and constitutive *ordo rerum*. These regulative ideas received their somewhat dubious validity from the feeling that without their validity human moral life would be impossible. The ensuing materialism, however, proved only too quickly that this argument lacks force, and that man can live, at least when human nature becomes a purely biological entity, without such regulative ideas. What a fall of the angels! At the beginning of the development lay Descartes' "angelism"; at the end emerged materialist naturalism: man the angel became man the higher animal. From a being whose reason is the supreme source of morality man became a powerless agent governed by the conditions of economic production.

John Locke (1632–1704) was as individualist in his social philosophy as was Hobbes, though he rejected Hobbes' glorification of the state as the "Mortall God" and denied that the Leviathan is the exclusive source of law. Although Locke, in opposition to Hobbes and Spinoza, depicts the state of nature as idyllic, as a condition of peace, good will and mutual help, he contends that the state, or rather government, is in practice indispensable. For Hobbes the function of the *status naturalis* and of the idea of natural law is merely to furnish a basis for the institution of the *status civilis* and the positive law, whereupon the natural law disappears. For Locke, on the other hand, the function of the state of nature and of the idea of natural law is to establish as inalienable the rights of the individual. But these rights by no means vanish in the *status civilis;* indeed, the true purpose of the latter is the more perfect preservation and development of such rights. Thus these innate and indefeasible rights of individuals afford an ultimate criterion for judging all acts of the government and all laws of the state. The rights to life, liberty, and estate or property make the law; the law does not create them.

Locke's philosophy of law does not view the law as an objective order of norms out of which individual rights flow by intrinsic necessity; the rights of the individual are prior, and in them originates whatever order exists. Order is consequently the product of contracts between individuals, who are induced by their rather selfish interests to enter into these contractual relations. The *status civilis* is thus not the objective result of man's social nature itself: it is not a realization, through man's moral actions, of the natural order in the universe. The state is the utilitarian product of individual self-interest, cloaked in the solemn and venerable language of the traditional philosophy of natural law. Locke substitutes for the traditional idea of the natural law as an order of human affairs, as a moral reflex of the metaphysical order of the universe revealed to human reason in the creation as God's will, the conception of natural law as a rather nominalistic symbol for a catalogue or bundle of individual rights that stem from individual self-interest. Any order of law is accordingly the product of the contractual will of the individuals concerned, and it has for its object the protection and promotion of individual self-interest. The characteristic note of individualism (the preponderance of commutative justice and of self-interest over distributive and legal justice and the common good) is obvious in Locke's thinking.

The hidden root of this position is, of course, an overconfidence, born of optimism, in the typically individualist presumption that the common good is nothing real, that it is merely the sum of the particular goods or interests of individuals. If this is true, the free pursuit of self-interest on the part of individuals who are restricted only by the like freedom of others must work like the "invisible hand" of Adam Smith and produce, as it were automatically, a sort of social harmony.

The concept of natural law had thus degenerated from an objective metaphysical idea into a political theory which sought to justify and promote definite political changes. But the uselessness of such a degenerate concept, once these political changes had been effected and consolidated, is evident. The idea of natural law, once the eternal objective norm of all social life, served Hobbes as a means of establishing the absolute rule of the state as the "Mortall God." It served Locke as a means of vindicating the "Glorious Revolution" of 1688–89 and of laying the juridical foundations of bourgeois society. It served rationalism as a means of promoting the codifications of law at the hands of princely absolutism, which was the destroyer of feudalism and medieval constitutionalism, and hence as a means of strengthening the bases of bourgeois society.

But Locke's empiricism in epistemology undermined the philosophical bases of the natural law at least as much as this political theory endangered its very idea. Thus Locke prepared the way for the destructive criticism of Hume and Bentham. Basically a skeptic in metaphysics, Locke could not attain to certainty in moral philosophy, a prolongation of metaphysics. His moral philosophy, had he ever worked it out, would have ended in a barren utilitarianism of the Benthamite type. But Locke, quite unaware of the implications of epistemological empiricism and oblivious of the consequences of his skepticism concerning metaphysics as the basis of any valid theory of natural law, contented himself with a belief in natural law as a dictate of common sense. His feeling for political realities, as well as the fact that the English common law retained many of the traditional concepts of the natural law, prevented him from drawing the conclusions to which Hume's acid criticism would later lead. In Locke, therefore, we have an excellent example of the revenge which common sense so frequently takes upon empiricists and philosophical skeptics. Locke allowed his common sense to affirm in practice what his philosophy implicitly denied. In this he was like Karl Marx, the most typical instance of such behavior. Marx was wholly intent upon destroying, as a merely instrumental ideology, the ideas of justice and truth. Yet at the same time he thundered like an Old Testament prophet against the injustices and deceits of bourgeois society and philosophy. He thereby implicitly affirmed justice and truth as objective and transcendent, and not as merely relative to and immanent in the conditions of socio-economic production.

The doctrine of Jean Jacques Rousseau (1712–78) stands almost diametrically opposed to Hobbes and his conception of the natural law. Hobbes' theory glorifying absolutism had aroused a strong reaction. Although this reaction, led by such thinkers as Locke, Montesquieu, and Hume, did not go so far as democracy, it was transforming the freedom of subjects in the unlimited monarchy into constitutionally guaranteed natural rights (power checks power and creates the condition of freedom). This line of thought attained its harshest expression in Rousseau.

Whereas for Hobbes the state of nature was a "warre of every man against every man," the Geneva dreamer preached a state of nature that resembled the biblical Paradise. For Hobbes the state, the legal order, and consequently goodness, are, in the interest of mere order, the goal of an historical philosophical movement that wishes to be rid of nature, of the *status naturalis,* and to attain to the *status civilis* in which the ruinous liberty of human wolves comes to an end. For Rousseau, on the contrary, the *status civilis* and the objective, enforced order of unfreedom in the state constitute precisely the condition of corrupt human nature, whereas the state of nature is, taking an optimistic view of man's nature, exactly what it ought to be. "Back to nature" was, in Rousseau's teaching, something more than a game played by a bored and snobbish nobility. Civilization, in the literal sense of becoming a *civis* (citizen), only then does not spell ruin when the original, natural rights of liberty and equality form the essential reservations of the social contract. Men do not have to enter into the social contract. They enter into it freely; they are driven by no mysterious impulse out of the war of all against all into the enforced peace of absolutism. But they can enter into it because it is their will, the will of everyone in the general will that now comes into being.

At bottom, for Rousseau the historical *status civilis* is the world after man's fall, whereas the *status naturalis* was the garden of Eden. Consequently, the state as such, as *ordo rerum humanarum,* is not a necessary, ethical institution; it is but the minister of human rights. It is for this reason that the right of revolution exists, if natural rights are violated by the positive law. Rousseau's fanatical passion for liberty, virtue, and right lived on in the men responsible for the Reign of Terror of 1793–94, in men like Robespierre. The highly emotional way Rousseau treated of liberty and man's unalterable rights accomplished more in this respect than the specific doctrinal passages of his books. Besides, he had less influence upon the thought of the age of natural law, upon the countless treatises of *ius naturae et gentium,* than upon the publicists and political writers of the time.

The era of natural law as a homogeneous epoch in the history of ideas was determined far more by the jurists and philosophers and their systems than by Rousseau's emotional philosophizings that were becoming the daily reading matter of the educated classes. Therefore the historical school of law directed its attacks chiefly against the former, whereas the conservative school and the writers inspired by the romantic movement (e.g., Burke, De Maistre, De Bonald, Goerres, Arndt) were more concerned with refuting Rousseau.

This period, celebrated in the history of ideas and of science as par excellence the age of natural law, is chiefly associated with the names of Pufendorf, Thomasius, and Kant. Side by side with these, however, innumerable scholars of lesser renown were active in the professorial chairs established at that time for the *ius naturae et gentium.* They were filling the libraries of educated people, government officials, and judges with numberless systematic but conflicting expositions of natural law. With few exceptions (e.g., Wolff, Zallinger, Schwarz) these men claimed that they were the first to discover the natural law or to free it from the fancies and verbiage of the Scholastics. It was precisely this break with tradition that was responsible for the confounding of this doctrine of natural law with the perennial idea of the natural law. So it was, then, that the nineteenth century could believe that, with the refutation of this doctrine, the natural law itself had been proved a chimera. This was an extremely fateful fact in the history of the philosophy of law as well as in the history of philosophy in general. Or was it not fateful that Pufendorf was well acquainted with scarcely a single Greek or Scholastic, and that Kant, the watershed from which flow so many and such varied streams of modern thought, knew Aristotle and St. Thomas only from a very imperfect history of philosophy?

The decisive differences between this newer natural law and that of the Scholastics are three in number. The first is the individualistic trait manifesting itself in the predominance of the doctrine of the state of nature as the proper place in which to find the natural law. The second is the nominalist attitude which found expression in the separation of eternal law and natural moral law, of God's essence and existence, of morality and law. The third is the resultant doctrine of the autonomy of human reason which, in conjunction with the rationalism of this school, led straight to an extravagance of syllogistic reasoning, of deductively constructed systems that served to regulate all legal institutions down to the minutest detail: the civil law governing debts, property, the family, and inheritances as well as constitutional and international law. And, in contrast with the imperfect historical law, these legal systems possessed the inestimable merit and value of emanating from the pure rational nature of man.

These differences especially characterized the leading figures of the new school of natural law, Pufendorf and Thomasius. The latter was particularly concerned with separating morality and law. He thereby stands out in the history of philosophy as a precursor of Kant.

Samuel von Pufendorf (1632–94), in his concept of man's nature, did not take man in his teleologically determined totality of human nature. Man is not essentially social, so that, as earlier thinkers had held, the essential forms of community living evolve by inherent necessity out of his natural tendency for society. On the contrary, he should develop sociality because it is of advantage to him. Man is an *animal sociabile,* not *sociale.* What had for earlier thinkers been but a sign of man's internal and natural tendency, a realization of his nature itself in time, became in the newer natural law mere capability, mere impulse. Accordingly, empirical nature and any impulse or capacity whatever (sociality or, as in the case of Thomasius, felicity) formed the starting point of speculation. The presupposition of such natural-law thinking is the individual as an isolated being in the state of nature, hence abstracting from the essential forms of human nature as such that find expression in the historical forms of state, law, marriage, and family. Wherefore Pufendorf proceeded to set forth how man in the original state of nature, abstracting from the historical *status civilis,* from positive law and from the legal order, has as an individual to behave toward God, toward himself, and toward his fellow men.

Pufendorf first draws up a list of duties toward God, i.e., principles of natural religion, and then, in a most exhaustive fashion, a catalogue of duties toward oneself and toward others. Such duties toward others are, for instance, that everyone must keep his word, must not swear falsely, must be sincere in speech. He shows what norms for the acquisition and use of property, for marriage, the family, and inheritance, can and must be deduced from reason alone. He describes the procedural law in the state of nature, and he indicates the norms of distraint which must find application in that state. Thus in reality the entire positive law, so far as it has to do with the civil law and its procedure in lawsuits, is straightway transformed into natural law. It logically becomes suprahistorical or prehistorical (in Pufendorf's case) and in itself unalterable. But the *status civilis* is a superadded *status* with laws that in final analysis are only formal.

Because of its revolutionary possibilities, however, the basically critical attitude shifted at once to a conservative one: the existing law is in itself good, and is merely in need of reform. The law of the state of nature is an ideal law, a model law; it is not a law that is actually in force. This follows from the determination of the relationship between positive law and natural law. The former is needed on account of the sinful propensities of men, who cannot adequately be kept in order through mere knowledge of the natural law and solely out of reverence for it. Hence the public authorities enact positive laws in order that the natural law may be observed. As soon, then, as the state is founded as *status adventicius* in virtue of the original contract, and as soon as a sovereign authority is set up by means of the governmental contract, man must comply with the positive laws by reason of the fundamental principle of natural law, "agreements must be kept." The distinction between the prescriptions which pertain to the prohibitive and directly binding natural law and the further norms of the hypothetical natural law (the *ius naturale permissivum* of the older writers) made it possible for Pufendorf to explain all positive laws as hypothetical natural law. In this way the whole body of concrete civil laws (the laws concerning debt, property, the family, and inheritance, in particular the modes of acquiring ownership, conveyance by will and succession, the monetary system and contracts involving monetary considerations), i.e., the entire contents of those positive laws which were viewed as necessary, became natural law. The preceding age, on the other hand, had conceded to only a few basic norms (Decalogue) the dignity and grandeur of natural law.

Pufendorf's theory of international law throws light on his doctrine of natural law. Princes and states live in the *status naturalis,* since no *status adventicius,* no *civitas maxima,* as yet exists. Hence international law consists merely of natural law. There is no positive international law because there is no sovereign authority. Measured by the contributions of Grotius and the Late Scholastics, this view marks a great stride backward along the path which Hobbes had already taken.

Those of his contemporaries who had not succumbed to the rationalist temper of the period charged Pufendorf with being "not much of a jurist, and a philosopher not at all" (Leibnitz) and with having totally abandoned tradition.[7] As a matter of fact, Pufendorf had never understood the traditional view that moral philosophy with its partial content, the *ius naturale,* is a continuation of metaphysics, the science of being, which, when applied to the free will of rational man, becomes the science of oughtness. But his unrestrained and unhistorical rationalism arises precisely from this fact. The doctrine of the eternal law he had never grasped. It is true that he encumbers his writings with formulas culled from his readings. Yet they have there a different meaning, because they are torn from their proper intellectual setting. The *ius naturale,* therefore, is not related to God's essence as a participation of the eternal law. It is rather, in typically nominalist fashion, placed in

7. Cf. A.-H. Chroust, "Hugo Grotius and the Scholastic Natural Law Tradition," *The New Scholasticism,* XVII (1943), 122–25.

God's will. It has to do with the external order of sociability as an actual fact. It is in force because God has so willed to create man; it was not in force, it did not exist, when man did not as yet exist. It is thus not a participation in the divine law, eternally present in God's essence. It is "eternal" only so far as it is of the same age as man; hence it has only been in force since man has been in existence, since God created him. This position is diametrically opposed to the view of Arriaga and Grotius, that the natural law would still possess some validity even if there were no God.

This position, however, formed the basis of extreme rationalism. For henceforth not God's essence, but human nature, viewed existentially as well as merely in the abstract, would be regarded as the source of natural law. Thence also originated the abstruse intellectual sport of a logically deduced law for man in the state of nature, as well as the widespread unhistorical attitude and the inability to comprehend Aristotle's everlastingly true proposition, that outside the state (not society) man is either a beast or a god. For this line of thinkers the idea of law does not live in the historical legal systems, nor was the eternally valid natural moral law recognized as the essential norm from its exemplification in the legal forms. Rather, the natural law was derived from a purely imaginary state of nature, or from a state of nature that was supposed to have once existed (theoretically and without regard for concrete historical exemplifications). In practice, indeed, the improvements and reforms of the historical positive legislation that were deemed good, useful, and necessary assumed the guise of natural law. That explains the significant politico-legal function of this brand of natural-law philosophy of the Enlightenment.

At the hands of Christian Thomasius (1655–1728) the sociality of Pufendorf received a utilitarian interpretation. The aim of ethics is mastery of the passions, because these endanger the temporal happiness, i.e., the peaceful existence, of the individual. The supreme, central principle is therefore this: "Whatever renders the life of men long and happy is to be done, but whatever makes life unhappy and hastens death is to be avoided." It is no longer sociality or an *appetitus socialis* that is the source of natural law, but rather, after the manner typical of the Enlightenment, it is the happiness of the individual. Instead, the forms of community life appear as mere *status adventicii*, not as essential perfections of man. Happiness consists in a pleasant, carefree life; and evidently it is attainable only through a virtuous, respectable, and just life. A man should live virtuously in order to preserve inner peace; respectably, in order that others may come to his assistance; justly, lest others be provoked and external peace be disturbed. Law is therefore something external and is unrelated to the *honestum*, to the morally good. It produces only external obligations, whereas morality produces only internal ones. Legal duties are enforceable duties; moral duties are subject to compulsion solely through one's own conscience.

This conception reacted unfavorably upon the doctrine of the state of nature. The latter was interpreted in a pessimistic sense: legal force can be exerted only by means of self-help and self-defense. Hence the state arose by way of contract, merely out of considerations of individual utility. An external power is a more effective guarantor of external peace than is the individual's right of self-help. Thus the absurdities mount.

The grandiose pessimism of a Hobbes possesses, by comparison, a consistency that is refreshing. Besides, Thomasius also drags in the old formulas, such as that of God as the ultimate foundation of the natural law. For him, however, this merely means that even the natural law owes its existence to God as the Creator of all things. But the ground of its validity is not God's will, since in particular cases we know what God's will is through revelation alone, not by means of natural reason. The principle of the natural law thus remains temporal happiness understood in a highly subjective sense.

The metaphysics of the natural law was by now altogether lost to sight. Deductive, autonomous reason could henceforth, without let or hindrance, evolve natural and detailed systems of law. Into such legal systems were admitted, of course, as unalterable and supreme postulates all those parts of the positive law which the individualistic spirit of the Enlightenment regarded as good, as well as whatever it considered worthy of enactment into law.

In the course of this evolution the individualistic trait grew steadily more pronounced. Pufendorf had already conceived of sociality, not as a category bound up with the nature of man, but as a capacity, a mere potency, a tendency. Marriage, the family, property, and the state are not institutions, derived from natural-law social forms, germinally present in the idea of social animal and proceeding of necessity therefrom (and hence in their essence independent of the will). They were viewed from the standpoint either of the advantage accruing to the individual or of their utility for a happy temporal life taken subjectively. As a consequence, too, it was not the family but marriage "relations" and the relations between parents and children, viewed as relations between individual and individual, that received attention. Such an approach was, of course, incapable of appreciating the position that the institution alone, considered in its essence, possesses natural-law character, whereas the juridical regulation of individual relations can be discovered in various ways from the evolution of society, and the positive law in turn from the whole complex environment; as in the case of paternal authority, forms of ownership, property rights in marriage.

Immanuel Kant (1724–1804) exhibits in his philosophy the individualist natural law in its final, highest form. Among German natural-law thinkers he was the most radical in making freedom of the individual the starting point of his system. Liberty or autonomy is the sole right that belongs originally to every man in virtue of his humanity. Man's innate equality and the entire list of the other primal rights are comprised in it. As the supreme law of right, emerges the formula: "Act externally in such a manner that the free exercise of thy Will may be able to co-exist with the Freedom of all others, according to a universal Law."[8]

This is likewise the basis of Kant's allegedly great achievement: the separation of ethics and law, of morality and legality. That law essentially concerns the external order was, however, a tradition of long standing. Equally ancient was the corresponding view that legal duties are, without any self-contradiction, enforceable by physical means, in contrast to such duties as love, gratitude, and reverence (love of country, for instance, is

8. Immanuel Kant, *The Philosophy of Law. An Exposition of the Fundamental Principles of Jurisprudence as the Science of Right*, Introduction, C, trans. by W. Hastie (Edinburgh: T. & T. Clark, 1887), p. 46. Kant further lays down (p. 45): "Every Action is *right* which in itself, or in the maxim on which it proceeds, is such that it can co-exist along with the Freedom of the Will of each and all in action, according to a universal Law."

unenforceable, whereas obedience to the laws of the state can indeed
be enforced). But both classes had always been conceived as moral
duties. Up to that time there were no merely juridical duties, even
though there existed merely ethical duties, e.g., gratitude. Yet no one
recognized any mutually exclusive opposition between ethical duties
and juridical duties, although people knew how to distinguish them.
Juridical duties are enforceable, and they are enforceable because without
such enforcement there can be no durability to the social order, through
which and in which the idea of man as a social animal finds completion.
Permanence is a special attribute of law. Violation of the law is a
negation of this order. But precisely because this order must exist, the
fulfillment of legal duties is likewise always a moral duty. Consequently
the state is not a pure apparatus for compulsion; it is always a moral
community, too. Moreover, it does not live by law alone, though it
lives in the law; it lives rather by the exercise of all the social virtues.
Accordingly thinkers had in the past always assigned to the state as its
essential task, to render the citizens virtuous.

Despite such accurate discrimination (precisely for the sake of morality as free fulfillment of duty), this inner connection was first torn
asunder by Thomasius in the separation of ethics (equivalent to inner
peace of the individual soul) and law (equivalent to external peace of
society). Kant, on the other hand, replaced inner peace by autonomous
freedom. Inner freedom, the moral autonomy of the individual person,
is the sphere of morality. "A person is subject to no other laws than
those which he (either alone or jointly with others) gives to himself."[9]
External freedom, according to Kant, requires coercive laws; on this
point he found himself in full agreement with tradition. Therefore,
Kant infers, the condition of external freedom (i.e., law) is something
purely external. Morality and law differ not so much by reason of the
diversity of duties (e.g., justice, love of neighbor, filial and parental
love) as because of the disparity of legislation. The motive of moral
legislation is duty, derived from the autonomy of reason and appearing
in the form of the categorical imperative and practically deified by

9. Immanuel Kant, *Introduction to the Metaphysic of Morals*, IV, 24, trans. by T. K.
Abbott, *Kant's Critique of Practical Reason and Other Works on the Theory of Ethics* (6th
ed., London–New York: Longmans, Green and Co., 1927), p. 279.

Kant. The motive of juridical legislation is not morality but the keeping of external freedom, the carrying out of the coercive measures that are necessary thereto. The legal order is devoid of moral character. "Hence ethical legislation cannot be external (not even that of a divine will)."[10] Thus the impersonal, formal, categorical imperative takes the place of the eternal law. The natural law, therefore, as part of the *lex naturalis,* is no longer connected with the eternal law, for the very reason that it can no longer be understood as part of the *lex naturalis,* of the rational moral law. Furthermore, not enforceability but external physical force is directly and necessarily included in the concept of law.

Freedom as a starting point and first principle of the natural law in its purely formal character renders impossible a material natural law, a natural law with a material content. This follows also from Kant's pronounced dualism of speculative and practical metaphysics, the coordinated knowledge contents of theoretical and practical reason. Theoretical reason affords no sure knowledge of the essence of things; it can posit the existence of external reality only as a postulate. Practical reason alone yields certitude about the metaphysical. Practical reason "believes" in God, freedom, and immortality, things which theoretical reason is unable strictly and necessarily to know and demonstrate from the world of phenomena; for without them morality would be impossible. This primacy of the practical reason parallels to some extent the nominalist contention that the will is a higher faculty than the intellect and that supernatural faith as well as the positive divine law is the positive rule of knowledge and action. As in the case of the nominalist Occam, on this primacy of practical reason rests Kant's ethical rationalism, his deductionism uncontrolled by the intellect and consequently by reality. For otherwise the intellect would have to perceive the ideas in things and to be able to present that which is to the will as that which strictly ought to be.

Kant's formalism, i.e., the theory of mere conditions of knowledge and of moral autonomous freedom, is the main cause of this peculiarity of his ethics. It did not allow him to develop a doctrine of material values, but only the doctrine of conditions under which values can be

10. *Ibid.,* III, 19, trans. by T. R. Abbott, *op. cit.,* p. 275.

"given." The principle of freedom is too formal and hence too unfruitful to permit a material *ordo,* whether of oughtness or of essential being, to find acceptance, in relation either to knowledge or to volition. Since metaphysical being can thus exercise no control with regard to thinking, deductive free thought loses itself in rationalist constructions. Only too frequently, moreover, it clothes empirical, historical contents with the sheen of pure and absolutely valid deductions from reason. Indeed, this can be verified even in the case of the Neo-Kantian theories of formal and pure law, as, for example, in the writings of Stammler and Kelsen. (However paradoxical it may appear, Karl Bergbohm would actually have uncovered, in virtue of his peculiarly keen scent, abundant traces of natural-law thinking even in Kelsen.) Hence every external mode of action whereby the arbitrary freedom of the citizens is not mutually impaired would have to appear as juridical. That is to say, the joint consent and approval of the citizens would necessarily be able to render, in a positivist fashion, any action whatever a juridical one, quite apart from its material moral quality (here the well-known strong influence of Rousseau upon Kant is discernible). Thus, on the sole condition of the formal freedom of others, it would be possible for such intrinsically immoral actions as usury, theft, and adultery to become juridical, which Occam, who taught the same dualism of theoretical and practical reason, had admitted even in the case of the *lex naturalis.* The inherently immoral character of an action is no longer of importance for its juridical qualification.

This formalism thereupon led to abstruse deductions that altogether disregard the social value of, for instance, marriage and the family as institutions. To Kant the entire world of law appeared exactly like a variegated, intrinsically uncoordinated aggregate of subjective rights. Marriage becomes for him "the Union of two Persons of different sex for life-long reciprocal possession of their sexual faculties."[11] The use of another's sexual organs is, in Kant's view, a gratification for the sake of which one party gives himself to the other. But thereby a man makes himself a thing, which is contrary to the law of the humanity in his person. Only because the other person similarly acquires another as a

11. *The Philosophy of Law,* Part I, no. 24 (ed. W. Hastie, p. 110).

thing does he regain himself and recover his personality. "The Acquisition of a part of the human organism being, on account of its unity, at the same time the acquisition of the whole Person, it follows that the surrender and acceptation of, or by, one sex in relation to the other, is not only *permissible* under the condition of Marriage, but is further *only* really possible under that condition."[12] The act of generation is "a process by which a Person is brought without his consent into the world, and placed in it by the responsible free will of others. This Act, therefore, attaches an obligation to the Parents to make their Children—as far as their power goes—contented with the condition thus acquired. Hence Parents cannot regard their Child as, in a manner, a Thing *of their own making*, for a Being endowed with Freedom cannot be so regarded. Nor, consequently, have they a Right to destroy it as if it were their own property, or even to leave it to chance, because they have brought a Being into the world who becomes in fact a Citizen of the world, and they have placed that Being in a state which they cannot be left to treat with indifference, even according to the natural conceptions of Right."[13]

In Kant's thought also the state of nature, which is contrasted not with the social but with the civil or political condition of mankind, plays the same great role that it did in the individualist conception of natural law. Kant held that the state of nature is already social, and that the norms of natural law have force in it as private law. Accordingly the whole body of law derivable from reason (the law covering marriage, the family, inheritance, contracts, property and the ways of acquiring it, as well as trial and verdict) is dealt with in this connection. The *status civilis* is looked upon as something superadded, not as equally original. It is the domain of public law, in which "through public laws the 'mine' and 'thine' [is] safeguarded," hence not created. It has the important function of presenting these norms of private law, which are projected upon or into the state of nature conceived as social, as sacred to the public or positive coercive law of the state. The rights and institutions existing in the state of nature are at most to be protected

---

12. *Ibid.*, no. 25 (p. 111).
13. *Ibid.*, no. 28 (pp. 114 f.).

by the state with its force; they are not to be substantially altered or to be abolished. For what did not previously belong to the law of nature cannot become matter of civil law.[14] The circle of subjective rights, which is continually widening, and the maintenance of these rights in the *status civilis* form together the contents of the natural law. They are projected into the state of nature in order to protect them from encroachment on the part of the state. In this way the state itself is merely an institution resting on a free contract: it does not result intrinsically and necessarily from the essence and reason of man. At most it arises from eudaemonist and utilitarian motives, so far as the passions, which were generally viewed by rationalism after the Stoic fashion as devoid of value, menace the state of nature in its very existence and hence render coercion necessary.

The era of the individualist natural law, conditioned by the theory of a purely imaginary, unreal world of the state of nature and adopting as a starting point any propensity or attribute whatever of empirical human nature, brought to light nearly as many supreme principles of law and resultant natural-law systems as there were chairs and professors of natural and international law. Such were sociality, external peace, urge for earthly happiness, and, finally, freedom. As Warnkoenig has shown, eight or more new systems of natural law made their appearance at every Leipzig booksellers' fair since 1780. Thus Jean Paul Richter's ironical remark contained no exaggeration: Every fair and every war brings forth a new natural law.

The reforming zeal of the eighteenth century considered useful, right, and good its ideal of civil liberty and equality, economic freedom as a condition of social harmony, and liberation from the rigid bonds of guild law and corporations. All this was taken, together with and in addition to the traditional contents, into the natural law and transferred to the state of nature. Thus the particular systems of natural law became compendiums in which the norms of the positive law (only now rationally demonstrated), vindicated by speculative thought and before the bar of reason, appeared side by side with proposals for improvement

14. Cf. *ibid.*, nos. 41 and 44 (pp. 155–57, 163–65).

arising from the criticism of the positive laws. Moreover, in these systems the natural-law norms handed down from the past were dealt with alongside both the ideas of political reform stemming from the spirit of the time and the subjective rights of citizens and men. With these last were combined, with more or less good fortune or skill, the personal and often abstruse *desiderata* of the individual teacher.

For these reasons Anselm Desing, O.S.B. (1699–1772), who as a Catholic, in contrast to the majority of natural-law teachers, was still in close contact with the Scholastic tradition, could rightly point out that the pretended natural law of his time was in no way a "dictate of reason"; that it was rather a rationalization of the positive law of the period, yes, even of the laws of the nation to which the author belonged; hence that it was not at all derived, as asserted, from reason alone, but was little more than "the civil law adorned with some spoils of philosophy and moral theology." How are we otherwise to explain the fact that, side by side with the natural right to liberty and equality, a natural law of feudalism was taught; and that, alongside the new French constitution, the constitution of the Holy Roman Empire was shown to belong to the natural law? Or that the postal system was converted into a natural-law institution? Nature, state of nature, natural reason, natural theology, and natural ethics were the dominant ideas and viewpoints of the age. Whoever was desirous of representing something as good and worth while had now to make of it a requirement of the natural law, and to show that it is a conclusion of reason and that it existed in the state of nature.

This individualist natural law of rationalism did not, however, owe its importance in world history to its absurdities. It owed this significance rather to its ethical and politico-economic aims, which were raised to the sublime dignity of natural justice and held in altogether singular esteem by the spirit of the eighteenth century. Through its acid criticism of society, it certainly served to dissolve the traditional and rigid forms of feudal and guild law in the reforming legislation of enlightened despots like Frederick the Great of Prussia and Joseph II of Austria. This causal connection is verified in the authors of these reforms, who lived and taught wholly under the spell of this natural law. Nor did it only smash these forms to pieces in a revolutionary manner, as the Jacobins inspired by Rousseau did in France. It also preserved from ultimate extinction a goodly part of the old national legal heritage by investing much of the latter with the splendor of natural justice. For example, Thomasius rejected the free testamentary disposition of Roman law and opposed to it, as a requirement of natural law, the Germanic system of succession according to blood. Moreover, in conjunction with the Enlightenment, it again did away with the belief in demons, which since the close of the Middle Ages had been working havoc in the sphere of law (witchcraft delusion); and it thus deprived torture of all justification arising from belief in demons, from the supposed "possession" of the criminal. Finally it upheld, in Germany by means of reform, in France through revolution, human and civil rights against a personal absolutism of princes that towered above everything; in this way it once more helped the idea of the constitutional state on to victory. Yet we should not overlook that it likewise vindicated to the point of chicanery the police-state of enlightened despotism along with its tutelage of the citizens.

On the other hand, the separation of morality and law, and the assignment of law alone to the state and of morality to the individual, aided materially in the suppression of the police-state. The state, it was held, is not to concern itself with the morality of the citizens, which is an internal matter. Among the consequences of this view in the moralizing century was not only the victory of civil toleration in matters of religious belief, but also the victory of the liberal constitutional state over the totalitarian educational state, whereof Maria Theresa's morals commissions still afforded evidence. For, supposing that the Church as a free community pre-eminently concerned with faith and morals is lacking or is not recognized, the identification of morality and law leads readily to a state which no longer respects a sphere of personal moral responsibility or a personal nature and goal which transcend the state.

We can, therefore, readily understand that the rationalist natural law should have lost ever more and more of its importance as its aims were progressively achieved in political life and in positive law. Yet it is a singular thing, and a sort of poetic vengeance for its own betrayal of tradition, that throughout the entire nineteenth century this natural law passed in the scientific world for the natural law par excellence, and that thus the battle against it was regarded as a fight against the natural law. Thus positivism, which was now beginning its triumphal march, obtained its laurels all too easily, since it was indeed able to vanquish this historical form of a philosophy of law which called itself natural law, but not the idea itself of natural law. The latter was carried along by the *philosophia perennis* even through the centuries flushed with passion for deduction. It sought for fresh confirmation in every historical setting of the problem until, with the exhaustion of positivism, with the resurgence of metaphysics, and with the collapse of the spirit of the nineteenth century, it came back renovated. It returned, not of course absolutely speaking, for it had always been cherished in the shadow of moral theology and the metaphysics of the *philosophia perennis,* yet return it did even into the realm of jurisprudence, from which positivism had attempted to banish it.

CHAPTER V

The Turning Away from Natural Law

The attack upon the idea of natural law came mainly from two quarters. It came, in the first place, from skeptics and agnostics like David Hume or from utilitarians like Jeremy Bentham (1748–1832) and their disciples. In the next place, it came from the leaders of the romantic movement, which was antirationalist and antirevolutionary and was based upon the philosophy of traditionalism as expounded by De Maistre and De Bonald.

Common to both groups, however, though for very different reasons, was a pronounced distrust of the power and abilities of human reason in individual men. This distrust resulted from a strong reaction against the overestimation of that same human reason in the era of rationalism. For both groups, law is not a system of clear rational conclusions from some axiomatic or self-evident principles. It is not a body of deductions which human reason can construct *more geometrico,* as Baruch Spinoza, in keeping with the predilection for the mathematical method which dominated the rationalist era, attempted to work out in his *Ethics.* On the contrary, law becomes the effect of habits, the product of the experienced utility of conventional behavior for individualist self-interest. Hume never tires of pointing out that reason is and ought to be the servant of the passions, and that consequently man is ruled by the passions and not, as the rationalist must contend, by reason. Similarly the romantic movement (in legal philosophy, the historical school of jurisprudence) would insist that law is merely the creation of the *Volksgeist* or spirit of the people which works in an irrational manner and reveals itself in the establishment of legal conventions and customary law. Law itself is constituted by such time-honored customary laws, which emerge from the mysterious soul of the nation that grows like an organism and is not deliberately fashioned. It is not the legislator of rationalism, deliberating in the rational clarity of consciousness, who makes the law; and it is not the will of the state, informed by abstract logical reasoning and vesting the natural law with the cloak of positive law, that makes the law. The law is the silent, almost subconscious, historical product of a particular *Volksgeist*, of the spirit of a particular people. The law is not made; it grows.

Both ways of thinking result in the rejection of the theory of natural law. Yet there exists between them a significant difference. The skeptics, agnostics, and utilitarians sought definitely and completely to undermine and destroy the very idea of natural law. The historical school of law, on the other hand, launched its attack rather against the antihistorical, abstract thinking of the age of rationalism. It leveled its guns against that passion for constructing systems out of the whole cloth of abstract reasoning which was so typical of the natural-law theorizing of the seventeenth and eighteenth centuries and was at the same time so destructive, as appears in the excesses of the French Revolution, which appealed to the idea of natural law in justification even of its most wanton injustices. This school of law was antirevolutionary and antirationalist, but it was not, like the agnostic school of thought, antimetaphysical.

It has been pointed out that the forces which would destroy the hold exercised over men's minds by the idea of natural law were already germinally contained in John Locke's empiricism. Locke began with a certain distrust in the power of human reason that was only slightly neutralized by his philosophically rather inconsequential confidence in practical common sense. The point has also been made that Cartesian rationalism, with its conception of the human intellect as practically angelic, contained within itself a fall of the angels by leading to relativist sensualism. In the philosophy of David Hume (1711–76) these forces became mature. "Reason is, and ought only to be the slave of the passions, and can never pretend to any other office than to serve and obey them."[1] Reason fails us, but only in order that nature herself (reason and nature are now opposed; no longer is reason the dominating element of human nature) may step into the breach.[2] What, then, is this "nature"? It is the passions, the propensities, and an assorted bundle of perceptions.

Hume's dissolving criticism leaves no method for determining what is intrinsically good or bad in these passions and in the acts that proceed from them. Whatever may be the moral principles that guide our actions, they are not founded on objective truth and on reason. Indeed, they are not principles at all. They are only names, symbols for emotions, i.e., for feelings of pleasure and pain. What the earlier philosophers called natural law is but a common name conventionally agreed upon for moral sentiments of approval or disapproval. Thus the morality of an action is determined not by its conformity with reason but simply by the sentiment of approval: "Morality is determined by sentiment." As a consequence, Hume defines "virtue to be *whatever mental action or quality gives to a spectator the pleasing sentiment of approbation;* and vice the contrary."[3] The reason for such sentiments is not the intellectually apprehended conformity of the action with objective principles. Such a conformity supposes powers of intellectual cognition which Hume, in his epistemology, denies to the human mind. The single remaining explanation and ground of these sentiments is the usefulness of the action to serve human needs, as repeated experience shows. The sentiment of approval is a sign that the respective action is useful, either directly to self-interest, or indirectly, inasmuch as the action is useful for the preservation of society in its function as framework for the realization of self-interest, which ultimately is the sole thing that matters. Out of repeated individual experiences which evidence the utility of an action, arises the presumption of standards of behavior and the fixing of habits.

The moral law is far from being intrinsic and objective; even the

---

1. *A Treatise of Human Nature,* Bk. II, Part III, § 3, ed. by L. A. Selby-Bigge (Oxford: Clarendon Press, 1888), p. 415.

2. Cf. *ibid.,* Bk. I, Part IV, § 1, pp. 180–87.

3. *An Enquiry Concerning the Principles of Morals,* Appendix I, i. *Hume, Selections,* ed. by Charles W. Hendel, Jr. (New York: Charles Scribner's Sons, 1927), p. 241.

utility of our actions is not an objective quality. It is consequently but a sum of societary conventions that are adapted to serve human needs and urges according to our experiences, which, however, may be superseded by different experiences at some future time. Thus the moral law has no basis in the intelligible rational and social nature of man; it has to do with no eternal, unchangeable verity rooted in the metaphysical order of the universe established by the Creator. Hume rejects the fundamental conception of St. Thomas that being, truth, and goodness are intrinsically linked together (*ens et verum et bonum convertuntur*). For Hume, being does not appear to the human intellect as the true because man's mind has no access to the thing-in-itself, to the essences or ideas of things. Similarly, being, which confronts theoretical reason as the true, cannot appear before practical reason and the will as the good to be realized, as the objective norm of human action. Conventions cannot, of course, claim intrinsic validity. Utility or usefulness, in addition to its inherently subjective slant, is a quality which changes with socio-political circumstances and with accidental and more or less arbitrary estimates of human needs.

All that remained after this analysis was empiricist positivism. The good and the just are what is here and now deemed useful to the self-interest of individuals and to their life in common. The latter, of itself and through educational enforcement, develops a social habit of considering a common interest, which, however, is not such in reality: it is but a nominalist symbol for the sum of tangible individual interests.

This "destruction" of the idea of natural law at the hands of Hume[4] was, in the Anglo-Saxon world, of less importance for the survival of the natural-law concept in jurisprudence than one might have expected. This fact must be attributed to the tenacity with which the spirit of the English common law retained the conceptions of natural law and equity which it had assimilated during the Catholic Middle Ages, thanks especially to the influence of Henry de Bracton (d. 1268) and

4. George H. Sabine, *op. cit.*, pp. 598–605, gives an enthusiastic exposition of Hume's alleged destruction of the natural law. He candidly admits, however, that Hume's destructive criticism of natural law stands or falls with his psychology and analysis of causation. But Hume's psychology and analysis of causation flatly constitute an affront to, and a mutilation of, the human intellect. Cf., e.g., Celestine N. Bittle, O.F.M. Cap., *The Whole Man*, pp. 316–21, 540 f.

Sir John Fortescue (d. *cir.* 1476). For a long time natural law remained the critical norm for common-law judges who, much like the Roman praetors acting under the influence of the philosophically minded juris-consults and their *responsa,* allowed the principles of equity to control the rigid formalism of the original common law. In addition, the decisions of the Christian courts or ecclesiastical courts, applying canon law which is imbued with the idea of natural law, constituted a vessel in which this idea could be handed down to later generations. The English religious revolt of the sixteenth century brought with it the grave danger that the resulting caesaropapism might pave the way for a revival on English soil of Byzantine absolutism. According to Byzantine legal theory the emperor as *lex viva* was above and not under the law, a conception which might be used by the king to establish his supremacy over the law. But the Christian elements of the common law continued to keep alive in the minds of the judges the traditional belief in the supremacy of natural law. Thus Sir Edward Coke upheld in *Bonham's Case* (1610) the general principle that statutes are void if they do not conform to the natural law.[5] Ideas such as these, inimical to arbitrary power and unlimited governmental prerogatives, found a peculiarly favorable socio-cultural environment in the New World, though here they came to receive a starkly individualist interpretation which, owing to the *Zeitgeist* of liberalism and to special economic and social condi-tions, culminated in so-called rugged individualism. It was mainly with the growth of the analytical method of John Austin (1790–1859) and with the progress of pragmatism that the dilution of the Christian legal heritage advanced to an alarming degree.

The other offensive against natural law was launched by the romantic movement and its legal offshoot, the historical school of law. The genius of jurisprudence became exhausted by the airy abstractions of the

---

5. In the following century Sir William Blackstone laid down explicitly that "the law of nature being coeval with mankind, and dictated by God himself, is of course superior in obligation to any other. It is binding over all the globe, in all countries, and at all times: no human laws are of any validity if contrary to this; and such of them as are valid derive all their force and all their authority, mediately or immedi-ately, from this original" (*Commentaries,* i, p. 40, cited by A. V. Dicey, *Introduction to the Study of the Law of the Constitution* [9th ed., London: Macmillan and Co., 1939], p. 62).

cosmopolitan natural law; it was sobered and shaken by the passionate rhetoric and the horrible, legally infamous sentences of the murderous tribunals of the French revolutionaries. Now it bowed before the vigorous life of the legal sense flourishing in the popular mind and committed itself to the strictly antirevolutionary sway of the historical process. Just as it had formerly been driven on by the arrogantly rationalist spirit of the Enlightenment, so now it was propelled by the conservative thinking of romanticism. But the historical school of law was not yet positivism, although it adopted a hostile attitude toward natural law. Karl Bergbohm (1849–1927), the diligent tracker of natural law, has made this point sufficiently clear. Yet what Bergbohm (and many others with him) overlooked is the fact that the historical school directed its attacks against the individualist natural law. The blame for this gross error is to be ascribed to the total ignorance of the great Western tradition of natural law, together with the antimetaphysical mood of the closing nineteenth century.

The historical school of law showed an affectionate regard for the past of peoples, especially for that of one's own people. "The motley world of legal forms, like language, art, and mores, does not evolve in virtue of deliberate natural reflection or reasoned considerations of utility; it springs rather from the common conviction of the people, from the like feeling of inner necessity which excludes all thought of fortuitous and arbitrary origin" (Friedrich Carl von Savigny, 1779–1861). The state does not create the law; it should only formulate it, just as in earlier times the national judge merely "found" the law and applied it. The consciousness of law and its contents are the law. Law is the general will of those living together under law. The spirit of the people is the source of human or natural law, of legal principles. Consequently the law of each people is as different from that of other peoples as is its language. "Hence to the German people corresponds a German law" (Puchta). Within law, as in language, are found provincialisms. Customary law is thus the first form of the law which emerges from the dim workshop of the spirit of the nation. Law does not originate through action of the state. On the contrary, the state presupposes a legal consciousness, a law, even though the state is a necessary complement of the latter.

In this way the historical school acknowledged three sources of law: customary law, statute law duly promulgated, and the science of law which brings the law, so to speak, into consciousness by the path of jurisprudence. In its view, moreover, these sources flow forth in chronological sequence. First on the scene is customary law which, as the legal consciousness of the community, also represents, as it were, the higher law. With advancing civilization, as the state becomes conscious of its special mission toward the law, the state regulates the various domains of life by means of legislation. Last of all appears the science of law, which gathers up the customary law, interprets the statute law, and, in conjunction with the judiciary and the legal profession, brings customary and statute law into agreement. The historical school thus upheld a sort of hierarchy of these sources of law. Customary law, which is in force among a people prior to the legislative activity of the state, ranks highest. The state does not enact law that is new and foreign to the people; it decides what in doubtful cases is to be considered the general will so that it may itself adhere thereto. The science of law, however, brings into consciousness principles of law which are, so to say, concealed in the abundance of the concrete and intuitively known legal rules acknowledged by the citizens as well as in the laws of the state. In the order of importance this law of jurists ranks lowest, for it is all too much in danger of becoming abstract. Wherefore both the genius of jurisprudence and the genius of legislation must seek to find the law where it abides par excellence, that is, in the general legal consciousness of the people. Furthermore, the law must be "found." It cannot be derived from unsubstantial principles by a process of abstraction and rationalist deduction, since it has but one principle: the obscure depths of the national spirit.

The historical school, therefore, acknowledged only positive law. "There is no law but positive law. What underlies the conception of a natural law are precisely those concepts and precepts of the divine order of the world, the ideas of law. But these possess neither the requisite definiteness nor the binding force of law. They are the motives for the perfecting of the commonwealth, not already valid norms. Hence there are indeed demands of reason on law, but there exists no law of reason." Thus wrote the philosopher of the historical school, F. J. Stahl (1802–61).

Consequently, he continued, "the human community whose function it is freely to give to the concept of law its definite shape, can convert the latter into its opposite and command what is unjust and unreasonable; and even in this condition of opposition to God the law retains its binding authority. The binding authority of law is nothing else than the divine order of the world, but its abode is the existing law which can come into conflict with God's order of the universe."

Such was the first reaction of the positivist spirit to the individualistic natural law, in particular and designedly to the idea of natural law. "For," as Stahl insisted, "the highest principles touching the binding force of the positive law—that one must obey the public authorities; whether there is a limit to this obedience and what the limit is; whether active resistance is permissible—lie beyond positive law. Yet this pertains not to natural law but to ethics, and hence everyone according to his conscience will judge for himself before God what stand he should take on the matter."

Structurally, however, this position is akin to the speculation characteristic of the law of reason. What we have here is, on the one hand, the higher law of custom which, though not set up by the state as a higher norm, rules prior to the state and over it; and on the other hand, statute and jurist-made law which takes its norm from customary law. Such at least is the way it ought to be. But in keeping with its conservative attitude, like the whole romantic movement antirevolutionary, the historical school, faced by the decisive question of a conflict between positive law and natural law (or ethics, as Stahl termed it), could only say: "Subjects may not, relying upon the natural law, set themselves singly or collectively in opposition to the positive law; that would be the crime of the Revolution." Besides, customary law is related to the statute law of the state as the conservative natural law of the state of nature was related, e.g., in the thinking of Christian Wolff, to the statute law of the prince. The sole difference, though it is a decisive one, is that customary law was historically existing law, not abstract law deduced from abstract principles. The historically minded romanticism of the antirevolutionary era stood no longer in need of such a natural law, for it felt no call to make laws as did the reform-minded age of the law-of-reason enthusiasts.

But there is one more striking point. For the historical school, too, the eternal law was not a genuinely binding norm, no more than it was for Occam. Just as Occam had raised the question of whether God (by willing it) can oblige a person to hate Him, so Stahl declared that a positive law which is contrary to God's law is none the less binding. Despite the historical metaphysics of the national spirit, law in the eyes of the historical school is will rather than reason. To state the matter more exactly, for the historical school law is a product of the vital, irrational impulse in historical development, a result of historical necessities and of the spontaneously working power of the popular mind, rather than a product of clear, cool, non-historical reason. Nevertheless, although the historical school was positivist, it did not disavow justice, but referred the latter to moral philosophy. Its object was to replace the eternal and unchanging natural law with its cosmopolitan appeal to enlightened reason by the rich and varied abundance of the positive, historical, national law. This it did in order effectively to oppose the demands, clothed in natural-law dress, of the revolutionary publicists and of the jurists who were clamoring for reform and pressing for the codification of the law. The historical school was neither able, nor did it wish, to dispute the right, in principle, of ethics to pass judgment upon existing historical law. Stahl, as has been indicated, expressly stated: "What underlies the conception of a natural law are precisely those concepts and precepts of the divine order of the world, the ideas of law." And he assigns to the philosophy of law the knowledge of what is just and valid independently of all recognition.

It is, then, no wonder that out of the same spirit of romanticism and in spite of the struggle of the historical school, the natural law forthwith reappeared in a purified form. With the victory of empiricism, scientism, and antimetaphysical thinking, however, it was once more driven back to the confines of Catholic moral philosophy and the adherents of the *philosophia perennis,* but only to return at once.

Thus the idea of natural law remained alive throughout the entire nineteenth century. Certainly, open profession of the doctrine through employment of the name itself was no longer so common. But the systems of philosophical right, of conceptual or pure law, and of law in itself are indicative of the vitality of the natural-law idea. They are likewise indicative of the fact that the nineteenth century was for the most part acquainted only with the individualist natural law of Pufendorf and his successors, especially with that of German idealism and that formulated by Kant. The natural law and philosophy of law of earlier centuries, with the exception of a few stereotyped formulas which were repeated *ad nauseam* and in their isolation had very little meaning, were wholly unknown to nineteenth-century legal thinkers. This remarkable telescoping of tradition to the period of from 1600 on had disastrous consequences, as no less a scholar than Rudolf von Jhering complained. As is well known, the latter asserted, amid severe reproaches leveled at contemporary philosophy, that he would probably not have written his work, *Der Zweck im Recht*, had he been acquainted with the philosophy of the past, in particular with that of St. Thomas Aquinas. For, he went on to say, "the basic ideas I occupied myself with are to be found in that gigantic thinker in perfect clearness and in most pregnant formulation."[6]

Noteworthy, however, is the fact that though this epoch, down to about the time of the victory of scientism and even earlier in the case of historical materialism, was often ashamed of the name "natural law," it did not repudiate the thing itself, that is, a real law before and above the positive law. We observe that this idea was upheld particularly in penology. Certainly it is much more difficult to maintain that murder, manslaughter, perjury, theft, and adultery constitute breaches of the law solely because the positive law so determines than, e.g., that a written form is required for the legal validity of a promise of gift or that, since a person can make free testamentary disposition of his property (in contrast to the right of succession) only in writing, this is law because the positive law so ordains. No, the positive law prohibits such crimes and threatens their perpetrators with the heaviest penalties because the deeds are wrong in themselves: no agreement or statute could make them lawful. In like manner the idea of natural law was further applied in the case of international law. Here, too, the norms

6. *Der Zweck im Recht* (2nd. ed.), II, 162, cited in Martin Grabmann, *Thomas Aquinas. His Personality and Thought,* trans. by Virgil Michel, O.S.B. (New York: Longmans, Green and Co., 1928), p. 162.

governing the international community did not consist of positive law alone, nor did actual practice suffice. In particular, the first principles of international law, e.g., the much-invoked fundamental rights of states, are rules of law, not because some congress of states has so decreed or because a usage may exist—political history proves how frequently this usage is overridden—but because here the legal conscience still strives with unyielding vigor to prevent might from making right.

The second reason for this continued existence of the natural law in the disguise of a pure, absolute law was the circumstance that the separation of ethics from law, inaugurated by Thomasius and Kant, could not be carried through. The great function of the idea of natural law, to preserve morality in the law, continued to be performed even during this period. That the importance of the natural-law idea was outwardly not so great is readily explainable. The great codifications of the early nineteenth century had taken over the moral, yes, "natural" principles of law almost without exception and explicitly in the form of general clauses. Consequently ethics was embodied in the law.

But down to the last decades of the nineteenth century the natural law maintained itself even outside the Christian doctrine of natural law which lived on in the native soil of a great tradition. It was taught, for instance, by the Aristotelian, F. A. Trendelenburg (1802–72), in his system of a natural law grounded in ethics.

Nevertheless, throughout all the centuries the tradition of natural law held its ground in the *philosophia perennis*. It is true that it was treated with contempt by Pufendorf and Thomasius. But this attitude is not difficult to understand. The adherents of the traditional natural law, even in the seventeenth century, had exposed the extreme rationalism of Pufendorf and others, just as later on, in the era of revolutions, they did battle with the revolutionary dynamic of individualism. They also stood in the front line when the notion again gained ground in international life that the fact creates right.

In his *Syllabus* of 1864, Pius IX condemned the following propositions: "Moral laws do not require a divine sanction, nor is there any need for human laws to be conformable to the law of nature or to receive their binding force from God" (56); "Rights consist in the mere material fact, and all human duties are an empty name, and every human deed has the force of right" (59); "The commonwealth is the origin and source of all rights, and enjoys rights which are not circumscribed by any limits" (39).[7] In connection with the revival of Thomistic philosophy under Leo XIII, Catholic scholars began afresh to occupy themselves with the natural law in the context of moral philosophy. As a result a large number of important and comprehensive treatises made their appearance under such titles as *Institutiones iuris naturalis*. Leo XIII himself, in his encyclicals on political and social matters, afforded a shining example of the strength of the natural-law idea, which precisely from that time on was exposed within the sphere of jurisprudence to the fiercest attacks at the hands of positivism.

The doctrine of natural law also proved to be extraordinarily valuable for constructing Christian social theory as well as for establishing Christian social policy. The social encyclicals of Leo XIII (*Rerum Novarum*, 1891) and Pius XI (*Quadragesimo Anno*, 1931) are themselves weighty evidence of this value. At the same time, these very encyclicals and the treatment of the social question undertaken in numerous and sometimes authoritative writings, together with the critical analysis of that fossil of the individualist natural law, individualist liberalism with its purely economic basis, constitute a strong proof of the vitality of this Christian doctrine of natural law. Other by-products of the same movement were the development of the so-called natural-law doctrine of the state and the grounding of sociology in social metaphysics, which received systematic treatment and a solid foundation in the natural-law doctrine. Further telling evidence of all this is found in the lifework of Heinrich Pesch, S.J. (1854–1926),[8] among others, as well as in the important part played by the natural-law doctrine in the theoretical and practical policies and reforms sponsored by the Catholic social movement and developed in its literature.

7. The entire text of the *Syllabus* in English translation may be found in Raymond Corrigan, S.J., *The Church and the Nineteenth Century* (Milwaukee: Bruce Publishing Co., 1938), pp. 289–95.

8. Cf. especially Franz H. Mueller, *Heinrich Pesch and His Theory of Christian Solidarism*. Aquin Papers: No. 7 (St. Paul, Minnesota: College of St. Thomas, 1941).

CHAPTER VI

The Victory of Positivism

The attack of positivism proceeded from several quarters along an ever-widening and enveloping front. It came first from scientific empiricism, which was generally lacking in a sense of the normative. The conflict of ethics with sociology opened, so to speak, a second front. The third point of assault was the spread of philosophical and historical materialism. For, in the "overthrow of the titans" of German philosophy, even the power of German idealism after Schelling and Hegel had been broken, notwithstanding the efforts of the post-Kantians (Feuerbach, Marx).

Empiricism, which dismisses metaphysics as epistemologically impossible (agnosticism), believed that, since it had won such great triumphs in the natural sciences, it is also the right method to follow in the so-called cultural sciences.[1] It penetrated into legal philosophy in proportion as the historical school, which in this matter had acted somewhat as a forerunner, came more and more to adopt what amounted to Kant's view of the connection of law with morality. According to K. Binding, for example, the sole way to true knowledge of the law is exact analysis of actually existing law, present and past. The philosophy of law should therefore not only rest upon mere external experience, but it should be restricted thereto. Every project of passing beyond it is rejected as metaphysics.

Philosophy of law, however, means understanding the ultimate and highest principles of law: it means understanding the essence or nature

---

1. See, in general, John Wellmuth, S.J., *The Nature and Origins of Scientism.* The Aquinas Lecture, 1944 (Milwaukee: Marquette University Press, 1944).

of law, the source of its obligatory character, the essential and intrinsic difference between right and wrong, justice and injustice. Experience teaches us nothing about all this. It merely tells us that such and such laws were enacted by the constitutional organs, that this or that rule was once recognized as law. But certainly all true understanding of law calls for something more. It demands to know just why in final analysis this law was right, and why this law could become binding in conscience. It is thus no wonder that empiricism led not only to relativism, but to skepticism as well. No right exists as an eternal idea. There are merely positive rights which are only to be known, not to be recognized. The *ignoramus et ignorabimus* ("We do not know and we shall never know") of the natural scientists invades legal philosophy. The will of the state, the formal general will of the citizens, is the source and criterion of law. Sociology thereupon explains by the mechanism of environment, by the struggle of interests, the further question of why this particular norm is chosen by the will. Lastly, historical materialism reduces law to the level of a mere reflex of the modes of production and the class struggles, or to a line of demarcation between classes.[2]

To be fair, therefore, we must distinguish two forms of positivism: first, positivism as a consequence of an empiricist narrowing of reality, as a method; secondly, positivism as a philosophy of life, as a conception of the meaning of the universe and of man's place in it, as a Weltanschauung. The crudest expression of this second form of positivism has been materialism, whether in its metaphysical (Feuerbach, Buechner, Haeckel) or historico-economic dress (Marx). Moreover, the second form of positivism has played by far the more important role.

Positivism as a method was already present in the historical school of law. It developed with the victorious advance of scientism, of natural-science modes of thought.[3] This approach to reality became the standard

2. For a brief but penetrating exposition and criticism of recent American schools of jurisprudence which pass for philosophies of law—sociological jurisprudence, economic determinism, and realism with its psychological, experimental or skeptical approaches— see Francis P. LeBuffe, S.J., and James V. Hayes, *Jurisprudence* (3rd ed. rev., New York: Fordham University Press, 1938), pp. 70–81.

3. On scientism and on the proper relations between natural-science modes of thought and philosophy, see John Wellmuth, S.J., *op. cit.;* Jacques Maritain, *The Degrees*

methodological pattern for all scientific thinking, as was once the case of deductive, mathematical rationalism which insisted on conceiving and handling ethics and law *more geometrico*. The essential feature of this view of reality is the prominence assigned to the empirical knowledge of individual things, and the restricting of the mental horizon to the empirical and the individual. Whatever else there may still be is ethics and not law, for it is not a law that is immediately experienced. This attitude held relatively little danger so long as moral philosophy itself did not become positivist. But when this occurred, there resulted from methodological positivism, which relegated the natural law to the background of ethics, either a world view that was frankly materialist or a self-denying skepticism which, with an almost ascetical self-restraint, merely gathered, compared, and verified. Or positivism simply referred to the newly emergent science of sociology what had hitherto been assigned to ethics; it tried thereby to rid itself of responsibility for answering the fateful question of the foundation of law.

The jurisprudence of materialism must boil down to mere positivism. Materialism regards man as nothing more than a highly evolved animal; the soul is a mere concept, required by the law of parsimony, for the manifold functions of the brain: it is not an immaterial, immortal substance. In place of a personal God, materialism is a doctrine of impersonal eternal force or of perpetually recurrent changes of matter in accordance with the blind necessity of the laws of nature. There thus exists no free will, and hence no morality in the Platonic and Aristotelian sense, or in that of the Roman jurists, or in that of the entire Christian tradition. Right as idea and the order of justice are things, concepts, which have as little relation to reality as have God, immortality, and free will. Positive law alone exists, i.e., coercive law, for only what is actually enforced is law; and it is merely a creation of the state. Moreover, the state itself is not recognized as a moral collective person, as a moral phenomenon. It is rather a necessary product of the evolution of social forces or, as historical materialism declares, of the

of Knowledge, trans. by Bernard Wall and Margot R. Adamson (New York: Charles Scribner's Sons, 1938), chap. 1; Jacques Maritain, *Scholasticism and Politics,* trans. by Mortimer J. Adler (New York: Macmillan Co.), chap. 2.

conditions of production. It is a natural product in the proper sense of the term. In this way it is, what it is in fact, merely a thing of the class that actually has the upper hand, the ruling class.

The positive law, on the other hand, is "the boundary, fixed for the time being by the social groups struggling for power and influence in the state, of their authority and their influence" (Gumplowicz). This boundary is continually shifting; a common body of ethical and legal ideas is wanting. Here the law of the stronger holds sway. Callicles had spoken of this long before, and he as well as Spinoza had identified it with the natural law because they regarded nature as the antithesis of mind. Consequently there is no eternal justice, nor is there an unalterable moral law. The state is the creator of morality and law, but the state in turn is merely a product of the struggle of social classes and servant of the class that rules at any given time. Hence "the political order is the moral order for the time being, and the self-interest of the state [which is itself a product of naked power] is an element of morality. . . . All the highest goods that man possesses—freedom, property, family, personal rights—he owes to the state" (Gumplowicz). Law is thus not a genuine norm. It does not tell what ought to be, but is merely an indication of how far the power, the material and psychological power, of the ruling class extends. The law indicates what the sociological situation is. This is the extreme form of materialist jurisprudence. In this view, the law is neither reason nor will: it is but the line of demarcation of the relations of social power. Therefore real force, whether physical or psychical, is of necessity the essential note of law. Law is merely what is actually enforced, not what is enforceable. Jurisprudence is an inept expression, handed down from a metaphysico-theological age, for the materialist sociology of a purely experimental science that tells how the power pattern of the groups within a society stands at the moment in the struggle for the machinery of political control.

In contrast with this crassly materialist positivism stands a moderate form of positivism. The latter simply acknowledges the positive law as legally binding, and believes it possible to forgo a philosophy of law, i.e., to avoid the question of the basis of the binding character of law. Law is the will of the state that is expressly declared to be such, is enacted in conformity with constitutional provisions, and is then duly promulgated. Any further criterion, as, e.g., the inherent justice or the moral lawfulness of the action commanded by the positive law, is rejected as irrelevant for the sphere of law. The legal sphere is identified with the creation of law by the state, the carrying out of the law by the administration and the citizens, and the applying of the law by the judges. This is the position taken by the so-called theory of will, which has gained numerous adherents in political science and international law. It has found its strongest expression in the idea of the absolute sovereignty or the juristic personality of the state. Such sovereignty is even greater than that of the absolute monarch of the seventeenth and eighteenth centuries, who considered himself bound by the natural and divine law. Indeed, upon closer examination, the doctrine of sovereignty transfers states, after the manner of Hobbes, into a pure state of nature with its single rule of self-preservation. Thus international law is dependent at every moment upon its actual acceptance or rejection by the states, just as parliamentary majorities in states like England may in theory pass any measure whatever. Law is consequently no true norm or something pertaining to reason, but mere actual will in the psychological sense. It does not depend upon the essential being of things or upon the nature of the case, which L. von Baer, following here the Anglo-Saxon judicial tradition, designated as the basis of law.

Such views can emanate from a tired agnosticism that admits no metaphysical foundation of law. They can also spring from a strong feeling against the rationalist deductions of the natural-law doctrine which prevailed in recent centuries. Often, too, they are the result of a hostility, stemming from a conservative outlook, toward the revolutionary components of the newer natural law. These components hold danger for the state, whose inspirational value and sublime dignity are held to need no further justification. Moreover, the reason for such views often lies in the typical attitude of the modern scientific mind: satisfaction with the mere ascertainment of what actually exists, industrious search for facts, idolatrous worship of the factual. On the other hand, many students of law are much concerned about the great blessing of legal certainty. These hold that even a poor law and its application are more conducive to the general welfare than the riddling of the positive law by appeals to natural law or moral principles. This contention is based on the importance of the secure expectation of the members of the community that they may count on a definite and, if need be, enforced mode of conduct on the part of the rest. They clinch this contention by pointing out that no uniformity of views and convictions concerning this higher law prevails either among the members of the community or on the bench or among jurists.

With the exception of the group of agnostics, these jurists in no way deny the value of justice or the validity of the ethical norm. What the older writers termed natural law they regard as an ethical norm. But such norms, so far as these are not contained in the positive law, they exclude from "law." In their eyes, law and justice, law and right, are not identical. The lawmaker, of course, should enact no unjust laws. Yet if he enacts a law of this kind, it is law in the true sense. One may not look upon it as non-binding from the viewpoint of a natural law, but only from the viewpoint of ethics. This matter, however, everyone must settle for himself with his own conscience. Legal dualism, the doctrine of a natural law functioning as real law concomitant with and superior to the positive law, is flatly repudiated.

The ultimate basis of this moderate positivism was and is the paralyzing realization of the unsettled condition of philosophy in the nineteenth and early twentieth centuries. This was and is quite apparent even in moral philosophy, which itself was not long in becoming positivist. For so must we designate an ethics which holds with Friedrich Paulsen, for example, that morals or mores "are, like instincts, . . . *purposive modes of behavior* for solving the various problems of life,"[4] or in the form of pragmatism identifies the good with what is useful and successful, and evil with what is detrimental and unsuccessful (biologism). This school of thought has been unable to find a distinction between a material, unalterable ethics and such positive, interested, historical moral codes as those of the nobility, the bourgeoisie, and the peasants. Thus, in the face of ethical relativism and the rejection of all metaphysics, it could see no other possibility than a self-denying positivism in law.[5]

4. *A System of Ethics*, ed. and trans. by Frank Thilly (New York: Charles Scribner's Sons, 1899), p. 346. Italics in the original.

5. In regard to ethical relativism, see the remarkably forthright admissions, and no less remarkable confusions, of Friedrich Paulsen, *op. cit.*, pp. 19–25, who reaches the

The great speculative outburst of German idealism had given way to a purely formal criticism of knowledge, to which the contents of thought were a matter of indifference or which was even frankly skeptical about the possibility of attaining scientific knowledge of the content of ideas. Stahl's work on the philosophy of law, which was representative of the thinking of the historical school of law, appeared in a final (fifth) edition in 1878, that of H. Ahrens, in a second (last) edition in 1860. Roeder's work on the natural law appeared in a second (last) edition in the same year, 1860, and the already mentioned treatise of the Aristotelian Trendelenburg on the natural law based on ethics appeared in a final edition in 1866. It is likewise significant that, toward the close of the century, the compiling of the first volume, dealing with legal philosophy, in Holzendorf's well-known *Encyclopedia of Law* was entrusted to A. Merkel, the first thoroughgoing positivist. The philosophy of law, the theoretical doctrine of the natural law, now became a general science of law, a nonmetaphysical science founded on generalization and comparison, in full agreement with the evolution in philosophy.

Positivism, of course, could be no more permanently satisfying than could the historical school of law with its one-sided preference for customary law and the purely historical element in a science which has to do with oughtness, with norms. This external mark of the formal will of the lawmaker can by no means answer the perpetually arising question about the intrinsic difference between right and wrong. "Legal statutes must be measured by some standard or other to prove that they are justified"; moreover, "the doubt whether the existing law is in conformity with reason cannot be simply pushed aside" (R. Stammler). The existing law must also be one that ought to exist. The much-acclaimed consciousness of right is not a creator of law but an intimation that a legal fact is perceived and acknowledged as one that also ought to be.

It is a continually recurring experience that, even when we are wholly disinterested in a matter, we keep trying to distinguish laws as good

---

following general conclusion (p. 25): "Every moral philosophy is, therefore, valid only for the sphere of civilization from which it springs, whether it is conscious of the fact or not." Cf. Jacques Leclercq, *Le fondement du droit et de la société* (2nd ed., Namur: Maison d'Editions Ad. Wesmael-Charlier, 1933), pp. 25–43; Walter Farrell, O.P., *A Companion to the Summa*, Vol. II, chap. 21.

and bad according to their purpose, but as just and unjust laws in accordance with an intrinsic criterion. Yet that is possible only if this intrinsic criterion is the very basis for the qualification of right and wrong. Hence pure positivism has at no time been carried through in actual practice, even in the countries that make the judges wholly dependent on the formal law. It is simply repugnant to the notion of a true judge to be merely a subsuming automaton. Even the positive law has again and again had recourse to morality, to natural-law norms. This it does since the presupposition of positivism, that is, the lack of gaps in the statute law, is not verified. Moreover, not only do legal codes refer to the natural principles of law (e.g., *Austrian General Civil Code, Code of Canon Law*), but even the law itself refers to good faith and to good morals. In these references there is no thought at all of that which is merely proper, of that which passes at a given period for respectable or conforms to the mores of a certain class of society. Frequently in such cases it is far more a question of the conclusions and further inferences from the natural law as well as of applying them. Nor does it do any good to explain, in a spirit of unshakable loyalty to positivism, that the lawmaker has precisely willed all this. For such an explanation presupposes not the actual lawmaker but an ideal one, i.e., a lawmaker who wills what is just.

"The individual experience of law is, when clearly grasped, dependent upon the universally valid concept of law, not vice versa. The concept of law cannot be derived from particular legal experiences (through induction or comparison), since these really become possible only through the former" (R. Stammler). Law exists prior to jurists and legal philosophers. They have not created law, but, inversely, law is the precondition of a legal profession and philosophy of law.

We have recorded the victory of positivism. But this must not be taken to mean that positivism won a definitive and total victory on all intellectual, moral, and political fronts. The victory, such as it was, was the outcome of the eventual undermining of metaphysics and the progressive dilution of the Christian heritage at the hands of both Kantian criticism and empiricism. The immediate result of these trends of modern thought was an agnostic and skeptical relativism, whose mock heroism showed itself in an almost ascetic, disillusioned search for "facts" and whose contempt for the theological and metaphysical era was pretentious and likewise ridiculous. Wherever these presuppositions of positivism did not prevail, the idea of natural law continued to live its now hidden life. It is true that most university professors and most practical jurists, to say nothing of the popularizers of shifting scientific fashions, spoke of natural law as a dead letter. Yet the idea of natural law once more found refuge in the *philosophia perennis* which, as we have repeatedly pointed out, had been its home whenever it was exiled from the secular universities and law schools. And the idea, divested of its academic dress, went on living also in common sense, in the minds of ordinary men.[6] Bergbohm, the Quixotic assailant of natural law, was forced to admit that all men are born natural-law jurists. How right he was! The spirit of skeptical agnosticism, which denies to the human mind access to transcendental truth and objective values and, doubting the inner logic of the universe, constructs subjective systems of thought, is more an attitude for the academic ivory tower or for the private study of one who enjoys economic security.

In real life this attitude is untenable. When he acts, and does not merely turn things over in his mind, even the skeptic acts as if such a thing as natural law or objective justice existed, as the common sense of ordinary men and women has always implicitly held. And the reason is obvious. If anyone were to attempt to realize a strict and consistent positivism in the everyday life of society, his sole possible attitude would be an unbearable cynicism. When he becomes interested in problems of economic, social, or political reform, the avowed positivist frequently turns, in practice and as it were unconsciously, to the idea of natural law and to standards of unchanging justice. The "scientific mind" may skeptically deny the existence of the natural law, but the heart, in which, as St. Paul says,[7] the natural law is recorded or inscribed, affirms it. It is easy to profess and proclaim positivism in a culture that is secure and is saturated with materialism. Positivism is the typical by-product of a solidly established, economically secure, and politically unendangered ruling class (*beati possidentes*). Yet man with his unquenchable thirst

6. On the important question of the relation between philosophy and common sense, cf. Jacques Maritain, *An Introduction to Philosophy*, chap. 8.

7. Rom. 2:14–16.

for justice cannot long be content with such an attitude. The hunger and thirst after justice are no less pressing than the ceaseless quest for truth. The idea of the natural law may thus be compared to the seed which, buried under the snow, sprouts forth as soon as the frigid and sterile winter of positivism yields to the unfailing spring of metaphysics. For the idea of natural law is immortal.

The Reappearance of Natural Law

The genius of the legal sciences could not be detained for long in the arid waste of positivism. Bergbohm, who tracked down the natural law into all the nooks and crannies in which it was supposed to have hidden itself from positivism, found everywhere, even among self-styled positivists, natural-law thought patterns. His intention was to dislodge it definitively. The year was 1885. Had Bergbohm repeated his hunt for the natural law about 1925, forty years later, he would have been shocked at the many new camouflages of his quarry. There is manifestly something invincible and eternal about that body of spiritual and moral ideas which for thousands of years has been called natural law and is once more coming back into honor. This is true even if those who admit these ideas in fact look back with false shame at the deductive extravagances of the rationalism of the seventeenth and eighteenth centuries and suppress the name of natural law. Not many concepts have had to endure so much violence as the notion of natural law. Yet few conceptions have had so proud and so great a tradition and a past, and are destined to have so great a future.

Positivism had no sooner achieved its position of dominance than men began to turn away from its Stoiclike self-denial. This first occurred, in a rather timid fashion, in the Neo-Kantian philosophy of law, of which the doctrine of Rudolf Stammler (1856–1938) affords a specific and typical instance. Stammler distinguishes between form and content of law—in the Kantian sense, of course, not in the Aristotelian. For Stammler, "formal" means the same as "conditioning," and he accordingly asks under what conditions positive law can be true law. Thus it is not a question of a legal content, but, as in Kant's ethical system, a question of a purely formal and empty concept which can receive various contents. Law thus becomes a "conditioning and determining form" of social life as the matter, the content. But this form hovers as far above every merely historical content as, in Kant's philosophy, the world of noumena soars above that of phenomena. Yet just as Kant did not attain to a material ethics determined by being, so Stammler fails to achieve a material jurisprudence. On the contrary, he arrives at a natural law with historically changing contents, for natural law is merely his concept of formal law. Such at least should be the case.

In reality, however, Stammler's doctrine of law does attain to contents—by way of the "social ideal" of the community of "freely willing men." By this path he arrives at universally valid legal principles which, because of their emptiness, are in part merely tautological. An instance in point is the principle that the individual should not be compelled to renounce interests to which he is fully entitled. But the whole question, of course, is to determine what makes him fully entitled to certain interests. Or "the unconditioned law for man is the good will, i.e., the direction and determination of empirical ends, which can present themselves as universally valid, abstracting from subjective selfish impulses." However, good will has precisely little to do with the rightness of a law; and whether or not the will is good, i.e., free from subjective selfish impulses, needs precisely to be ascertained by comparison with objective, legitimate, unselfish impulses. In this way, then, Stammler ascribes to his formal law contents that are "right," measured by the social ideal which likewise is not without a content that supplies a standard. The community of freely willing men implies, according to Stammler, rejection of slavery, polygamy, and despotism. But the rejection of adultery, perjury, theft, and intentional killing of an innocent person is equally well founded. It is no wonder that the positivists have charged that Stammler's natural law with a changing content still retains a sort of sediment of unchangeable "old" natural law.[1]

Many jurists separate the juridical and social aspects. Jellinek, for instance, in his political philosophy makes a distinction between legal theory and social theory. The legal theory is constructed along positivist lines; and then in social theory the old natural law at times breaks through. It is altogether surprising how often recourse has been had to the natural law, i.e., the idea of unalterable norms, in social philosophy and sociology for the building of social institutions, after it had been banished from jurisprudence. And yet this should not be wondered at, since social philosophy has from of old been closely connected with moral philosophy, as may be seen in every table of contents of the great *Institutiones iuris naturalis* of Theodor Meyer, Cathrein, Costa-Rosetti, Taparelli, Schiffini, and others. It is astonishing solely for the social doctrine that really wishes to be purely empirical and yet judges the empirical world of social phenomena by an unexpressed but ever-present social ideal of a just social order as a standard. The same is true of ethics. Even in the more recent systems of ethics, as in that of Nicolai Hartmann, we find principles aplenty which contain good old natural law. The institution theory of Maurice Hauriou (d. 1929),[2] the eminent French jurist, likewise contains, as even his respect for St. Thomas Aquinas would indicate, principles corresponding to the old natural law.

On the whole, in this advance of the idea of objective order as opposed to conditions and relations arising from the arbitrary will of individuals, we can and must see a sign of an intellectual revival that is open to the natural law. German legal scholars sometimes speak of the flight of certain natural-law principles (such as good faith, good morals and what we have the right to expect somebody to do or to tolerate) into the general clauses of the German Civil Code. This fact is most embarrassing for the formal jurist, particularly for a jurist who simply regards as an ideal the

1. For an exposition and criticism of Stammler's Neo-Kantian philosophy of law, cf. Erich Kaufmann, *Kritik der neukantischen Rechtsphilosophie* (Tuebingen: J. C. B. Mohr, 1921), pp. 11–20.

2. Cf. Jacques Leclercq, *Le fondement du droit et de la société*, pp. 276–78.

obligation of the judge to adhere to the formal law. But this is merely one more clear indication that alongside the positive law stands yet another law which often exactly resembles the old natural law. Indeed, it is an experience repeatedly verified that natural law makes its appearance whenever, through an altering of the circumstances, to use St. Thomas' expression, the positive law would work material injustice if it were applied. This situation occurs when the ontological foundations of the law have undergone a substantial change or when improved understanding reveals the inadequacy of this positive law. Ever since the dogma of the absence of gaps in the positive law was overthrown, natural-law concepts have been pushing in more and more; and the necessity of a moral quality in the law is receiving recognition in continually widening circles. The French Civil Code threatened with punishment the judge who would refuse to hand down a decision on the plea that the law is silent on the matter. When the judge finds no positive rule in the code, he is to make use of the principles of natural equity in reaching a decision.

From still another angle legal positivism has proved itself utterly inadequate. Positivism has only one criterion for law: the will of the sovereign formulated in accordance with the legislative process prescribed by the constitution. This formal criterion, consisting in the observance of the method and form of legislation as provided by the technical constitutional rules, is all; any material criterion (conformity of the law with the ethical end of the state, with the objective common good, with the objective moral law) is repudiated by positivism. The latter acknowledges only formal legality; it has no place for material legitimacy. Now either the will of the legislator, formulated with legal correctness, must be taken as a mere psychological act, or the will, i.e., the law, is to be regarded as the act of rational beings which has, or must be presumed to have, a content determinable by reason. Yet even the positivists agree that, for the jurist at least, the will of the legislator is no mere psychological act. The jurist has to concern himself with the intent of the law, with the *ratio legis;* that is, he has to concern himself with the normative intention of the lawmaker, not with the psychological facts of formulating and declaring or enouncing the intention. As applied in juridical and administrative practice, therefore, the psychological will disappears, and rightly so, and a new idea makes its appearance, namely, the rational intention of a normative character. In this way, what matters is not the psychological will enunciated in a legal document which represents the sole fact, but the normative intent of an abstract legislator who deliberates and resolves in a rational manner. The latter is substituted by the courts and administrative agencies for the factual lawmaker.

The law thus acquires an objective mode of self-existence which is independent of the psychological acts or of all persisting acts of will. Practically speaking, the law contained in the statute books is no longer any conscious and enduring will. It is construed as a regulative norm, as the result of the deliberations and reasonable intentions of a legislator who is presumed rational as well as prone to regulate certain social relations in a reasonable manner. The jurist imputes reasonableness to the will of the lawmaker; he is little concerned with the psychological process of willing. The law as a norm frees itself from the psychological will as soon as it is inscribed in the statute books and interpreted in the courts. Very often, indeed, it even frees itself from the actual intentions of the concrete legislators and acquires an existence of its own in virtue of the end or purpose in the law. It is not the subjective intention that matters, but the objective intention of an abstract reasonable legislator, whom the jurists assume to have, as a rational being, intended a reasonable regulative norm. The formal text of the statute is construed in this sense, and not by a study of the subjective, psychological moods, intentions, and wills of the accidental members of the legislature whose action may have been very unreasonable. This liberation of the law as an objective, reasonable norm from the actual concrete psychological will of the legislator proves that law is essentially reason and not arbitrary will.

In the second place, no positivist can get around the problem of limitations of governmental authority or limitations on the will (sovereign will) of the legislator. It is a common conviction that the law limits the will of the legislator, that the latter cannot will what he pleases. In effect, limitations of this sovereign will represent a dilemma for the positivist, who contends that the duly formulated and promulgated will of the legislator makes the law. Jellinek thought to resolve this dilemma of the positivists by saying that the lawmaker limits himself (theory of auto-limitation). But this theory does not solve the juridical dilemma, even though in practice the legislator may feel himself bound by promises of auto-limitation. For as long as the auto-limitation is itself dependent on the will of the lawmaker, those who are subject to this will are at the mercy of the uncontrolled arbitrariness of the lawmaker.

It may indeed be objected that at least under a representative form of government such an auto-limitation is workable enough in practice. Since in the system of representative government the will of the legislature is the product of a rational deliberation and ample discussion of pros and cons, it may safely be considered to represent the general will. In other terms, the legislative will is identified with the will of the citizens: the lawmakers and those subject to the law are in some way identical. But this contention is superficial and untenable. In actual practice, the general will, because representative government is almost necessarily party government, is always at best a majority decision against which the minority will ever claim the protection of the law. For the formal will of the numerical majority cannot logically be asserted to be always reasonable and just, however great the presumption may be that the majority has more and better reasons for its decision than has the minority. This claim of the minority to protection by the law against the will of the majority functioning as the positive law clearly shows that there exists prior to the positive law an a priori element of a material character which qualifies the legislative will as just or unjust. It is strange but common to see many jurists who adhere to positivism bow before this a priori limitation of the will when they turn social reformers. On these occasions they do not condemn the existing law as technically inefficient, as failing to achieve its juridically and morally indifferent purpose. On the contrary, they condemn the injustice of the purpose itself, the immorality and unreasonableness of the will itself. They thus acknowledge and establish pre-existing conceptions of justice, morality, and reasonableness as limitations of the legislative will and as material criteria of the positive law, in place of mere political prudence that seeks to avoid armed resistance on the part of a strong minority which has been defeated at the polls.

The influential French jurist, Léon Duguit (1859–1928), was quite conscious of this necessity of limiting the legislative will through the law. Nevertheless he stubbornly maintained that he was a positivist, and he labored to refute the idea of natural law. But how can the legislator's willing be limited by the law, if the latter is the creature of his will? According to the positivist school the state as legislator is the omnipotent creator of the law; but Duguit certainly did not agree with such a juridical deification of the legislator. If the state is the omnipotent creator of the law, a conflict between the law and the lawmaker is, as positivism indeed affirms, obviously out of the question. The will of the legislator may be economically unreasonable, financially disastrous, socially inefficient and futile, and morally perverse, yet juridically it is, if duly enacted, the law. The real problem, however, is that of the limitations on such legislative fiats by means of the law.

Duguit vehemently rejects all identification of law with the duly enacted will of the legislator. He protests strongly against the tendency of the majority of German jurists to regard any enactment duly emanating from the legislative organ as a legal norm before which the jurist has simply to bow and which he has to accept without subjecting it to critical evaluation.[3] Duguit insists that, on the contrary, there exists a rule of law that imposes itself upon rulers and governed alike, upon the state and its subjects. He contends that this rule of law exists and is valid apart from any intervention of the state, and that it is not the creature of the state's will. Yet he denies the seeming consequence that this rule must originate in a superior principle of the metaphysical order.[4]

What, then, is the nature of this rule of law? It is a social norm which has become juridical in virtue of the fact that the mass of individual consciences has come to understand that the material sanction of this norm can be socially organized.[5] Thus the rule of law does not contain a moral and juridical obligation of conscience; it is a mere indication that it will be wise for the individual to observe the rule lest he incur the organized resentment of the group. Yet it is the undeniable essence of law, of the juridical and moral norm, that it involves an imperative and binds the conscience, as Duguit himself is forced to concede.[6] Law by its very nature places an obligation on free rational beings, irrespective of the fear of

---

3. *Traité de droit constitutionnel* (2nd ed., 5 vols., Paris: E. de Boccard, 1920–25), I (3rd ed., 1927), 174 f.

4. Cf. *ibid.*, I, 97.

5. Cf. *ibid.*, I, 81, 93. Notice that Duguit says that the material sanction can be, not ought to be, organized.

6. Cf. *ibid.*, II, 169 f.

retaliation at the hands of the group or social milieu. Yet what is it that
obliges in the strict sense, and does not merely counsel on the basis of
utilitarian motives or prudential considerations? What, in final analysis,
legitimates the juridical norm? Duguit denies that a superior norm, a real
or hypothetical basic norm, such as the natural law, which he rejects, can
provide this legitimacy. However, he concedes that "the mass of individual consciences does not create the juridical norm." The bare fact that
such a norm is held or accepted by the mass of individuals does not, of
course, necessarily give to this norm an imperative character which binds
consciences, however much, by threat of ruthless enforcement, it may
compel people to outward conformity.

At this point in his argument Duguit, after the manner of Jhering,
introduces the teleological concept. The social norm is a "law of purpose"
which governs the cooperation of the individuals who form the social
group, limiting their actions and imposing certain acts while it leaves
intact the substance of their will.[7] Thus the end or object of the norm
becomes the criterion by which acts are judged right or wrong: acts which
are conformable to the end are right, those which are not conformable
thereto are wrong. But then the same problem recurs. For the question
inevitably arises: What ends are to be approved of as right, or disapproved
of as wrong? It appears obvious, indeed, that not all ends actually intended
by a concrete group are intrinsically right or good. To this Duguit replies
that social solidarity is the universal end. Right is what strengthens social
solidarity, wrong is what weakens it. But this criterion also is too formalistic. How may we distinguish a state or commonwealth from a robber
band? To attain their ends both need social solidarity. As St. Augustine
said, "Take away justice, and what are realms but great robber bands?"[8]
Duguit is fully aware of this objection. Hence he adds that, besides the
solidarity experienced as necessary by the mass of individual consciences,
these consciences must also have a sentiment of the justice, both commutative and distributive, of that sanction.[9] Thus the rule of law is character-

7. Cf. *ibid.,* I, 80 f.
8. *De civitate Dei,* Bk. IV, chap. 4. Cf. C. H. McIlwain, *The Growth of Political
Thought in the West from the Greeks to the End of the Middle Ages* (New York: Macmillan
Co., 1932), pp. 154–61.
9. *Op cit.,* I, 124 f.

ized by the end of social solidarity and by the justice of the sanctions of the rule. Consequently the justice of the sanction, not the justice of the end, would be the superior rule, the criterion of the rightness or wrongness of the positive law, of what the legislator wills. To this rather formalized justice, to this "rule of law" Duguit ascribed an over-all general validity for the law of all countries and for all branches of the law, private as well as public. They all obey the superior norm.[10] At the same time, he asserts that the spirit with which one has to approach the study of law, of all branches of the law, is the spirit of justice. In truth, Duguit seems to have come to the vestibule of natural law. His next step should have been a discussion of the rightness and wrongness of the concrete ends as measured by the objective ends in the metaphysical order.[11]

The work of Duguit leads to the inevitable conclusion that either positivism is sound—a contention which Duguit ably confutes—or the time-honored doctrine of natural law must be accepted in order that the legitimacy of the positive law can be founded on a superior norm of material justice, unvarying and general. The juridical norm cannot be based on the accidental historical fact of the will of the legislator; it must rest ultimately on being. Oughtness and being must in final analysis coincide. Normative oughtness must be grounded in metaphysical being. By attacking legal positivism Duguit had, as it were in spite of himself, to open the way to the idea of natural law.

It is true that a refutation of positivism does not lead straight to the idea of natural law. Yet it opens the way thereto, inasmuch as it raises the problems of the higher law, of the legitimacy of the positive law, of the intrinsic limitations of the power and will of the legislator. A rejection of positivism means a refusal to solve these problems by simply referring to the psychological motivation in the subjects, a motivation that makes it wise and profitable to comply with the demands of authority in view of the undesirable consequences of non-conformity. As a result, the con-

10. Cf. *ibid.*, I, 685 f.

11. For a good exposition of Duguit's theories of law as well as for a criticism of the same from the inadequate standpoint of an analytical jurist, see Westel W. Willoughby, *The Ethical Basis of Political Authority* (New York: Macmillan Co., 1930), chap. 21. Cf. also Charles G. Haines, *op cit.*, pp. 260–72.

temporary criticism of the modern concept of sovereignty must logically turn against legal positivism and thereby break down one of the greatest obstacles to the revival of the natural-law idea.

Numerous jurists have criticized the positivist concept of sovereignty. Positivism conceives sovereignty as legal and political power limited only by physical or psychological facts, not by the natural and divine law. This modern concept of sovereignty, which became particularly poisonous in combination with an essentially materialist rationalism, was not the brain-child of Jean Bodin. It stemmed rather from Hobbes, who allowed the idea of natural law, which was still held by him, to disappear in the will of the state. Bodin, on the other hand, stood for centralized state authority against feudalist pluralism and decentralization of political authority, but he never doubted that all such authority is subject to and limited by natural and divine law. Therefore the modern concept of absolute sovereignty could appear on the scene only after positivism (as a general philosophical trend) had freed sovereignty from the limitations which Christian tradition and the ideas of natural and divine law had placed upon it. These restrictions had in earlier times made Bills of Rights relatively unnecessary; the modern positivist conception of sovereignty has rendered formal and positive declarations of human rights a practical necessity.

For the past half-century this positivist concept of sovereignty has been vehemently criticized. Léon Duguit, H. Krabbe, Otto von Gierke, Hans Kelsen, and Harold J. Laski have led the attack. The sovereign authority must itself be subject to the law as a higher norm. The state, i.e., the political will-power, whether the latter is invested in an individual or in a majority group that can enforce conformity to its demands or to its will, is not the source of law; that is to say, will is not the essence of law. The irreducible source of law is, according to Krabbe, the sentiment and conviction of the members of the community as to what is law. The positive law thus becomes a mere declaratory agency which gives expression to the law residing in the people's consciousness and sentiment of right.[12]

Kelsen contends that it is impossible to found a normative oughtness

---

12. For the theories of Krabbe, cf. Westel W. Willoughby, *op. cit.*, pp. 410 ff.; Charles G. Haines, *op. cit.*, pp. 274–77.

upon a fact, upon being. A norm must always be founded upon another, a higher norm. The notion of sovereignty wrongly implies that a fact, a psychological being, the actual will of the legislator plus his socio-psychological power of coercion, is looked upon as the source of law or of oughtness. But every norm must be based on and derived from another, a higher norm, and, since this process cannot go on *ad infinitum,* Kelsen postulates a formal basic norm or original norm. It seems that his thoroughgoing agnosticism prevents him from anchoring his basic norm in a fundamental being of the metaphysical order. Hence his basic norm is a mere hypothetical construct, even if it is not inappropriately called *civitas maxima,* which of course is again a being.[13]

Had his agnosticism not stood in the way, Kelsen could have attained to the idea of natural law. In this conception rational nature, viewed in the Thomistic sense as a metaphysical being, is the rule of oughtness for the concrete being, and essence is the final cause of existence. Kelsen, however, does not make this latter distinction since for him being is simply existence. Yet it is interesting and significant that Kelsen's view of the relation between the positive law and the basic norm, however indistinct the character of the latter may be in his theory, shows a similarity of formal structure with the philosophy of natural law. But for his agnosticism this thought structure would have led straight to the conclusion that the basic norm must be the law of God, in whom being and oughtness are identical and who has revealed His law in the order of being, in the *ordo rerum,* from which through intuition or by discursive thinking we derive the precepts of natural law.

It is readily understandable that natural-law principles are for the most part being applied in the spheres of social life where the law itself is in the process of formation (e.g., social legislation, labor laws). The new legislation may set down, for instance, the principle of the social responsibility of the entrepreneur for his workers or the principle of mutual fidelity governing those engaged in a common business enterprise. These princi-

13. For a forceful criticism of Kelsen's theory, see Erich Kaufmann, *op. cit.,* pp. 20–35; Herman Heller, *Die Souveraenitaet, ein Beitrag zur Theorie des Staats- und Voelkerrechts* (Berlin and Leipzig: W. de Gruyter & Co., 1927); Heinrich Lenz, *"Autoritaet und Demokratie in der Staatslehre Kelsens," Schmollers Jahrbuch,* L, 4, pp. 93–124.

ples were overlooked in an age which out of an excessive concern for individual freedom would not allow ethical duties to be made strict legal obligations. Yet precisely because it is law in a formative stage, the new legislation has left undetermined the specific facts and conditions to which and in which these principles have to be applied. In such cases the legal determination and adjudication of facts and conditions have been made on the basis of natural-law concepts, by means of judicial decisions and with the help of such formulas as "from the nature of the case" and "in virtue of natural equity." Compare, e.g., what the papal social encyclicals, following in the footsteps of tradition, call natural law and what the courts designate from the nature of the matter as mutual legal responsibilities, duties, and rights in the field of labor relations. It will be found that the decisions of the courts and the demands of the encyclicals not only have much in common but are practically identical in content.

Furthermore, the ideas of the autonomy of nation and nationality in relation to the state have furnished a powerful inducement to criticize positivism. These ideas were already alive in the period before World War I, but they have since attained great force. From the standpoint of the right of a nationality to an autonomous life, it proved impossible to uphold the principle that law is what the state wills; and this is true in a state composed of a single nationality as well as in one that comprises several nationalities. The special value of the nationality had of necessity to become its special right which exists prior to the state and constitutes the natural-law limit of the state's centralized power. The "spirit of the nation" was at one time conjured up to do battle with the natural law. But now the same national spirit, with its natural-law claim to respect for its special value and therewith for its prerogatives, is rising up against the modern centralized administrative state with its continually expanding control of all domains of life. Here too, then, being has become the source of an ought. Liberal and nationalist thought maintained the identity of state and nation (viewed as a society of individuals). But this identity is being exploded by an appeal to the difference of values and thereby of the natural right of the nationality. The omnipotent state of positivism is turning into the instrumental order of the autonomous nation or people, whose members are not citizens or individuals but rather families, kindred and national groups with their culture growing out of blood, native province, and intellectual life.

International law is likewise law in process of formation. It is in this field that the old natural law is most noticeably returning to life. International law cannot be based solely on the mere self-obligation of sovereign states. A positivist foundation of international law is impossible because an international lawmaker is wanting. Consistent positivists logically deny altogether the legal character of international law. On the other hand, Franz von Liszt (1851–1919) asserts: "The international legal community rests upon the concept of the co-existence of different states with reciprocally delimited spheres of sovereignty, with a mutually recognized sphere of power. From this fundamental concept [more properly, from this essential being of the state exemplified in sundry states] follows immediately a whole series of legal norms, by which rights and duties of states are reciprocally determined, that need no special recognition through agreements to possess binding force" (whose source is therefore not the will of the states that form the union, but rather reason which derives these norms from the nature of the international legal community). ". . . The rights which result from this fundamental concept are due forthwith to each and every state as a member of the international legal community. . . . So far as these 'basic rights' form the object of special agreements between two or more states, these have either exclusively declaratory character or it is a question of carrying out in an individual case the principle which is self-evident."[14] Statements such as these could stand word for word in a natural-law treatise of the Late Scholastics, Vittoria, Suarez, or Bannez.

The protection of national minorities should also be mentioned in this connection. Since this protection ought to be the concern of international law, and not a mere matter of municipal law solely for reasons of internal policy within states which have minorities, this right to protection has come as a matter of course to be founded upon the natural-law preroga-

14. *Das Voelkerrecht systematisch dargestellt* (10th rev. ed., Berlin: Verlag von Julius Springer, 1915), p. 65.

tives of national minorities. That is, it has come to be based on rights which already had juridical existence prior not only to the purely declaratory positive constitutional principles of states with minorities but also to international legislation touching the protection of minorities. Writers of repute, like Wolzendorf, thus find it quite natural to speak openly of the natural law governing national minorities. If a foundation in the natural law is indispensable wherever law is in process of formation, this is certainly true today in the case of international law.

But all this does not yet, and without further ado, mean natural law. But it surely signifies one thing: There are still other sources of law besides the positive will of the legislator. The will of the state is not the sole source of law. Of equal importance as a source of law, and prior to it, is the "nature of the case," which is synonymous with what the older writers used to call the *ordo rerum*, the essential order of being. And, through the breaches thus effected in positivism, jurisprudence is subject to continual invasion on the part of ideas whose relationship with the old natural law grows steadily more apparent. Frequently, to be sure, because of the discredit into which the individualist natural law brought it, the old natural law goes under such designations as "sentiment of right," "a priori foundations of law," "consistent cultural norms."

In 1925, Niemeyer published in his review, *Niemeyers Zeitschrift fuer Internationales Recht*, the results of a questionnaire submitted to a representative group of professors of international law and jurists. These had been asked whether Grotius' theory of natural law (whose close connection with tradition has been pointed out) has validity today for the interpretation and completion of the positive international law, which rests upon the legal will and consent of states, so that international and national courts as well as arbitration tribunals ought to follow the principles of this theory. Of the forty-one best-known teachers of international law and jurists who replied to the query, fourteen answered with a flat "yes" and only eleven professed positivists gave a negative answer; the remaining sixteen adopted, it is true, a neutral position with respect to the natural law, but, on the other hand, they did not declare in favor of positivism. Of the last group one, for instance, rejected Wolff's conception of natural law, but he demanded that the judge effect just settlement of matters in dispute; another declared that positivism is impossible, that it has now passed its peak, and that international law may not be torn from its ethical roots; a third affirmed that Christian morality, as the native soil of the natural law, must have force even in international law.[15]

Many signs, therefore, point unmistakably to a renascence of natural law. Such renascence, moreover, concerns the metaphysical natural law, the *ius naturale perenne,* not the individualist natural law. It has coincided with a return to a doctrine of material values in ethics, and with a return to metaphysics in philosophy. This recent revival of the natural law is a fresh proof of its perpetual recurrence.

Despite appearances, the rise and spread of contemporary totalitarianism do not invalidate the contention that a distinct revival of natural law is occurring today. Modern totalitarianism is an end product; it is not the opening period of a new era. It is indeed the final outcome of positivism as a general philosophy, as an intellectual atmosphere, as a scientific method raised to the level of the absolute and divine. The position that law is will has come to mean that the human will is freed from all universal ideas, from any objective moral order beyond class interests, beyond nationalist or racial programs, beyond economic considerations, beyond unlimited evolutionary progress. But modern totalitarianism has provided the *reductio ad absurdum* of the axiom, *Voluntas facit legem;* indeed, it has revitalized in its victims and adversaries the idea of natural law. For resistance to totalitarianism, in which the end results of positivism appear as ethical and intellectual nihilism, had to look for support beyond any mere national tradition or *status quo ante* and base itself on something superior to history, race, class, scientific method, and the like.

In the first place, the nationalist form of totalitarianism arose and flourished most in the two countries where juridical and moral positivism had obtained a dominant position in the universities, in the legal profession, and in the official philosophies of law which conditioned or determined the outlook and practice of courts and government. For in Italy and Germany, more than anywhere else, positivism had filled

---

15. For a rather full account of the results of Niemeyer's questionnaire, see Charles G. Haines, *op. cit.,* pp. 294–300.

the void created by the dissolution of the idealistic philosophies of the nineteenth century. In the eyes of this juridical positivism the mythical will of the state, formally established in accordance with constitutional norms, was the sole, exclusive, and sufficient source and foundation of law. When, therefore, the totalitarian revolutions had succeeded by formally legal methods, whence could a positivist, whether judge or jurist, derive a critical norm that would enable him to pass judgment on the legitimacy of the legally correct totalitarian revolution? Or how could a positivist determine the intrinsic injustice of a formally legal act of the now totalitarian government? An appeal to former legal traditions, to juridical ideas that formerly were commonly accepted, could be of no avail since, according to positivism, these possessed validity only because they had been the then will of the state. Any criticism of, or resistance to, totalitarianism had consequently to find a deeper juridical basis of criticism or resistance than the mere actual will of the state formulated with legal correctness and enforced with an irresistible power. Is it far-fetched to contend that the predominance of positivism among judges, high government officials, and teachers of jurisprudence robbed them of any juridical support against the will of the now totalitarian state?

It is worth observing in this connection that the resistance which Catholicism has offered to totalitarianism and its pseudoreligious political creeds is not based exclusively on dogmatic theology but above all on natural law. Nathaniel Micklem has rightly pointed out[16] that the Confessional (Protestant) Church in Germany, under the influence of Barthian theology, which rejects a natural theology and with it the idea of natural law, has had a less advantageous basis for its resistance to Hitlerism, whereas the Catholics have had the natural-law doctrine to lean on in addition to their religious principles.

It is further deserving of mention that totalitarian propaganda, aware of the recent revival of natural-law thinking, has abused the term "natural law." Such abuse of revered terms is indeed typical of totalitarianism: witness today the sorry abuse of the term "democracy" at the

---

16. *National Socialism and the Roman Catholic Church* (New York: Oxford University Press, 1939).

hands of totalitarian leftist regimes. As if out of reverence for them, terms like "natural law" and "natural rights of the nation" have been frequently used in propaganda and even in serious books.[17] But it is quite evident that the term "natural" has here undergone an even more wanton disfigurement than it suffered at the hands of Hobbes, Hume, or the utilitarians. "Nature" no longer refers to the rational nature of each individual man or to man's endowments of intellect and free will, on which rest the dignity, liberty, and initiative of the individual person;[18] nor does it refer to the universal order of being and oughtness, to the transcendent reality of reason. On the contrary, nature is transformed into an altogether materialistic concept. It is viewed as the blood, the hereditary biological mass of animal nature, deprived of its personalist and spiritual values. Thus metamorphosed, the law of nature has but one principle: Right is what profits the German folk-community—just as a deformed proletarian natural law would yield the single principle: Right is what profits the proletariat. This vicious alteration of the meaning of the terms "nature" and "natural" makes it possible for Huber on one page to abuse the venerable terms in the interest of the blood-and-race ideology and on another to maintain that "there are no personal liberties of the individual which fall outside the realm of the state and which must be respected by the state. . . . The constitution of the Reich is not based upon a system of inborn and inalienable rights of the individual."[19]

As a consequence the internal and external opponents of totalitarianism have had to base their defense and their criticism on the perennial idea of natural law as it has been preserved in the *philosophia perennis,* in common sense, and in the juridical tradition of Western civilization. Moreover, they have had to take this stand in spite of and against the prevailing evolutionary materialism, philosophical positivism, or the refined historical materialism of the Neo-Marxist and pragmatist schools of thought. Thus the natural-law doctrine became willy-nilly the ideological basis of the struggle against totalitarianism. Totalitarian

17. Cf. Ernst R. Huber, *Verfassungsrecht des Grossdeutschen Reiches* (Hamburg: Hanseatische Verlag, 1939), pp. 194 ff.

18. Cf. St. Thomas, *De potentia,* q.9, a.5.

19. *Op. cit.,* p. 361.

regimes are in their very nature the ultimate consequences of the positivist denial of natural law, i.e., of a transcendental and universal moral
and juridical order valid for all nations, races, classes, and individuals,
of an a priori for all legal institutions and for any will of the state. The
growth of totalitarian regimes, far from checking or reversing the revival
of natural law, has on the contrary contributed mightily to this revival
in ever wider circles. For totalitarianism has opened the eyes of more
and more thinking people to the ultimate consequences to which the
denial of the natural law must lead. Such consequences were not obvious
or clearly predictable so long as modern society, though infected with
positivism, continued to live on, beguiled by an optimistic faith in an
inevitable and automatic evolutionary progress and under the protection
of a constitutional form of government which was still feeding on an
inherited Christian substance. People and their leaders were therefore
not yet sufficiently aware of the depths of evil and perversion to which
the evolutionary product, man, supposedly determined by blood or
mere economic conditions, could sink, if once the age-old moral and
intellectual molds and floodgates were shattered.

In the next place, totalitarianism and the struggle against it have
also brought to light the weakness of a more refined form of juridical
positivism. This subtle form of juridical positivism (sometimes referred
to as juristic monism or analytical jurisprudence), though it does not
deny the absolute character of the moral law, maintains that legally
the state can do anything, since positive law as the will of the state
does not find a legal limit in the moral law. Juridically, it holds, there
exists only the self-limitation of the state's will. But this contention
rests on an illicit separation of positive law from its matrix, the natural
law, which is simultaneously ethical and juridical. The Kantian separation of morality and legality, which was a reaction to Hobbes' effort
to identify morality and legality, may underlie this position. Yet the
consequences are the same.

The formula according to which the state can legally do anything
(which recalls the description of the emperor as *lex animata* in Late
Roman jurisprudence) appears to be equivocal. If by the phrase "can
do legally" is meant that the state, i.e., the persons in authority or
holding power, controlling the legislative organ and the enforcement

machinery of a totalitarian regime, can declare anything law and can by physical force and psychological threat compel subjects to active obedience or at least to passive conformity, then this is merely a statement of experimentally verified fact. Totalitarianism has indeed proved how far a modern tyrannical regime can legally go in declaring lawful any act which it deems advantageous to its arbitrary aims, from the suppression of religious freedom to the shooting of guiltless hostages and the killing of innocent persons in the interest of scientific research or of purity of the racial stock. By applying all the means at the disposal of the modern state with its intricate compulsory mechanism (propaganda, terror, fear, indoctrination and control of economic life), the totalitarian state is comparatively or even practically certain of the obedience and conformity of its subjects. For the life and fortune of these would be at stake should they fail to conform. In addition, the totalitarian state will always find, among the citizens, individuals who by reason of indoctrination, perversion, or brutalization will serve as its agents and actively compel all others to conform.

But this actual fact of being able legally to do anything or of being able to declare any act lawful is not the real problem. Actually, when we use the term "can" we mean "may." We have in mind the moral problem: How far is the state permitted to go? By "state" we here mean the persons who have at their disposal the means of compelling conformity of the citizens and active obedience of the law-enforcing agencies to their commands, duly declared legal or lawful. The problem is thus whether resistance to the state on the part of the citizens and refusal to obey on the part of the executive organs become lawful if the commands clothed with legality go beyond the line which separates licit and illicit use of legal power, of the legal "can." It seems clear that the question cannot be solved by saying that the line is where the state is certain to find open and violent resistance and insurmountable mass disobedience. For this is a matter of mere psychological fact or experiment; it is a matter of expediency. An answer is possible only if a paramount law is acknowledged that serves as a measure and critical norm both for acts which are formally declared legal and for the lawfulness of resistance and disobedience. Furthermore, what is to be said of the execution of orders of superiors, orders which in a totalitarian state are indubitably lawful inasmuch as the will of the state is always lawful? Is the minor war criminal, who hides behind the lawful orders of the supreme war lord as head of the state, free from moral and legal responsibility for execution of a lawful act of his superior, of an act that is obviously in conflict with natural law and reason though not with the laws of his state?

To put these questions is to answer them. "Every positive law, from whatever lawgiver it may come, can be examined as to its moral implications, and consequently as to its moral authority to bind in conscience, in the light of the commandments of the natural law."[20] It is inadmissible to separate the legal "can" and the moral "may," the formal legality of the positive law and its material morality (the agreement or disagreement of the positive law and its material morality, i.e., the agreement or disagreement of the positive law with the natural law). Totalitarianism has merely verified once more the profound wisdom of St. Augustine's dictum: "Take away justice, and what are realms but great robber bands?"[21] The natural law binds all men collectively and each one separately: the sovereign lawmaker, the executive or administrative official, the judge or juror, the citizen and subject. Duguit as well as the Roman jurists had a higher opinion of the jurist's office and function than merely to bow before all acts of the state clothed in due legal forms.

To repeat, such theories as this can flourish only so long as their sociological and political presuppositions prevail: a consciousness of political unity in spite of a pluralism of groups; free associations in religious, economic, and cultural life; a limited sovereignty under an unquestioned constitution which includes a bill of rights, some division of powers, a procedure to protect officials against arbitrary acts of repression on the part of their superiors, and, above all, a truly independent judiciary. As soon as these institutions are suppressed *de facto* or *de jure* by totalitarian regimes, the weakness of this subtlest form of juridical positivism and the necessity of a moral basis for positive law appear with unmistakable clarity and force.

20. Piux XI, Encyclical *Mit brennender Sorge* (1937), cited by Michael Oakeshott, *The Social and Political Doctrines of Contemporary Europe* (Cambridge: Cambridge University Press, 1939), pp. 53 f.

21. *De civitate Dei*, Bk. IV, chap. 4.

PART TWO

Philosophy and Content of the Natural Law

CHAPTER VIII

Being and Oughtness

The history of the natural-law idea shows that there are many ways of clothing any system of ideal law with the appeal of the natural or the rational. In periods when the positive law, grown rigid, is no longer the order of justice that people believe in, but rather a means in the struggle of the ruling class to maintain its social and political power which can no longer be justified in the name of the general welfare, revolutionary and reforming groups, unwilling or unable to appeal to the "good old law," have to appeal to the natural law. On such occasions, however, the natural law all too readily appears as something impure, as almost inextricably entangled with juridical demands arising from the concrete sociological situation: demands whose bases are not solid from every point of view, whose support lies in passion rather than in reason.

Yet one point history does make clear. The idea of natural law obtains general acceptance only in the periods when metaphysics, queen of the sciences, is dominant. It recedes or suffers an eclipse, on the other hand, when being (not taken here in Kelsen's sense of mere existentiality or factuality) and oughtness, morality and law, are separated, when the essences of things and their ontological order are viewed as unknowable.

The natural law, consequently, depends on the science of being, on metaphysics. Hence every attempt to establish the natural law must start from the fundamental relation of being and oughtness, of the real and the good. Since the establishment of the natural law further depends upon the doctrine of man's nature, this human element has also to be studied, especially inasmuch as the question of the primacy of intellect or will in man is related to being and oughtness. In the next place, justness, or right as the object of justice, needs to be considered if we are to grasp the distinction between *lex naturalis* and *ius naturale*. A brief survey of the order of the sciences will thereafter be in place. Only then, finally, will it be worth while to go into the details of the natural law, in order to explain, from the theoretical side as well, the actual historical fact of the perpetual recurrence of the natural law.[1]

If moral philosophy and, in moral philosophy and with it, legal philosophy are to have a solid foundation, they must be a continuation of metaphysics. At least this is true of a natural system of ethics and jurisprudence, though not of a positivist one which is grounded only in a will as such. In this connection "being" does not denote simple existence, the imperfect form of being. It means essential being, the *esse essentiae*. Kelsen, who repeatedly asserts that oughtness has nothing to do with being, with the factual, and that the science of law must be constructed in a purely normological fashion, has not heeded this distinction which is basic for the metaphysics of realism. His rationalism, therefore, leads him to a theory of law devoid of contents and constructed apart from the factual, the existent. Yet since his atheistic relativism prevents him from acknowledging with Occam a supreme omnipotent will of God as the source of all norms, Kelsen's rationalism ends by bringing him to the position that factual reality is indeed the ultimate, primordial norm, that is, the existence of the order of the

---

1. In his otherwise valuable study, *The Revival of Natural Law Concepts*, Charles G. Haines resolutely forgoes dealing "with the philosophical and psychological processes which underlie natural law thinking" (p. viii). Yet this self-imposed limitation, psychologically very difficult if not impossible of observance, does not prevent the author from freely criticizing and evaluating the natural-law doctrine in its various forms—which only an epistemology and a metaphysics would rightly allow him to do. E.g., the exposition of natural law by Viktor Cathrein, S.J., is unjustly but altogether typically taxed with being religious and supernatural (pp. 286 f.). This merely means, of course, that the thinking of the Jesuit moral philosopher is theistic and not utterly secularist, does not view nature as a self-subsisting, closed whole, and does not eschew ultimates so far as they are attainable by the natural powers of the human mind. Benjamin F. Wright, Jr., is similarly unphilosophical-minded. He concludes his volume, *American Interpretations of Natural Law*, with the words: "Natural law, in its essence, is the attempt to solve the insolvable" (p. 345). But such a conclusion stands or falls with its particular frame of reference, characterized by metaphysicophobia.

civitas maxima, the factually existing world legal order. But this position is downright paradoxical in view of his ideal of a science of pure, normative law built upon the unbridgeable opposition between being and oughtness. Thus for Kelsen, precisely because he lacks Occam's supreme will which lays down the positive norm, existence and oughtness ultimately coincide. Thus he arrives at an extreme empiricism. Had he had a metaphysics, the doctrine of essential being, he would have avoided this contradiction.

For being and oughtness must in final analysis coincide. Or to express it differently, being and goodness, the ontological and deontological or moral orders must at bottom and ultimately be one.

Accordingly, the first prerequisite of an unalterable, permanent, standard natural law is the possibility of a knowledge of being, of a knowledge of the essences of things; in other words, a realistic epistemology or theory of knowledge. For Pufendorf, Kant, and others, who have no realistic epistemology, not being but some impulse or other, a special property like sociality or a postulate of practical reason like freedom, is the source of oughtness, the principle of ethics and of natural law. Deductive reason is thereby freed from control by reality and consistently indulges in an increasingly hollow rationalism which, to be meaningful, borrows continually from the actual political and sociological ideals of the age. Natural law in the strict sense is therefore possible only on the basis of a true knowledge of the essences of things, for therein lies its ontological support.

Thomistic philosophy lays the foundation of the natural law in the following manner: Man perceives individual things through the imagination and the senses, and he is thus able to apply the universal knowledge which is in the intellect to the particular thing; for, properly speaking, it is neither the intellect nor the senses that perceive: it is man who understands by means of both. The intellect alone does not understand; that is to say, objective reality or the things of the external world do not release in the soul ideas of things which are already innate. Nor do the senses alone perceive: it is not individual things alone that exist, and the concepts of essences, which the intellect forms in a quasi-authoritarian manner from motives of economy of thought, are not without foundation in reality, as both nominalism and sensism maintain. Again, it is not the intellect alone that understands, as rationalism pretended when it placed the conditions and the measure of knowledge in the intellect as subjective forms of the latter, and when it failed to make things or reality the measure and condition of knowledge. As a result, the deductive intellect, for which the essences in real things remain unknowable, can no longer control itself by reference to reality. But man understands by means of senses and intellect. Consequently, through intellectual activity he knows the essences from the things. Things in their reality, i.e., that which actually is, are the measure of knowledge. The entire domain of that which is (and is therefore knowable) in the context of the first principles and ultimate particulars constitutes the intellect's field of investigation.

The things themselves are the cause and measure of our knowledge. The speculative intellect is moved by the things themselves, and thus the things are its measure. The being of the thing is the measure of truth. We constantly meet with these and similar propositions in the writings of St. Thomas. It further follows that there is nothing in the intellect that has not first been in the senses.[2] For the senses are the gateway through which things or reality pass, according to the mode of the intellect, into the latter's immaterial possession. But the senses always portray only the particular. Phantasms, the images of things, transmitted by the senses constitute material for the intellect, and this material has to be transformed from sense perception into intellectual knowledge. Knowledge, however, is the apprehension of essences. A thing is not known through the senses, but through the intellect with the aid of the senses, since the intellect apprehends or takes into itself the thing in its essence, in that which it is. At first, then, the intellect is passive. Reality exists prior to the intellect. The mental image is a copy whose original is the real. This real, moreover, presupposes for its actuality only God the Creator, the first creative intellect, who as the All-actual and All-operative gives things their measure. But reality is independent of its being thought of or noticed

2. It is amazing how frequently this fundamental proposition of Aristotelian and scholastic epistemology, *nihil est in intellectu quod prius non fuerit in sensu*, is described as John Locke's contribution to psychology. Locke's sole claim to fame on this point is to have emphasized this axiom against Descartes' doctrine of innate ideas.

by the finite intellect. It exists whether or not the finite intellect thinks of it.

The human mind is at first passive, receptive, open. It is not, however, as though the intellect were affected by the senses and, looking into itself, perceives innate ideas released through sense impressions. Nor is it as though there were in the intellect a thought-mechanism which now in accordance with subjective conditions works the images into ideas, independently of the being of the thing represented. On the contrary, the human mind is able to understand only by remaining in contact with reality: by continually adjusting its knowledge to reality. For true cognition is the agreement of the thing as known with the object of knowledge, the thing itself. Or, according to the recent way of stating the matter, it is the agreement of the assertion expressed in the judgment with the actual reality, of the logical with ontological truth, of the intellectual equation with a real equality. Hence the great importance of experience, the incessant self-orientation toward reality which is the norm of thought. Continual experience of reality, not a sort of geometrical deduction from a principle, is the adequate method. This is all the more important, too, the farther thought wishes to proceed with its deduction. St. Thomas himself requires experience in particular for moral philosophy and the science of law. Not doctrine, but experience over a long period of time proves the goodness of a law. The difference between realism and an empiricism that glories in experience does not, consequently, lie in the preference of empiricism for experience (induction) whereas realism, so to say, prefers speculation (deduction). The difference consists rather in the fact that empiricism remains content with what is in the foreground, with actual reality, whereas realism, with its delight in knowledge, holds it to be both possible and necessary to push beyond the cheerfully affirmed actuality to that which is in the background, to the metaphysical, to the essences and their laws of being in the actual facts.

The object of rational knowledge or cognition is therefore not the particular or the individual as such; this the senses lay hold of. The object of cognition, what judgments assert of the individual thing in the predicate, is what the thing is: the essence of the thing which lies hidden in the core of phenomena as an idea in every thing of the same kind; in a word, the form. The intellect does not attain to the core of the being by way of intuition, by the immediate contemplation of the being, but by way of abstraction. This brings us to the famous dispute over universals and to the distinction, basic for the possibility of all metaphysics, between essence (quiddity, whatness) and existence (haecceity, thisness).

Sense perception grasps only the particularity of the existent being, of the individual thing, as, e.g., this man or this concrete state. But cognition is founded on the perception of the universal, of that which is in all things of the same kind as their quiddity or essence. The thing is that which the abstract concept of the thing, the object of intellectual knowledge, represents, signifies, means; and this object of intellectual knowledge is really in the thing. Being belongs to a nature, e.g., to the nature of a stone, in a twofold manner: existential being, so far as the nature is in this stone and that one, which it therefore possesses in the individual thing; and intentional or mental being, which the nature attains in the individual intellect, in mine and in yours, so far as it is thought of by us. But the nature becomes universal and hence representative of the essence, the quiddity of the thing, when it is abstracted, as St. Thomas says, *ab utroque esse*, when it is viewed apart from existence in things of the external world as well as from existence in the thought of some intellect. It is this nature, considered absolutely and in itself, which is predicated of all individuals as their quiddity, their form, their essence, their nature.

The universals are not substances.[3] They do not live in a heavenly region, nor does the soul, affected by sense impressions, remember them from its premundane sojourn in that region, as Plato held. Nor are they mere names or vocal utterances (*flatus vocis*) which, lacking a foundation in reality, were arbitrarily devised by human agreement for the purpose of bringing order into the welter and chaos of sense impressions; hence they are not arbitrary products of the human intellect or of the human will. Finally, neither are they types derived by a process of pure induction from individual things: certain uniformities which lead only to an empirically probable general validity, so far as our

---

3. I.e., not primary substances in the Platonic sense. See, e.g., K. F. Reinhardt, *op. cit.*, p. 43.

experience has gone. On this distinction rests that of existence and essence; upon it also is founded teleological thinking as well as the unity of being and oughtness in the metaphysical order.

This essence in the thing is the measure of our knowing. It is the universal predicate in the judgment which establishes the truth of our knowledge. For a judgment does not say that the abstract concept in my mind is the thing, but that the objective content, which is independent of the mere fact that I am thinking of it, of the abstract concept is perceived by me in the individual. For example, a state in itself does not exist. Concrete states alone exist. But a social unit, a territorial corporation, I call a state because and so far as it is a realization of the idea "state." Accordingly the intellect alone does not know, nor do the senses alone know, but man knows by means of both.

To be sure, as has been stated, things as bearers of essence can be the measure of our knowledge only because they themselves in turn receive measure from the supreme creative intellect of God, who measures all things with wisdom. The divine reason by thinking creates the essence of things. The divine will brings them into existence either immediately as first cause or indirectly through secondary causes. This is basic for the possibility of the natural law, because it means that the essential forms are not dependent in their quiddity on the absolute will of the almighty Spirit, but only in their existence. The essential forms of things are unalterable because they are ideas of the immutable God. Occam's question of whether God must be able to will that His rational creatures hate Him is the foundation for his moral positivism. Conversely, the doctrine of the immutability of the natural law, of the natural goodness of certain moral actions that follows from the nature of things, has meaning only if the unchangeableness of essences is acknowledged. These lines of thought are of importance because the principle that law is positively something pertaining to reason and not mere arbitrary will depends upon this realistic epistemology. This is also shown indirectly by the fact that the principle that law is arbitrary will (*auctoritas facit legem,* and other equivalent formulas) is founded upon a nominalist or purely empiricist theory of knowledge.

The principle that being and truth coincide is a further consequence of the foregoing considerations. Intellect and reality stand in a threefold relationship to each other. From the viewpoint of the intellect we speak of knowing, of the thing, of the real, of being known, and the unity of both is called truth. To know a thing, however, means to apprehend or assimilate the essence of the thing or its form. In contrast to creatures which lack cognition, the intellect is capable of having, and even of becoming, the form of another (every created) thing. The knowing mind is in a certain manner everything. Knowledge is possession of forms. "The intellect in act is wholly, i.e., perfectly, the thing understood."[4] The attainment of the abstract concept, of the universal, whose content is the essence, is the function of the active intellect. The latter gathers from the real, which is given in the mental image of the sense impressions, the immaterial essential core, intelligible being itself, which however is identical with the natural being in the real. Hence a being, so far as it is intelligible, is also true. All that is is true, because it is knowable.

But the essence (form) which constitutes the real thing in its being is also the end, the final cause, of the thing. The Aristotelian-Thomistic theory of knowledge starts essentially from the actual fact of motion, of self-change or of being changed, in short, from the attempt to comprehend becoming. Thence came the distinction between an inner, enduring core, the form, and a changeable element, the matter, that which is formed or molded in every material thing. The prototype of such thinking is the creative activity of the artist, who fashions the form out of the material or matter, as well as organic growth in the realm of animate nature, as in the case of plants: in seeds the incorporeal form, acting after the manner of an entelechy, unfolds itself in the matter. The form is not only the proximate efficient cause of the thing; it is also its end. All beings aim at, strive after, desire, their own perfection. But goodness is that which all things aim at, strive after, desire, since the essence of goodness consists in this, that it is in some way desirable. Therefore perfection and whatever leads to it are good.[5] Becoming, the proper condition of all created being, is the way to perfection, to fullness of being. Hence the more perfectly a created

4. St. Thomas, *Quaestiones duodecim quodlibetales,* VII, art. 2. Cf. also Joseph Pieper, *Die Wirklichkeit und das Gute* (Leipzig: Jakob Hegner, 1935), pp. 31 ff.

5. Cf. St. Thomas, *Summa theologica,* Ia, q.5, a.1.

being becomes its essence, and the more its thisness approaches its quiddity, the more does the essence overcome the imperfection in the existence. In God, the most perfect Being, essence and existence are consequently identical. God is pure Act; He is absolute, most perfect Being. The creature, however, is its quiddity in an imperfect manner only; yet it is intended to become this quiddity, to realize its idea. Becoming is the condition of the creature; being is the nature of God. The full realization of its nature, of the idea, is the end or goal of a thing, ever greater realization of the quiddity in existence. This holds true of inanimate nature, so far as it is moved from without, as the artist fashions more and more perfectly the form of the statue out of the material. But it also holds good of animate nature, which in the process of becoming realizes more and more perfectly the form which is germinally present in it. Whence the axioms: every being, as being, is good; being, truth, and goodness are convertible.

Let us take an example or two. The so-called marriage that legally existed for a while in Soviet Russia was rejected by the more or less Christian West because it was not distinguishable from concubinage. But this position did not rest on a comparison of the Soviet view of marriage with the marriage law of the French Civil Code, or with the *matrimonium* of Roman law, or with the marriage legislation of Germany or of the Anglo-Saxon countries. It was based upon a measurement by the idea of marriage which is expressed and exemplified in the positive legal institutions of these codes. We speak of the imperfection of a piece of marriage legislation by measuring it against the idea of marriage. Moreover, in the history of marriage legislation we distinguish stages according as the positive, historical, legal forms realize the idea of marriage in a more or less perfect manner.

Again, a territorial corporation or a tribe does not become a state by the fact that international bodies or other states recognize it, as though international recognition were constitutive of right. No; this recognition takes place, and the territorial corporation has a right to this recognition, because an actual case is present which realizes, however imperfectly, the idea of state; in this way a state can become known, and it thereupon has a right to formal recognition. The basis of the obligation to recognize this state lies in the degree in which the idea of state is realized. Incidentally, the school of comparative law leaves us unsatisfied because, for fear of natural law, which nevertheless makes its appearance, it avoids taking the final step to the nature, to the idea, of legal institutions. Its work thereby becomes interesting, instructive, informative. But it enters only the vestibule of the philosophy of law, where its skepticism detains it.

The teleological conception, grounded in the metaphysics of being, is therefore the basis of the essential unity of being and oughtness, of being and goodness. The entire past had to be forgotten before the theory of pure law, the normological school, could maintain that being has nothing in common with oughtness. It was right when it was unwilling that empirical existence should be regarded as a root of oughtness. The factual cannot become right in virtue of mere factuality. There is no factuality of right. A basis of right exists only when in something factual an essential being is striving for realization. Right can never arise from a violation of right. Yet even laws of an illegitimate ruler can bind in conscience, not in virtue of the illegitimate power, but by reason of the actual fact of the common good realized through the laws, irrespective of their factual source, and so far as they realize it. The distinction between essence and existence would have preserved from its antimetaphysical formalism the theory of pure law, whose criticism of the thesis that the fact creates right is so effective. It would likewise have saved it from its ultimate relapse into the thesis of the factuality of right in the case of the *civitas maxima* or great society.

The essence of a thing is the norm and the goal of its becoming. But the creature is always in the state of becoming or development, whether toward the goal, toward goodness, or away from the goal, toward evil, that is, toward the lack of being. But goodness is the final embodiment or realization of the essence in existence, of the tendency of the existent being toward its essence. The fullness of being is the goal. Every being (everything that is real) tends naturally to become its essence, to realize its idea. But that toward which a nature has always an essential bent is a good; for it is an inclination toward perfection. Every real thing moves toward its essence. The perfection of being is the end, the good, the essence. Fullness of being is the real in the repose of the goal of becoming, of self-movement, or of motion from without.[6]

Thus in the essence lies the norm, the end or goal is in the quiddity, and the good is the full being. Therefore all that is, so far as it is real being, is good. But since the good also ought to be, it follows that in the domain of metaphysics being and oughtness coincide.

These ideas lead further to the conception of an order of reality, that is, according to the degree of being which things possess. This order rises from purely potential being which is not yet real through the stages of created actual being with a greater and greater content of being and with less and less mere potentiality. It mounts from the inanimate creation through the world of animate beings to the living rational being that is man as the norm of creation. It culminates in God, the most perfect Being, who is both infinitely superior to the whole of creation and essentially different from it. In God all distinctions between being and becoming, motion and immovableness, potency and act, essence and existence, become meaningless. For God is purest Being, purest Act, unmoved Mover of all things, and therefore most perfect Goodness, deepest Truth, ultimate Norm and highest End, in whom there is no distinction between essence and existence. Hence God as the supreme Good is also the goal of all created being, as indeed the latter is being solely in virtue of its participation in the divine Being, although merely in an improper, analogical sense. God is the final end of all human life and activity. His glory is the goal of creation.

The world is order. The order of creatures according to the differentiation of their natures and their gradations proceeds from God's wisdom. Chance is not the origin of things, nor is the world a chaos into which our intelligence had to bring order. The law of order corresponds to God's wisdom, which first conceived it in idea prior to God's will calling it into existence. This order is therefore an order in accordance

6. See in particular Gustaf J. Gustafson, S.S., *The Theory of Natural Appetency in the Philosophy of St. Thomas*, pp. 68–90, and, for an excellent psychological analysis of appetency on the sensuous and rational levels, Celestine N. Bittle, O.F.M. Cap., *The Whole Man*, pp. 242–46, 354–59.

with the essence of God. Whatever is real is an imperfect exemplification of the ideas of God which are embodied in things. Man recognizes this order as directed to one final end, to God Himself, who at one and the same time is origin and end of the order. For the rational creature endowed with free will, who cooperates in shaping the world, the order of being thus becomes an order of ends, culminating in the final and highest end, the glory of God.[7]

7. A brief but clear treatment of the important concept of God's eternal glory, fundamental and formal, as the end or purpose of the created universe (so frequently misunderstood) will be found in John F. McCormick, S.J., *Scholastic Metaphysics.* Part II, *Natural Theology* (Chicago: Loyola University Press, 1931), pp. 201–05; Ignatius W. Cox, S.J., *Liberty—Its Use and Abuse* (2 vols., New York: Fordham University Press, 1936–37), I, 9–11.

CHAPTER IX

Intellect and Will

The order perceived by reflective thought is not, however, a rigid, static order of motionless things. It is not external compulsion, a clocklike mechanism which, once wound, runs according to mechanical laws. The order conforms to the natures of the things. It is indeed an order of necessity for inanimate as well as for living but irrational creatures. But it is an order of freedom, a moral order, for beings endowed with reason and free will. Therefore, so far as man perceives that he is a creature possessed of free will who is not subject to blind necessity but to the law of freedom, he also perceives that this order, in accordance with God's will, ought to be. The ontological order becomes, in relation to man endowed with free will, the moral order. The order of being confronting the intelligence becomes the order of oughtness for the will. Since, therefore, from knowledge of the essences of things the order is perceived as established by God in conformity with His essence, this order necessarily appears to the will of the rational and free creature as likewise an order to be attained and preserved and as a norm of the finite will. But this order is naturally and really "given." It is not projected by human reason, in keeping with subjective, regulative forms, into an external world which in itself is unrecognizable as order. It is objective order, independent both of our thought and of its being thought of here and now.

In its essence this order is established by God's wisdom; in its existence it has proceeded from God's will. In its meaning and end it is again directed to God, the highest end. Teleologically also there is but the one order, because being is both true and good.

The law of order, then, does not lie in the bare, positively promulgated will of God, but in the nature of things as God's wisdom ordains them. The order of being can be a moral order only if its essential basis is God's wisdom, only if in God the intellect is, humanly speaking, the nobler faculty. Otherwise we could never derive a norm from the essential order of the world, but solely from the revealed will of God.

It has already been shown how in moral philosophy this thesis of the will as the nobler faculty led, and had to lead, through Duns Scotus to Occam, i.e., to the most one-sided moral positivism, for the doctrine of the will as the nobler faculty is itself the root of nominalism. But nominalism, directed only to the individual, particular thisness, to the existence which is related to the will, arrives in its extreme forms at the denial of the clear and distinct knowability of the essences of things, of the essence which is related to the intellect. The universals are but vocal utterances. Reality, since in its quiddity it is not unmistakably knowable for us, is likewise not the measure of our knowledge. The order of being cannot of itself become a norm of the will; the absolute, omnipotent will of the Supreme Being can alone become that.

The entire doctrine of the eternal law and natural moral law is undermined by such a view. Just as the theory of will in municipal and international law cannot admit a law beyond the positive one (or, more precisely stated, beyond the factual will as a persisting act), so Occam, for instance, could not admit a morality that does not have its first, proximate, and sole norm in omnipotent will, in the absolute power of God. If, then, the idea of God and therewith the supreme personal will are lost to sight or rejected, nothing is left as the source of norms but the concrete will of the earthly lawmaker. Or, as in the case of Spinoza, the deep impulses of nature (here taken as contrasted with mind) are regarded as the natural norm. The biological as well as materialistic ethical systems and theories of law have here their roots.

From this it follows that the doctrine of the priority of the intellect over the will in God as well as in man is a prerequisite of the possibility of a natural moral law and hence of the natural law in the narrower sense. It is significant that traditionalism is congenial both to the historical school of law and to the conservative thinking of Donoso Cortes, De Maistre, and A. von Haller, a consequence of the deep feeling against rationalism. The principles of morality, it appeared to them, are not to be discovered in being. They are a positive revelation, a primordial revelation, mysteriously handed down through the centuries and millennia in the hearts of men.

The objective, the real, is the measure of knowledge. The order subsisting in reality is perceived by man. At first it is known in a speculative, purely intuitive way. Reason is thus for a long while absorbent, receptive. But man is not only pure reason; as a free agent and part of the order, he is himself called to realize it. As reason turns from pure, merely receptive knowledge, from the idea as end, to existent being, it becomes practical reason which is directed to doing and making. Being is perceived as oughtness; the idea is perceived as goal and norm of making and doing. Realistic metaphysics sets out from artistic activity as a model as it does also from self-consciousness, from man's self-knowledge. Man does not act blindly. There are not two reasons in man. On the contrary, the rational soul, while it apprehends being as truth, directs the known truth to action. The position that the practical reason is the extension of the theoretical reason corresponds to the position that moral philosophy, the science of moral action, is an extension of metaphysics, the science of being. The speculative intellect becomes practical. First the theoretical reason knows, and the real exists prior to it. The known truth thereupon appears to practical reason as truth to be accomplished through the will.[1]

---

1. "It is at this juncture then that moral philosophy assumes its specific role, linking action to being, doing to thinking, ethics to metaphysics, and posing the all-important question as to how rational animals can guide themselves to their proper ends. And if . . . all activities, including all human acts, flow from the natures of created beings, then it is the order of being and reality which establishes an unshakable norm for the order of action or the moral order. And it is that same order of reality which exacts sanction and retribution whenever its laws are violated in the sphere of human action.

"This primacy of the laws of being and reality over the rules of action or conduct extends to every kind of human activity: it applies to individuals and groups, to the spheres of law, politics, and economics, to national and international life. In every field of human behavior and endeavor the ontological order or the order of being sets the rules and norms for the *practical or moral order*. The nature of a thing (its being) determines the modes of its activity, and the supreme categories of being . . . retain their validity in the sphere of action" (K. F. Reinhardt, *op. cit.*, p. 109). That is, action

In this priority of the real or of being over knowing, and of knowledge over willing, lies the basis of the possibility of a natural moral law. The structure of moral action is built up from the knowledge, through the theoretical reason, of the idea as goal of the being by way of the recognition, through the practical reason, of this being as a good. This good is then proposed to the will as something to be striven for.

Knowable being is the principle of oughtness. The supreme principle of oughtness is simply this: Become your essential being. For the rational, free nature of man this signifies: Act in accordance with reason; bring your essential being to completion; fulfill the order of being which you confront as a free creature.[2] The order of all being has its principle in God: as order of essences in God's essence, as created existing order in God's will. The essences of things, as first creatively conceived by God's intellect, are, once established, unalterable.[3]

---

or operation necessarily follows being (*operari sequitur esse*): all beings act in accordance with their specific natures.

2. In other words, man's basic and prime duty is to become (in fact, actually, fully, completely) what he is (in idea, potentially, germinally, essentially) through the consistent and persistent use of his reason and free will in the light and direction of his natural inclinations.

3. The primary norm of the natural moral law, "Do good and avoid evil" (i.e., act for your rational end in conformity with your total nature), must be understood and applied in the light of human nature adequately considered, i.e., in terms of man's individual and social constitution, ends, and essential relations. Indeed this intrinsic finality of human nature is the proximate criterion for determining effectively not only the good or perfection proper to individual men but also the common good of humanity as such. Now the finality of human nature necessarily expresses itself in man's natural inclinations or tendencies in which reason discerns the proper ends of all human acts. But these natural inclinations are themselves essentially bound up with man's natural faculties and their proper objects or ends. Hence the natural law generally obliges man to order each of his faculties, in each of their operations, in conformity not merely with the finality of the unitary whole which is man or of the common good, but also with the intrinsic finalities of the single faculties themselves according to the hierarchy of values discoverable by reason. As St. Thomas puts the matter, "it is good for everything that it obtain its end: and its evil is that it turn from its end. This applies to the parts as well as to the whole: so that man's every part, even as his every act, should attain to its due end" (*Summa contra Gentiles*, Bk. III, chap. 122). Natural morality, based on intrinsic finality in the first place, consequently demands that no single faculty or operative power of man be used except in consonance with its finalization adequately understood. That is, the natural law prescribes not only the end or ends to be achieved by man as his good but also the specific means thereto, i.e., the

This order of the world is the eternal law. The purposiveness of things, their continual pursuit of their ends, which reveals the order, points to the supreme Lawgiver. Accordingly the eternal law is nothing else than the exemplar of divine wisdom, as directing all actions (of rational creatures) and all movements (of irrational creatures) to their due end.[4] Or as St. Augustine had defined it, "the eternal law is the

---

proper exercise of his faculties. For reason constrains us to view in the hierarchically ordered faculties of man and their proper exercise, adequately considered, the means judged best by the Author of both the finality and the law for the attainment of His purposes in regard to man. Hence the moral law *per se* forbids the perverse use of a human faculty, i.e., a use of the faculty plus the positive frustration of its direct and necessary effect or, again, a use which involves the positive and direct frustration of the very good to which the faculty is intrinsically ordained. This is so because the ends or objects of the natural inclinations or appetites to which the faculties are related constitute the primary criterion of man's moral judgments. This criterion, however, is not applicable in all cases with the same ease and accuracy, nor is it the sole criterion of moral good and evil; it is of the greatest service in connection with the most fundamental problems of ethics. Nevertheless, as man may, for sufficient reasons, completely subordinate the intrinsic finality of an animal organism or faculty to his own good (e.g., in scientific experiments or artificial breeding) without being guilty of really abusing or frustrating the animal's nature viewed adequately, so, too, a person may, for proportionately serious reasons and within reasonable limits, in any way utilize, exercise, or sacrifice, without incurring the note of real abuse or frustration, a lower human faculty or organ for the good of the individual as a whole or of another person. For every faculty in man "has its own end or object, but is subordinate to the wider faculty which contains it and to the whole organism, since the end of the whole organism includes the end of each part" (Michael Cronin, *The Science of Ethics*, I, 138). But it would be utterly contrary to the order of man's rational and social nature itself for a person directly to frustrate in their very use the intrinsic good of his rational faculties and especially those faculties whose end or function is primarily social and directed to the common good (speech and sex), even at behest of the public authorities; yet induced temporary suspension of a rational faculty for a sufficient reason would not constitute frustration. In certain instances, moreover, faculties appear to be used outside rather than against their proper finalization, inasmuch as no loss of a good seems to be involved in such use. Cf. St. Thomas, *loc. cit.;* Michael Cronin, *op. cit.*, I, 127–74; John A. Ryan, *The Norm of Morality Defined and Applied to Particular Actions* (Washington, D.C., 1944); especially James B. Sullivan, O.M.I., *The Principle of Finality and the Problem of Contraception*, unpublished dissertation of the University of Ottawa (1943), chapter 3.

4. Cf. St. Thomas, *Summa theologica*, Ia IIae, q.93, a.1. As St. Thomas likewise observes (*ibid.*, q.93, a.5 ad 1), "the impression of an inward active principle is to natural things what the promulgation of law is to men; because law, by being promulgated, imprints on man a directive principle of human action."

divine order or will of God, which requires the preservation of natural order, and forbids the breach of it."[5] But order results from the steady pursuit of their ends on the part of the various natures, from the natural activities implanted in things by God in conformity with the natures of the things. "All things partake in some way of the eternal law, in so far as, namely, from its being imprinted on them, they derive their respective inclinations to their proper acts and ends."[6] But they participate in it in keeping with their natures: the unfree, irrational creatures in an unfree manner, blindly obeying the compulsion of their nature; the rational, free beings in the freedom of oughtness. The order of the world is an order of absolute necessity for unfree creatures, but it is an order of oughtness, a moral order, for rational and free beings. In the former case the eternal law is a law of necessity; in the latter, it is a moral law of freedom.[7]

5. *Reply to Faustus the Manichaean*, XXII, 27 (trans. R. Stothert). Elsewhere St. Augustine more loosely states that the eternal law *"ea est qua iustum est ut omnia sint ordinatissima." De libero arbitrio*, I, vi, 15.

6. St. Thomas, *op. cit.*, Ia IIae, q.91, a.2.

7. "No theistic and teleological system of philosophy that acknowledges an intelligent supreme Being can omit the concept of a supreme and eternal law" (Hans Meyer, *The Philosophy of St. Thomas Aquinas*, p. 463). Man's general obligation, then, is to live according to right order adequately considered. The natural law does not merely command us to avoid whatever may harm ourselves, our fellows, or society; it commands us rather to observe the natural order of things, imposed upon us by the Author of nature as means to the end, lest such harm ensue. Indeed, we are not bound by the natural law to attain certain ends so much as we are bound by it to observe the order of nature as the means to their attainment. Since, therefore, it is not so much the immediate and proximate duty of man to attain the various ends of his nature as it is to observe the order itself which has been established for the sake of such ends, a person may not consider himself no longer bound to observe the natural order simply because some end is in a given case accidentally unattainable. God does not, by means of the natural law, impose obligations upon human nature through the individuals who share in it; He rather imposes obligations upon individual men through their human nature itself. Take, for example, the case of fornication on the part of a man or woman who has been sterilized, or the case of two parties who solemnly and sincerely bind themselves to take good care of any offspring that may result from their illicit relations. Does the natural-law prohibition of fornication lose its force or become unmeaning in the premises? Not at all. The natural law does not merely enjoin the due multiplication of men upon earth and the proper education of offspring; it rather obliges men to observe the order of rational nature, namely, the orderly and controlled satisfaction of their sex cravings in the marriage union alone, which has been instituted precisely for the attainment of these important ends. Hence any violation of that order

The natural moral law is therefore the eternal law for rational, free beings. The ontological law becomes a moral law; the order of being becomes an order of oughtness. The natural moral law may be defined[8]

---

viewed adequately, no matter what the results may be, is already an infringement of the natural law, a sin against the end of nature to which man is *intrinsically* ordered. And a substantial violation of the essential order of things constitutes a serious infringement of the natural law, a grave sin—which occurs in all extramarital use of the sex function as well as in certain marital abuses, for complete and unconditional restriction of human sexual activity to natural use in lawful wedlock is, especially but not solely in view of the disastrous operation of the wedge principle in sexual matters, absolutely required for individual and social well-being. Yet it must be frankly admitted that it is far from easy always to discriminate in the light of reason alone, in a very complex situation or very complicated set of circumstances, between what the natural order of things strictly requires, what the natural law precisely forbids, and what it permits as a genuine aid or supplement to nature itself adequately considered, i.e., in its constitution, end, and essential relationships. In such cases even the most intelligent, upright, and balanced moralists can and do disagree. Certain borderline cases have defied, and perhaps will continue to defy, clear and certain rational solution.

8. Or, in the clear words of Hans Meyer (*The Philosophy of St. Thomas Aquinas*, p. 466), the natural law is "the complexus of all those prescriptions which flow from human nature, which are directed to the fulfillment of man's ultimate end, which are known by the light of reason, and which appear in the consciousness of man armed with a claim to absolute obedience." According to Jacques Maritain, "natural law is the ensemble of things to do and not to do which follow" from the principle that we must do good and avoid evil "in *necessary* fashion, and *from the simple fact that man is man*, nothing else being taken into account" (*The Rights of Man and Natural Law*, p. 63). Natural law, says J. P. Steffes, comprises "all those binding norms which are valid for the whole of mankind on the basis of nature itself and not just in consequence of the authoritative expression of some will or other, which may however be added to finished nature, whether on the part of God or man" ("Das Naturrecht im Rahmen einer Religionsphilosophischen Weltbetrachtung," *Philosophia Perennis*, II, 1020). The essence of the natural moral law consists in three elements taken in some way collectively: man's natural inclinations, the light of reason with which he is endowed, and the resultant dictate or proposition of reason; more precisely, however, it consists in the third element, the dictate of practical reason. "Like all other animals, man has natural inclinations; unlike all others he has the faculty of reason which recognizes these natural inclinations naturally; and the result of these two is a natural dictate or command of reason. . . . Separately the inclinations of man or the light of reason do not at all answer to the description of *law;* separately the dictate of reason does not answer to the qualifications of the *natural,* for it is not born in us. With the three elements taken together all difficulties about the Natural Moral Law vanish. This dictate is natural, necessary as flowing immediately and inevitably from the two preceding elements, dependent upon them." (Walter Farrell, O.P., *A Companion to the Summa*, II, 379 f.). Cf. also: *The Natural Moral Law According to St. Thomas and Suarez*, pp. 82 ff.

as "the light of reason inherent in us by nature, through which we perceive what we ought to do and avoid; or also: the knowledge, communicated to us by the Creator through nature, that we must strictly observe in our conduct the order which corresponds to our nature."[9]

9. Viktor Cathrein, S.J., *op. cit.*, I, 344 f.

CHAPTER X

The Structure of the Sciences

The realistic theory of knowledge is the basis both of the unity of knowledge and of the internal coherence and organic structure of the sciences. Despite all distinctions of objects or ways of experiencing and looking at the one reality, and notwithstanding all the differences of methods, the sciences form an integrated system. Not only do they all rest upon metaphysics as the foundation of knowledge in general, but they also find their crowning in metaphysics as the philosophy of being, the science which affords the deepest knowledge concerning the principles and causes of being itself. The individual sciences deal with being from specific viewpoints. For instance, ethics deals with the norms which determine the deeds and actions of free persons, with the oughtness which springs from being; and physics treats of material things in their causal connection, their mode of existence, their motions. At the end of every science, moreover, there stands, not the value of the science for practical use, but its discharge into knowledge as such, the most profound impulse of the human spirit. Indeed, man is so dominated thereby that we must affirm that his deepest urge is to know as much as possible about everything. Wherefore Genesis has quite rightly designated pride, the desire to be like God ("You shall be as Gods, knowing good and evil"; 3:5), as the greatest sin. And the modern age merely betrays its shallow, vulgar, and unphilosophical mentality when it ascribes the temptation of the first human pair to concupiscence, as though sexual love itself were not at bottom a kind of impulse to know.[1]

Metaphysics is the logical foundation of all science. All science is a system of general, necessary judgments touching the existence or essence of their objects, and to that extent they constitute true and genuine knowledge. Thus jurisprudence is a systematic formulation of judgments about the general and particular positive institutions of the legal order: their existence, essence, sources, principles, normative coherence, validity in space and time. The history of law is a systematic exposition of judgments relating to legal arrangements that were formerly in force. International law is a system of judgments about the legal ordering of the community of states. But the formal element of every judgment is contained in the verb "to be": jurisprudence is a normative science. Hence the science of being (of its forms, principles, and modes) is the basis of every other science. Being is universally "given" simultaneously with every act of knowledge: knowledge is true knowledge through its agreement with a being. Being, however, is reality differentiated according to act and potency, according as being is determined or is capable of determination. Being is reality before the intellect and truth in the intellect; it is goodness before the practical reason and in the will.

Certain fundamental laws result from being: the principle of contradiction (nothing can both be and not be at the same time under the same respect), the principle of sufficient reason, the principle of causality. They are absolutely universal; they are always valid, even in regard to purely conceptual possible being, provided it is something conceivable by reason. Yet this does not mean that metaphysics as the first science must necessarily be also the first in time, as though the cultivation of other sciences were rendered possible only through it. It merely means that its essential principles first render science possible. In this way we positively hold in our secure, habitual possession the principles of contradiction, causality, and differentiation between being which determines and being which is capable of determination: and this possession is unconscious because it is continually experienced. These principles guide our entire thinking.

---

1. The very Hebrew idiom for denoting sexual intercourse, "to know a woman," lends color to this view.

They are valid for every object of knowledge, so far as it must possess a minimum of being in order to be apprehended or known at all. The first principles of theoretical reason are self-evident. Even an actual theoretical doubt about them proves their axiomatic validity: to doubt them is to affirm them in the very act of doubting.

"Philosophy does not inquire about particular subjects in so far as each of them has some attribute or other, but speculates about being, in so far as each particular thing *is*. . . . Physics studies the attributes and the principles of the things that are, *qua* moving and not *qua* being (whereas the primary science . . . deals with these, only in so far as the underlying subjects are existent, and not in virtue of any other character)."[2] The various kinds of being, participations of universal being by the many particular beings, particular reality in contrast to universal reality: all this conditions the diversity of the sciences. Nevertheless the different sciences are interconnected and they have a single object: that which is, and a more and more comprehensive and profound knowledge of it. How well and aptly, then, the creative spirit of all languages speaks of the craving for deep knowledge, for what lies beneath the surface, for the obscure that lies under and behind the clear and obvious! Realistic philosophy has no tendency to separate the sciences in place of distinguishing them; it has no tendency toward a fanatical excessive specialization.

Just as the speculative intellect by extension becomes the practical intellect, so metaphysics becomes moral philosophy. That which is, so far as it is, also ought to be. The essences or natures of things ought likewise to be the goal of the development and active formation, through the secondary cause, of the existing organic thing as well as of the thing to be produced by art. And the order of the world, as it exists ideally in the natures of the things ordered, is for the free will an order that ought to be realized. Likewise the essential nature of rational and free man ought to be. Realize your essential nature: such is the primary norm of moral action, the perfecting of the idea of man.

There are in man, however, as the slightest reflection makes plain, different modes of being. Man belongs to the corporeal world, to the

2. Aristotle, *Metaphysica*, K. 4, 1061b 26–32 (trans. W. D. Ross).

world of sentient creatures, and to the world of rational, free, and social beings. To this complex reality correspond various sciences which concern themselves with man inasmuch as he belongs to these worlds. But as a rational, social being endowed with free will, he is the object of the sciences that are properly human: of psychology, as a rational being; of social philosophy, as a being that is essentially social; of sociology, as a being that exists in concrete social forms. Yet as a creature that shapes his own rational and social life and being in freedom and not through compulsion, man is the object of the moral sciences which lay down norms of action in the light of the idea or essential being of man.

The first principle of ethics, that good is to be done and evil avoided, obtains its material content (the determination of what is good) from the essential being of the rational, free, and social nature of man. Thence result a natural social ethics, which also rests upon social philosophy, and, as part of it, a natural law, the natural law in the strict sense. When they were not treating of law in the narrower sense, the Scholastics and their successors frequently called their entire moral philosophy *institutiones iuris naturalis.* This served a good purpose: the unity of morality and law was thereby safeguarded. Moreover, law, through its inclusion in moral philosophy, was given its metaphysical basis. The science of law received its foundation, the philosophy of law its objects, and positive legal institutions their legitimation in the natural law, which in its turn rested upon social philosophy and hence upon the metaphysical doctrine of man. The oughtness or obligation of legal norms also obtained thereby a material foundation in the essential being of man's social and rational nature. Thinkers thus escaped positivism, which believes that it has to acknowledge and recognize only a factual willing of the norm by a lawmaker who has force at his command. Positivism has always originated in philosophical skepticism, or it is a purely arbitrary short cut in the matter of determining the structure and interconnection of the sciences. It renounces inquiry into the reason of the norm.

The essentially social nature of man means that his mode of being is social being, and that the idea of man is perfected in the community and its gradations. This is not a requirement of some impulse or other, but a reality which in ever increasing human experience shows itself as "given." Social being, the necessary communities of the social animal, is the object of social philosophy. Social being is *in* reality. Therefore continual contact with reality and observation of social life are needed in order to be able to make assertions and form judgments about the nature of social being. Only then can we discern what is permanent amid the changing situations, amid the alterations of outward forms in the course of history. With regard to social science, then, social philosophy plays a role similar to that of metaphysics in respect to the sciences in general.

It follows, consequently, that in this case also essential being becomes oughtness to the practical reason. In this case, too, essential being becomes the goal and norm of what is taking shape through the free activity of the human will. Social ethics and the philosophy of law are extensions of social metaphysics. As the mind by cognition draws out or abstracts the nature of social being from the social data, from reality, it discovers the first social ideas and principles. It does not itself construct them or postulate them from some abstract principle or other, such as freedom.

There is a philosophy of law, a doctrine of juridical oughtness, to the extent that law and every legal order constitute a peculiar order of social oughtness, a coordination of the various social relations and connections among men from the loose and ephemeral to permanent and firmly established forms of community living, since there exists a legal form of social being. The philosophy of law cannot be detached from ethics, since it is part of the latter. Furthermore, to the extent that it exists, it is as oughtness and norm grounded in essential being, in the nature of social being. Its first principles and the further conclusions form the content of the natural law. The laws of being become norms of doing and acting for the creative will. The eternal law, the law of the world's being, becomes the natural law in relation to the rational and free creature. Whatever necessarily appertains to the perfecting of a nature which is essentially social ought also to exist and to be realized by the will. What necessarily belongs thereto, no more, but also no less, is by nature right and moral.

As social philosophy is distinguished from sociology, and social ethics from historical moral systems or codes of an epoch or class, the positive science of law is distinguished from the philosophy of law, and the positive law from the natural law. The natural law embraces the contents of both the science of law and the philosophy of law. As in metaphysics the first ideas of being in general are presupposed, so here the ideas of individual person, community, morality, and of law are "given" beforehand. "The individual legal experience depends for its clear comprehension upon the universally valid concept of law, not vice versa" (R. Stammler). Moreover, this concept of law is immediately present to us who grow up in the legal community of family and kindred-group, of professional group and village or town, and of the state with its officials, judges, and courts. This holds true even if only in the form of the general normative appurtenance of certain things, and in the form of the relation of certain persons and their action to us as individual equal or unequal members of the community. Indeed this concept of law is so present to our minds that, upon attaining the use of reason, we at once become immediately conscious of the basic juridical and moral principles and we apply them in practice. Such fundamental principles are: Good ought to be; what is mine ought to belong to me, what is yours, to you; no one may molest me in what is mine. It is precisely the same as in the case of cognition where we immediately possess the intuition of certain principles, such as the principle of contradiction.

The science of law and the philosophy of law accordingly differ in their specific objects. The science of law views its objects, legal ordinances, from the precise standpoint of their positive validity and practical application in the administration of justice, their historical evolution, their logical coherence and consistent interpretation, and their positively established legal institutions. The philosophy of law, on the other hand, has for its object the necessary universal norms; and the legitimation of every positive legal ordinance implies an attempt to realize such norms. Hence its object is what has for centuries been known as *ius naturale*. For this reason, too, every attempt to philosophize about law bears willy-nilly a natural-law character. For without this going back to ultimate, necessary, and permanent norms, there exist only empirical generalizations, systems of legal types, genetico-historical explanations of the factual development of a legal institution (e.g., the loan), but not knowledge of the real grounds for the universally existing principle that what is borrowed ought to be returned.

The essential nature of man, the idea of man as a rational, free, and social being is, as the normative goal, the principle of social ethics and of the natural law. The legitimation of all law must ultimately be a moral one. This is possible, however, only if the normative oughtness of practical reason is ultimately *being* perceived by the theoretical reason. The circle of the mind and the sciences is thus closed. The given reality and the ideal core in it, as measure of man's knowledge and the object of theoretical reason, appear now to the practical reason, the extension of theoretical reason, as a valuable good and end, as a task to be realized. But the concrete realization does not get its legitimation from the will that does the realizing, but from the end or goal of the realization, the idea. Metaphysics is the presupposition and the crown of the philosophy of law, whose object is the natural law.

CHAPTER XI

The Nature of Law

It may be said with some exaggeration that the era of individualism was the first to pursue a philosophy of right or rights (in the subjective sense), whereas the preceding age had rather developed a philosophy of law. That would be especially justifiable were one to conceive right more as a subjective permission and power to demand, and law as objective order and the basis of duties and rights. The *suum* would then be first, while the norm, through which the *suum* would be determined and guaranteed, would come later.

The Christian doctrine of natural law, however, does not first posit the *suum* and the person, and only afterwards the law. But as the community is perceived simultaneously with the person, because it is "given" with the latter, so the norm which determines it is simultaneously posited with the *suum*. Man is continually viewed in an order that is simultaneously given, whose natural laws, arising from the nature of the essential order, require observance. Thus since thinkers did not set out from the isolated, abstract individual and did not begin by asking what are to be considered his inalienable rights, but always regarded man as a member of an order instituted by God and manifesting itself in man's essential being, attention was paid more to the law, to right in the objective sense.[1] Besides, whoever is of the opinion that

---

1. "The story of the spectral analysis of the law of nature into the prismatic colours of 'natural rights' is a long one. The chief influence was undoubtedly the Christian religion" (J. H. Muirhead, "Rights," *Encyclopaedia of Religion and Ethics*, edited by James Hastings [12 vols. and Index, New York: Charles Scribner's Sons, 1924–27] X, 771). Moreover, as Francis P. LeBuffe, S.J., and James V. Hayes explain, "all rights come from law and they come from law because it places a duty on the subject. But the fundamental law from which all other laws derive their force and efficacy is the Natural Law. Now the Lawgiver of the Natural Law is God, who has the right to

law and morality may not be separated, and hence that positive law and moral law belong together, will be especially capable of appreciating this view. Laws have then an ethical aim or end. They are not merely a safeguard or protection of previously given rights. They have in addition the positive ethical function of making men better, more virtuous. But this implies that the positive law is inwardly connected with the object which the moral law has in view.

In St. Thomas Aquinas we find at first an entirely general concept of law. "Law is a rule and measure of acts, whereby man is induced to act or is restrained from acting."[2] This rule or law is an ought, not a blind necessity. It applies to creatures possessed of free will while it leaves their freedom intact. It is not physical compulsion. (Hence the laws established for the movements—*motus,* not *actus*—of irrational nature, the laws of nature in the present-day meaning of the phrase, are laws only in an improper sense.) Law is thus a norm for human actions which proceed from free will and are therefore actions of a being who is master of his deeds and omissions, of a being who is a person. But free will presupposes reason, in keeping with the priority of the latter. Consequently it pertains to the nature of human actions that they are somehow determined by reason and are in agreement with it. It is thus nature, and, more explicitly, rational nature, which provides the proximate criterion in passing a judgment of values on a specifically human (morally free) action. But reason, as practical reason, further regulates action since it apprehends the connections and relationships of ordered things among themselves and in relation to their end, because order arises through common direction to an end. Again, all action occurs for the sake of an end. Without purpose, action would be meaningless; without purpose, the will has nothing to strive for.

---

man's obedience. Immediately consequent upon this right of God is duty in man. Hence, prior to every right in a man is his duty, general or particular, and prior to every duty is God's right to the ultimate purpose of creation and to the submission and service of mankind" (*Jurisprudence,* p. 136). Accordingly, man's primary right is the right to do his duty, i.e., to achieve his end, to perfect himself, to realize his essential nature, and thus to attain true happiness, his subjective end, in this life and in the next.

2. *Summa theologica,* Ia IIae, q.90, a.1.

But reason alone can grasp the appropriateness of the actions for attainment of the end; it alone can conceive the means and the series of intermediate ends that lead to achievement of the final end. This activity of reason, through its decision for or against a proposed course of action, precedes the will, the converting of the deliberation and the judgment into act. The content of every norm, therefore, as well as all that has in any way a normative character, is related to reason as essential nature and as principle of knowledge.[3]

It follows from the foregoing that law is "something pertaining to reason."[4] To the concept of law belongs "an ordinance of reason,"[5] not (as it is occasionally thought) an ordinance for reason, although law is this too. For law does not speak to the blind will as such, but to the will guided and informed by reason.

Man acts for an end. Hence every action has an immediate goal. It is evident, however, that the immediate end, e.g., writing, is subordinated as a means to a higher end, e.g., the communication of thoughts. Ever wider investigation brings to light an ultimate end, to which the subordinate ends are related as to a final cause. Their relation to the final end is that which is common to them all. It belongs to the nature of law to serve a supreme purpose that is ultimate in the respective order. The purpose or end is a creative element in law and right. The final end of all human action and at the same time the principle of such action is *felicitas*, happiness.[6] But universality belongs to this end:

3. For men "an action is natural only in so far as it harmonizes with the law of reason. This agreement with reason is not only the mark of naturalness, of humanity, it is the stamp of virtue; our actions are virtuous or good exactly in so far as they harmonize with the commands of reason, or, in other words, precisely in so far as they follow the directions of reason and move towards the goal of man" (Walter Farrell, O.P., *A Companion to the Summa*, II, 382).

4. St. Thomas, *op. cit.*, Ia IIae, q.90, a.1.

5. *Ibid.*, a.4.

6. "The first principle in practical matters, which are the object of the practical reason, is the last end: and the last end of human life is happiness or beatitude" (*ibid.*, a.2). Cf. *ibid.*, q.1, a.6; q.2, a.7; q.3, a.1; q.69, a.1. What man's last end or happiness does and does not consist in, how far and in what way it is attainable in the present life, and how we are to conceive the final and perfect happiness of the next life, St. Thomas deals with, *ibid.*, q.2–5; *Summa contra Gentiles*, Bk. III, chaps. 1–63.

it is the common good of all who strive for it. To that extent law is directed to the common good in the general sense, from which it receives the property of universality. Law is thus a general norm of reason which directs the actions of free man to the common good, not to a private or particular good.[7] This may not be restricted to the general welfare of the state, although this is its foremost application, but holds good for every higher community with an end of its own, in particular for the Church and the international community, but also for the family and the larger kindred-group.

To law pertains also a lawgiver. For a group of people, order among the individuals who compose it and their direction to the common end are essential. The group first receives its unity and concrete form, its sociological and juridical individuality, through the unity of order and through the end. However, the production of this unity and the enduring realization of the common good through the direction of the acting members to this goal presuppose one or more directors in the specific sense of that term. Chance or accident is not the creator of the community. For this reason the lawmaker pertains to the notion of law, which must be directed precisely to the general welfare. Consequently, too, he is the lawmaker upon whom devolves concretely the care for the common good, whether it be the corporate body itself, the people, or the constitutionally determined holder of the public authority.

Furthermore, since law is the rule of action for rational and free beings, it has of necessity to be made known to them, that they may direct their actions in keeping with it. Promulgation likewise belongs to the nature of law.

Accordingly law is a general rule of reason which is directed to the common good, emanates from public authority, and is duly promulgated.[8] The will, too, is included therein. For the framing of a legal decree is just as essentially an act of the will, but only on the basis of a precedent rational weighing of the ends and means which concern the law. A rule that does not issue from the activity of reason, an

---

7. Cf. *Summa theologica,* Ia IIae, q.90, a.2.

8. Law is "an ordinance of reason for the common good, promulgated by him who has the care of the community" (*ibid.,* a.4).

arbitrary rule or an arbitrary decree, "would savor of lawlessness rather than of law," says St. Thomas categorically.[9]

Law, then, is primarily not will, although it owes its positive concrete existence to a volitional act of the lawgiver. Materially considered, it has to be a rule of reason and for reason (in the one subject to the law). That is, only thereby can it obtain the decisive qualification of true law. For rational nature must be directed and guided in accord with reason, i.e., it must be in conformity with truth. That has been common intellectual property ever since the Greeks established the truth of the *nomos:* law is truth (*veritas facit legem*).

Closely connected with this idea is the doctrine that the end or aim of law is to make those who are subject to it good.[10] Law as a rational norm for the free activity of man must have at bottom this objective; it is not a mere safeguard against the antisocial impulses in man which menace the community. The dignity of the laws rests on this consideration. Wherever, as already among the Greeks, law had this ethical aim, law became something sublime and venerable. This idea corresponds likewise to the ethical character of the community, especially of the state. All law wishes to educate the members of the community. All true politics is education of the people. It has required the entire emptying and disparagement of the state at the hands of individualist liberalism to bring about the denial of the educative function of the law, and to assign to law merely a protective function in behalf of the autonomous, even morally self-sufficing, individual.

9. "Reason has its power of moving from the will . . . ; for it is due to the fact that one wills the end, that the reason issues its commands as regards things ordained to the end. But in order that the volition of what is commanded may have the nature of law, it needs to be in accord with some rule of reason. And in this sense is to be understood the saying that the will of the sovereign has the force of law; or otherwise the sovereign's will would savor of lawlessness rather than of law" (*ibid.,* a.1 ad 3). "Command is an act of the reason, presupposing an act of the will, in virtue of which the reason, by its command, moves to the execution of the act" (*ibid.,* q.17, a.1); see also the commentary of Cardinal Cajetan upon this article of the *Summa theologica.* The way the intellect and will mutually react and interact at all stages of conceiving, formulating, issuing, and executing a command is convincingly depicted by Walter Farrell, O.P., *A Companion to the Summa,* II, 49–62.

10. Cf. St. Thomas, *Summa theologica,* Ia IIae, q.92, a.1.

Such is the nature of law. It is universal and holds good for all laws: for the moral law and the positive law, whether the latter is a statute of some corporative body or a law of state or Church.

The natural moral law, too, bears the character of law. Indeed, as has already been mentioned, a heated controversy over this point took place among the Late Scholastics. It reached its climax in the dispute between Vasquez and Suarez. The argument turned on the nature of law: Is law an act of reason, or is it an act of the will? Vasquez was in agreement with tradition when he said that law is an act of the intellect on the basis of an act of the will. Materially, therefore, he regarded law as an act of the intellect; formally, as an act of the will. Therefore Vasquez was unwilling to characterize the natural law as law proper, simply because the law of nature as an intimation of that which is good in itself, i.e., in accord with reason, and of what is bad in itself, i.e., at variance with reason, contains no element of will. Some had on this account termed the natural law a *lex indicans*, in contradistinction to *lex praecipiens*.

The idea that rational nature as such is the natural law, and that the latter has force even in the impossible hypothesis that there be no God, was carried forward by Arriaga and Grotius almost to the point of the autonomy of human reason. The contrary position was the Occamist doctrine that law is but an act of the will: hence the natural law is divine positive law, and the basis of the goodness and rightness of certain actions is not found in their conformity with nature, but in the absolute will of God, who is completely free to prescribe even the opposite course of action. That meant the dissolving of the concept of natural law. Therefore Suarez was at pains to point out that, as the light of natural reason indicates by way of judgment the inner agreement or internal contradiction of actions with rational nature, it likewise indicates in the very same act that this corresponds also to the will of God, the Author of nature.[11]

11. Yet it must be insisted that the obligation of the natural law does not depend for its efficacy on a knowledge either of God as legislator or of the divine will. For in the impossible hypothesis that God might not will the natural law, the latter would nevertheless become known to men and would oblige men in the same way as now

All law is first and foremost an act of reason. Even technically the deliberation precedes the decree. Yet law is also a decree of the will.[12] The answer to the question about the nature of law is thus the answer to the question of the relationship between intellect and will. And the answer to this decides the question of whether a natural law is possible at all. The historical theories of the nature of law down to the present

because human nature would be constituted in the same way as now by command of the divine reason, and both human nature and its acts would be ordained to the last end—a truth glimpsed by Grotius. "The essential order of things, more particularly the rational good of man, is the proximate source of the obligation of the Natural Moral Law. It is a secondary but true cause in the moral order, producing a true effect, a true obligation." Ultimately, of course, the efficacy of this secondary cause of moral obligation, which simply results from the necessity of an act in relation to an absolutely necessary end, depends on the first and supreme cause, God and His eternal law. Obviously, if there were no God, nothing would exist, and hence there would be no natural law of any kind. Yet "the obligation of the Natural Moral Law no more demands a knowledge of God as legislator for its efficacy than do the first principles of the speculative order for their validity. This obligation follows from a first principle, the principle of finality, which like the other first principles has ontological value." To command is the function of law, however, and obligation on the part of the subject is but the inseparable corollary or consequent of command. Since the act of command is immediately and substantially directive or ordering (and not intimating and moving), obligation is primarily a product of the intellect; yet since the act of command is fundamentally and radically motive or effective, obligation is also a product of will. Thus the natural moral law implies the existence of God and His eternal law, and all men are in some degree aware of its obligation as a dictate of practical reason concerning necessary means to an absolutely necessary end, namely, personal perfection and happiness. For nature itself imposes this end upon man by physical necessity—he cannot but will it; and, on the other hand, reason can perceive that certain particular goods and actions suited to man's rational nature pertain to that end as necessary means or conditions of this perfection and ultimate happiness and that certain others do not. The natural moral law is no mere ideal to be pursued or not in accordance with one's whims or temperament; it imposes a strict obligation. It simply involves the obligation to apply the supreme moral principle, "Do good and avoid evil," to every deliberate human course of action. Cf. Walter Farrell, O.P., *A Companion to the Summa*, I, 383–88; *The Natural Moral Law According to St. Thomas and Suarez*, pp. 6–13, 54–61, 130–41, 148 ff.; "The Roots of Obligation," *The Thomist*, I (1939), 14–30; Michael Cronin, *The Science of Ethics*, I, 211–30; O. Karrer, *op. cit.*, pp. 52–57, 233 ff.

12. Law as it is in the legislator consists in an act of command. But "command is immediately and substantially from the intellect, radically it is from the will; it is an elicited act of the practical reason, presupposing an act of the will" (Walter Farrell, O.P., "The Roots of Obligation," *The Thomist*, I [1939], 17).

time cover the whole range of the antithesis: Law is reason—law is will. Besides, the nature of the law provides the basis for differentiating forms of government, and it renders philosophy of law possible or impossible.

In the United States, the judge, in virtue of his right to review the law, inquires whether an act of the legislative body is unconstitutional. Actually, however, he examines whether the act is reasonable, and he disallows it if he finds it arbitrary. The judge, or the Federal Supreme Court, thus becomes in the United States the first chamber, wholly unprovided for in the Constitution, with absolute right of veto.

The demand for a public consideration of the laws in parliament or congress, i.e., for the discussion of the reasonable grounds pro and con, is likewise understandable only on the basis of the view that law must be reason. Furthermore, paradoxical as it may sound, the same view underlay even the absolutism of a Louis XIV of France. For, as the latter passed not for a mere man but for a vicegerent of God, the reasonableness of a law which emanated from him was by inference a presumption of law and of right. The same is true of the enlightened despotism of the following century, which rested on the view that the ruler, because of his superior, enlightened reason, can manage the state to the advantage of the people.

Only Occam's positivism in moral philosophy and that of the closing nineteenth century in jurisprudence, by clinging to the principle that law is will, held fast to the theory of will. The unfruitfulness of this theory is at the same time the reason for its rejection.

Law must be reason, too, for the sake of man's dignity. The human person is not a means for the ruler's use. Obedience, to be ethical, must be reasonable obedience. This requires a certain insight into the reasonable character and the purpose of the norm. Hence the lawgiver, precisely in those governments in which the laws do not originate in public deliberation, almost always adduces, generally in a detailed and solemn form, the motives of the law.

Somewhat different is the question of whether the unreasonableness of a law or an actually deficient insight into its reasonableness exempts one from obedience. Here the Christian doctrine and individualist liberalism part company. The latter optimistically considers that the individual is always sagacious enough to have the requisite insight. In addition, it proceeds from a preconceived notion that the law, as a restriction of freedom, is rather a necessary evil than a means for making the citizen good. Lastly, it is filled with a distrust on principle toward the lawmaker, whether he is a single tyrant or a hundred tyrants, i.e., a parliamentary majority. The legislator should lay down only the formal rules of procedure. The individuals themselves determine the material content of law through their contracts, which, moreover, constitute the principal form of individualist jurisprudence.

The Christian philosophy of law, however, absolutely demands the positive law. And if it declares reasonableness to be an essential note of the concept of law, it can still, with St. Thomas, characterize only the absolutely unreasonable law, i.e., one that is at variance with the natural law, as savoring of lawlessness rather than of law. But since order is a very great good, just as is the will of the state which realizes and preserves this order, so along with the demand, addressed to the lawmaker, for the reasonableness of laws goes a demand addressed to the subjects to preserve the great good of order even when a particular law cannot be entirely justified before the bar of reason. The continuance of any order at all, however mixed it may be with injustice and arbitrariness, is of greater value than the utter lack of order, than total disorder. The Christian philosophy of law can demand this because in its eyes the nature of the state is not exhausted in the legal order, although the state must be essentially a constitutional state: it must be in the law. But the state is more than that, for it does not live by law alone; it also lives by the acts of all the social virtues through which the idea of man is perfected.

We have this antithesis: law is reason (*veritas facit legem*); law is will (*auctoritas facit legem*). The Christian philosophy of law holds that, although *auctoritas* alone can enact the law, *veritas* so pertains to the nature of law that law is quite as essentially reason, i.e., an act of the intellect; indeed, from the standpoint of the precedence of the intellect, law is primarily reason. For only then can human law feed on the eternal law and be truly a norm of rational nature. The dignity of law is founded on the fact that it is "an ordinance of reason for the common good," that it is a "dictate of the practical reason." As norm of human conduct, i.e., of rational behavior, law must be a reasonable norm.

For the same reason, too, coercion cannot enter into the definition of law, even though, in contradistinction to moral law, physical enforce-ability is proper to the positive law of the state. "Hence compulsion is rather an element of wrong than of right, since the latter, so long as it functions normally, has no need at all of forcible execution" (F. von Martens). Coercion is the consequence of the dignity and necessity of the positive law. The rational end or goal of the positive law is the ethical legitimation of compulsion.

The genius of legal reason cannot, therefore, rest content with self-denying positivism. It keeps returning to the natural law, to reason and truth in the law.

CHAPTER XII

Morality and Law

It is a universal conviction of mankind that morality is a higher norm than the positive law. This conviction is so universal that lawmakers and judges continually appeal to morality; and every revolutionary relies upon a moral, higher law of justice in his opposition to the positive law. But morality itself must then be absolute; it must cause the order of values to be terminated and at the same time grounded in a supreme value and good (*finis et principium*). Morality bases its norms upon the hierarchy of being and of goods, which obtain their rank and proper value in their instrumental relationship to the highest good. The highest good is the Godhead, purest Being. God's honor and glory, to which the whole of creation bears witness, are also its highest end. Therefore human morality consists in the preservation and execution of the order of being: in the perfecting and ennoblement of the unique godlike being not only in the domain of his altogether individual personality but also in the ever more perfect rightful development of communities, and this too from the first community, the family, up to the state and even up to mankind itself. This requires the more perfect development of the spheres within which human life unfolds: economics, labor, and technology quite as well as the arts and sciences. They are the great *Benedicite* of creation and of human culture as a whole. From the highest good they all receive due measure and their rightful place in the order of essential being. Hence it is an immoral state of affairs when economics, an instrumental department of life, becomes the dominant one: when the economic category of profit and utility is placed above man, that is, above sovereign and autonomous personal values, whether in the case of individuals or in that of national political communities.

Therefore, ethics, the doctrine of absolute morality, ranks higher than the other normative sciences such as art, medicine, hygiene, politics, legal and social philosophy. But this does not signify any narrow-minded moralization of the spheres of human life and activity. For the laws of art, hygiene, and legal organization remain for all that specific, independent laws which result from the very being of these subjects. This truth is founded upon the confidence, derived from the philosophy of being, that the realization of the specific modes of being, e.g., biological being, is at the same time a fulfillment of morality. Morality calls for fidelity to the laws of biology, whose ultimate coincidence with morality is capable of easy and ever fresh demonstration.

Every system of ethics which acknowledges a Deity distinguishes three orders of duties: duties toward God, toward one's self, and toward one's fellow man. The Greeks, the Roman jurists influenced by Stoicism, the entire period of the Middle Ages, Pufendorf and Leibnitz, and Christian moral teaching down to the present day have all accepted this threefold division of duty.[1]

Without a doubt right is correlated with the third class of duties, with social ethics. There exists no right against oneself; the right to oneself means a right against others. Right or, to use a term familiar since Aristotle, justice (whose object is right)[2] is "directed to another":[3] "it denotes essentially relation to another."[4] For justice "directs man in his relations with other men."[5] In relation to God and to oneself there exist moral duties, but no rights and legal duties in the proper sense.

But the rest of the specifically social virtues are also directed to another: love of neighbor, friendship, liberality, charity, and gratitude. How is right or justice distinguished from these? The simplest answer is: By the fact that it is derived from, and is enforced by, the will of

1. Strictly speaking, one cannot directly have duties to oneself. But "one has duties indirectly to himself inasmuch as he is bound by Natural law to attain certain ends" (Charles C. Miltner, C.S.C., *The Elements of Ethics* [2nd rev. ed., New York: Macmillan Co., 1936], p. 154).

2. Cf. St. Thomas, *Summa theologica*, IIa IIae, q.57, a.1.

3. *Ibid.*, q.58, a.5.

4. *Ibid.*, a.2.

5. *Ibid.*, a.5.

the state, the factual will of the lawful legislator. The state admits an action at law to obtain the fulfillment of certain duties and enforces the decision of the court. Since a duty arising from gratitude or friendship is not actionable, it is consequently an ethical duty. For the most part, as is well known, a lawsuit destroys friendship. Yet this positivist explanation is inadequate. It contradicts mankind's conviction of right: all peoples distinguish between law and right. The English Parliament is in theory sovereign: it can, to quote an expression which has become almost proverbial, "do everything but make a woman a man, and a man a woman."[6] Yet even though it is held to be able to make the wife of A the wife of B, it can never declare adultery lawful (Lord Hale, 1701). A saying attributed to the eleventh-century writer, Wippo, corresponded to the old Germanic law: "The king must learn and hearken to the law, for to keep the law is to reign."[7] The *Sachsenspiegel*, an early thirteenth-century treatise on the law of the Saxons, expressly differentiates the natural law, as genuine and true law, from the positive law of the state.

The proposition that law is a mere product of the factual legal will has long been flatly qualified as heresy. The contrast between legality and legitimacy, an altogether critical difference in political philosophy, would otherwise be but a play on words, and justice would be but an empty sound. Furthermore, there is assuredly a Church law (canon law) which, applicable concurrently with the law of the state on the strength of a concordat, is autonomous with respect to the state. Besides, the doctrine that the whole body of international law is derived solely from the will of states could not be upheld in view of the inherent injustice of the peace settlements of 1919 dictated in the suburbs of Paris. Since these treaties actually came into existence through consent on the part of the will of the states, their qualification as unjust must necessarily come from another source of law than the consent of the states. Lastly, is not the will of the state much more concerned with the ascertainment or finding of the law which is already in use among the members of the community than with the making of law? It would

6. Cf. A. V. Dicey, *op. cit.*, p. 41.
7. Cited by Carlyle and Carlyle, *op. cit.*, III, 128.

be much closer to the truth to say that right, as it were, antedates the law than to term the law of the state the sole source of right.

A specious attempt to solve the problem has been the distinction between internal morality and external legality (Thomasius, Kant). Certainly the law is for the most part satisfied with the outward fulfillment of the legal norm—for the most part! Often, however, inner motives also come into question, especially in criminal law where premeditation or cold-bloodedness is more severely punished in cases that otherwise are objectively the same. The situation is similar also in private law, where good and bad faith or the actual will of the parties to a contract, which is surely something internal, is the decisive factor, and not purely and exclusively the external document containing the contract unless, of course, the higher principle of legal security and of ability to count upon the semblance of law decides the matter. That acting *in fraudem legis,* i.e., with the intent of evading the law, receives no legal protection, points to the same thing. Perhaps the supposition that the distinction mentioned above is explainable by the political conditions of the time is not far wrong. The restriction of law to external conduct may well have arisen from the need to limit absolutism in the interest of a sphere of freedom for the individual. "Grant liberty of thought," the Marquis of Posa, in Schiller's *Don Carlos,* adjures King Philip II of Spain.[8]

However, the limitation of morality to inner peace, to that which is internal, is wholly unsatisfactory. Ethics embraces the total activity of man, his inner and outward acts. Acts of obedience toward parents, of truthful speech, and of fidelity to one's given word certainly do not lose their moral character merely because through their externalization they become legal acts. Since they are good in themselves, even without a law they are righteous actions; and their opposite is unrighteous, even though no positive norm explicitly lays this down. It is not difficult to believe that the same motive prevailed here as in the other case. The domain of law, in the concrete sense of absolutism, was to be restricted. Only external facts and circumstances were to fall under it. The state

8. Act III, scene 10.

was to be able to enjoin security, external order; but, beyond this, nothing. It was to have no ethical function. It might in this way be possible to circumvent, in the interest of liberty, moral education at the hands of the police-state.

St. Thomas teaches that justice "directs man in his relations with other men" in a twofold manner: "first as regards his relations with individuals, secondly as regards his relations with others in general, in so far as a man who serves a community, serves all those who are included in that community."[9] All this is brought out in the age-old saying, "Give to everyone his own" (*suum cuique*). But that is termed a man's own which is directed to him, which must be regarded as due or owed to him, from the standpoint of his essential idea. It is therefore that which must be left to him. The objectively and subjectively teleological or purposive character of things, goods, and actions, as the existential basis of persons, is, in the form of "being owed," of being necessary and hence of being enforceable, the specific feature of law. Man has a natural legal dominion over external things because he can, in virtue of his reason and will, make use of external things to his own advantage. "One's own" denotes not merely the physical tie, the causal connection, though it can also mean this, but rather the destination for the person. "To have a right means: there is something here that belongs to us, and the will of the state recognizes this and protects us" (R. von Jhering).

"Mine," however, presupposes an "I," a person, i.e., a subject whose aims and end things serve and whose advantage is a goal of the actions of others, solely by reason of being a person. Right does not consider the inner, moral quality. The citizen does not owe obedience to the head of the state because of the latter's interior moral goodness, but because he has charge of the common good. It is therefore profoundly significant when the legal reason sees only in the person a subject of right and confers legal personality upon groups of persons or associations which serve permanent human goals as bearers of rights and duties. The person exists for himself and for his own sake. He is the coordinating center of things and actions. The legal reason confers juridical

9. *Summa theologica*, IIa IIae, q.58, a.5.

freedom upon man and the human association in consequence of man's psycho-ethical liberty, i.e., independence or autonomy. Here also being is the ultimate ground of one's own, of a legal *suum*, and therefore of what ought to be done or respected by others. Hence to every right corresponds a duty. For the same reason, too, every man is legally competent. The person, the subject of right, can never by natural law become a thing, i.e., a mere means, either for another individual or for the community. That the Christian legal reason overcame slavery[10] is one of the most important achievements in the history of culture.[11]

Love also embraces the other, but in the form of complete union, of two-in-oneness. Justice, however, embraces the other for the precise purpose of accentuating and maintaining the otherness. Separateness, the delimitation of spheres of control, the closing of the latter to others, is an essential trait of right; not fusion, but clear separation. Law gives man an absolutely private sphere, a fixed place of independence in respect to others as well as to the community. The "I" and the "you" appear before the law as separate equals, distinct first of all in themselves and only then related to each other. "Mine" and "thine" appear as the *debitum juridicum*, as clear, firm determinations in the same plane. Therefore my sphere of rights is separated from that of the other, and it forms the boundary of his legal competence and the goal of his duty, and vice versa.

Not all of human activity falls under the law. Only what strikes the senses, only what is meant to be manifested, is matter for the law. It has been well said that "human law does not order this to be done for the sake of that, but simply that this be done," and that "the purpose of the law does not fall under the law." The possibility of applying force is thus a necessary consequence of the notion of law. With ethics law has in common the power to direct. But the power to compel

10. In conjunction, of course, so far as the actual fact of abolition is concerned, with fundamental socio-economic changes.

11. On the ethical problems raised by slavery in its varying degrees and with its different origins, see in particular Jacques Leclercq, *Les droits et devoirs individuels*, Part I, pp. 158–83; Luigi Sturzo, "The Influence of Social Facts on Ethical Conceptions," *Thought*, XX (1945), 97–99.

pertains exclusively to law. Every act or omission which relates to another, so far as it can be enforced without intrinsic contradiction, is a legal matter. The juridical character of an act is evidenced by the perception and recognition that this possible use of force is not in conflict with the inner nature of the act in question. The actual employment of coercion, therefore, in no way alters the inner quality of the legal action. On the other hand, a moral decision obtained by force is inwardly voided as a moral action or decision by the very fact of compulsion. Gratitude and *pietas* impel a son to care for his feeble and aged father. If he fails to do so, the law uses its force to compel him. The son's support of his father is then a fulfilling of a legal duty, but so long as the constraint is needed the moral law remains unfulfilled.

In the sphere of law there is no place for an arbitrary decision. The legal order is essentially different from the order of love or friendship. As there is no such thing as forced love, friendship and love freely embrace the special quality of the friend or loved one: the core of his person as wholly unique, as this "you." Law does not penetrate so deeply. It embraces the individual, i.e., a personal unity, only to the extent that he can be known by the legal mind, and then not in the uniqueness of his individual personality but in his universal nature as a person. Law presupposes a certain equality. That is the boundary of the order of justice. This leaves the inner core of the person free. Nay more, it affords him the prerequisites of free activity and guarantees such freedom. The legal order forms a network of rules around the person without regard for such individual qualities as peculiar and distinctive character traits: things and actions are thereby related to the person or are subjected to his control and competence. It compels one to cooperate or to refrain; but it likewise constrains the others to cooperate or to refrain. It erects and upholds the structure and organization of such social units as the state. It further regulates the activity, and confines within due bounds the unreasonable arbitrariness, of the holders of political power, and it turns this into moral power in the service of the general welfare. Here again, however, it is not a matter of the special, individual quality of the concrete person. The moral quality of a holder or organ of public authority does not enter into the question of his or its lawful position and of the legitimate exercise of his or its power. Catholic social philosophy was right in maintaining this view in opposition to all the sixteenth-century antimonarchists who wrote under the influence of Calvinist sectarianism. The moral necessity of living within the legal order coincides with man's inner goal, namely, to become a moral person. Wherever law binds, absolute power is impossible.

The law is an external, objective norm. My subjective right is attached solely to my quality as an independent being, a being with a goal that is altogether its own. Especially is it independent of the coming and going of my moral qualities. It guarantees the permanence of a community as well as of the individual person. The law is not an end in itself. It organizes the community for the sake of the latter's essential goal, and it gives me my rights for the purpose of rendering socially possible the achievement of my innate end as man. Thence comes its power to coerce.

But even though no enduring community can live without law— neither the family nor the state nor any association whatever—yet such communities do not live through the law but in the law. The married couple, the family, lives through love. Love grips the spouse in the uniqueness of his innermost being. The law touches merely his general quality as spouse. Wherever this is forgotten, wherever attempts are made to force into juridical categories each and every relation of man to man, the meaning of life is being lost. When in its panjurism, to coin a word, the natural-law doctrine of the Enlightenment sought to embrace everything with juridical categories and to explain the community as a mere product of legal conveyances, the great driving forces of society languished or became perverted. Formlessness was the final outcome in all departments of life. At least this was the case wherever the mere conservation of the existing order of things for the sake of the continued existence of society itself did not simply carry the day. The idea of the state dissolved when the state was made into a pure legal order. The idea of the family suffered an eclipse when people began to speak only of the right to self-enjoyment. The law cannot engender life, nor can it take the place of love. It can and should be but an inherently limited order that exists for the purpose of protecting life.[12]

In this connection one cannot fail to perceive the greatness of the *philosophia perennis*. It does not consist in linear thinking which, as fanaticism is accustomed to do, detaches a single notion from the ordered universe of ideas, thinks it completely through, and then becomes an ism of some sort. It is, as it were, spherical thinking. All essential ideas, which struggle with one another in their mutual interdependence, are beheld in a due and prudent equilibrium. Indeed fidelity to reality distinguishes this system of thought.[13] This means that such thinking is a kind of second intellectual creation which imitates the original creation of God, the supreme Intellect, who has willed order by creating reality as a cosmos. Accordingly no prison of norms that are essentially alien to them is erected for the spirit and the irrational vital forces. These forces are first perceived in an intuitive, experiential act. (It should not be forgotten that St. Thomas, for instance, was at the same time a composer of hymns and a liturgist.) But reason thereupon constructs for the vital forces the forms in which they ought to function. It gives them the clear rational norm which is a reflection of its essential being. It gives them the rule, the framework wherein, in conformity with their nature, they can alone exist. For essential being and oughtness

12. "Life and law are as closely intertwined as motion and its direction to a goal. Stating the nature of life in saying that it is a motion to a goal, we have also stated the nature and purpose of law; for law is exactly the direction of the motion which is life to the goal of life. It deals only with the direction of life; it does not constitute life, nor does it establish the end of life. . . .

"The identification of human life and moral life is an immediate indication of the close connection of law and morality. Indeed morality is nothing more than conformity with the rule which regulates human life—the rule of reason or law.

"Human life is reasonable life, morality is accord with the rule of reason, and law to establish that morality and rule that reasonable life must be the product of reason. It is not the result of caprice, even of divine caprice; it is not the decree of a superior will. The power of command is a power of the reason and not of the will. It is an ordination, a direction of motion, an effective directive motion; so it is an act proceeding immediately from the intellect on the presupposition of the movement of the will. . . .

"Our view of life will determine our view of law. If life is a motion to a goal and law the direction of that motion, of course our view on the goal of life will determine our view on both life and law" (Walter Farrell, O.P., *A Companion to the Summa*, II, 386 f.).

13. Cf. K. F. Reinhardt, *op. cit.*, pp. 13–26.

are correlative. The form, the law, is not life; it only guides the unruly vital forces (e.g., self-interest, the sex drive, the will to power, the acquisitive urge) in order that man can really live as man.

This explains the necessity and importance of the clear, cool rationality of law as such. But it also explains why law is insufficient for complete human living, and why law is meant to be enforced.

But law and morality are not separated. Of course, since it is the peculiar property of law to be enforceable, the boundary line of the distinction is a shifting one in history. It has shifted according as whether or not the fulfillment of definite moral duties was regarded by public opinion as necessary for the preservation of the concrete being of the community, and according as whether or not these duties were clothed in legal form. The Middle Ages were not intolerant out of mere narrow-mindedness, but by reason of the spiritual fullness of the uniform Christian culture. The heretic was not punished by the secular power because he had committed the moral sin of heresy. He was punished because in and with heresy he was doing harm to the internal stability of the community, to Christendom.[14] Juridical or civil toleration, which must be carefully distinguished from dogmatic tolerance,[15] had to be put into effect when the one Christian faith ceased to be a fact, when it had given way to differing creeds or denominations. Henceforth unity of faith could be looked upon as no longer necessary for political homogeneity. Whether or not disadvantageous legal effects are attached to illegitimate birth depends on whether the moral disqualification is viewed as necessary for the maintenance of the idea and institution of marriage and the family and hence as deserving of enforcement.[16]

These very examples show forth the nature of law in its inner connec-

14. In the same way the modern national state does not punish the traitor or the disturber of national unity because he is guilty of a sin against the moral virtue of patriotism, but because he is endangering national unity.

15. See especially Jacques Leclercq, *L'État ou la politique* (2nd ed., Namur: Maison d'Éditions Ad. Wesmael-Charlier, 1934), pp. 82–90; Karl Adam, *The Spirit of Catholicism*, trans. by Justin McCann, O.S.B. (rev. ed., New York: Macmillan Co., 1935), pp. 196–201.

16. Cf. Jacques Leclercq, *Marriage and the Family. A Study in Social Philosophy*, trans. by Thomas R. Hanley, O.S.B. (2nd ed., New York: Frederick Pustet Co., 1942), pp. 381 ff.

tion with morality. There is no law without morality. An immoral law is a contradiction in terms or simply a statement of fact, namely, that this positive legal norm conflicts with the moral law and hence can impose no obligation, though the state may have the physical power to enforce it. All law requires a moral foundation.[17] The will to achieve an ever greater approximation of the positive law to the norms of morality is so deeply rooted in man that even the positive law is always referring to morality. Often enough the judge, as was already the case among the Romans with their doctrine of *aequitas,* is not content with a mechanical subsuming of particular instances under the general norm but allows equity to play its part. In extreme cases, however, he goes back to the will of the lawmaker, who is assumed to will only what is moral; or, if the literal meaning is impossible, he puts forward an independent interpretation of the meaning of the law, on the ground that the lawgiver could not have willed anything unjust.

Yet all this does not exclude the fact that there is also a law on the periphery of law which is pure law without a materially moral character. Nor is every law necessarily a moral norm. Many police ordinances (e.g., traffic regulations), which serve merely a subordinate purpose of means to an end, exhibit no materially moral content. The same is true of the technical rules governing legal procedure or the organization of law courts. These norms bear such a technical, formal, and utilitarian character that the qualifications of moral or immoral cannot be applied to them. Questions touching a monarchical or democratic constitution, lay courts or a professional judiciary, collegiate or bureaucratic organization of offices, fall likewise into this category. Hence it is plain that these norms bear only an instrumental character in relation to the material law. The legislative process serves the law, not vice versa.

It devolves, however, upon the idea of natural law, as part of the natural moral law, to verify the morality in the law. And the high professional ethos of the true judge and of every custodian of the law also evidences it. Ulpian has given immortal expression thereto. Speaking of those who

17. "No human law can violate the Natural Moral Law and still claim to be a law, because it cannot still pretend to aim at the ends of nature, the common good of the state and the individual" (Walter Farrell, O.P., *A Companion to the Summa,* II, 378).

apply themselves to the study of law, the art of knowing what is good and just, he wrote: "Anyone may properly call us the priests of this art, for we cultivate justice and profess to know what is good and equitable, dividing right from wrong, and distinguishing what is lawful from what is unlawful; desiring to make men good through fear of punishment, but also by the encouragement of reward; aiming (if I am not mistaken) at a true, and not a pretended philosophy."[18]

18. *Digest,* I, i, 1, trans. by S. P. Scott, *The Civil Law* (17 vols., Cincinnati: Central Trust Co., 1932), II, 209.

CHAPTER XIII

The Content of the Natural Law

From a purely factual standpoint the history of the natural-law idea teaches one thing with the utmost clearness: the natural law is an imperishable possession of the human mind. In no period has it wholly died out. At least since the advent of Christianity, it has always had a home in the *philosophia perennis* whenever it appeared to be temporarily banished from the secular wisdom of the jurists. Even in jurisprudence it has never entirely lost its efficacy. No one has better established this fact than Bergbohm, who was tireless in uncovering traces of the natural law. He discovered natural law everywhere, even in the thinking of the strictest positivists of the late nineteenth century. Ironically enough, Bergbohm, who had set out to banish natural law once and for all from jurisprudence, lived to hear Joseph Kohler say of his formidable attack on the natural law that he had merely demonstrated the utter untenableness of legal positivism, i.e., the complete untenableness of the doctrine directly opposed to the natural law. Indeed, even in Bergbohm's own lifetime a distinct revival of the natural-law doctrine was observable.

But history teaches still another lesson. Whenever the sole possible foundation of the natural law vanished on account of doubts about metaphysics, not only did voluntarist ideas bring positivism to the fore, but rationalism itself discredited the natural law through its passion for deductions uncontrolled by being. For this abuse of deduction, together with the resultant absurdities, produced a skeptical attitude toward the idea of natural law.

The natural law is not in the least some sort of rationalistically deduced, norm-abounding code of immediately evident or logically derived detailed rules that fits every concrete historical situation. And this statement holds equally good of the natural moral law, of which the natural law is but a part. Yet the natural law is also no purely ideal, regulative norm which hovers over the whole of history. It is no objective mind which, as pure form, may receive ever-changing contents from the real situation. Hence it is not a norm that would not in any strict sense be valid, would never have legal validity, but would leave binding force and reality to the positive law alone.

The truth, like virtue according to the age-old Aristotelian-Thomistic axiom, lies in the mean. It lies midway between the excess of deductive rationalism and the self-denying defect of a practicalness that is held prisoner by purely external facts. St. Thomas points repeatedly to the fundamental importance of experience for the normative sciences themselves. "What pertains to moral science is known mostly through experience."[1] He unequivocally demands a long-continued study of positive legal ordinances and of customary law. Experience is far more necessary than a doctrinaire approach for those who would be experts in the normative sciences.[2]

A deep chasm exists between the treatises of the sixteenth and seventeenth centuries supported by tradition (e.g., *De legibus De iustitia et de iure*), as well as the nineteenth-century works which are products of the natural-law doctrine of the *philosophia perennis* (the *Institutiones iuris naturalis*), on the one hand, and, on the other, the comprehensive treatises of the individualist and rationalist schools of natural law compiled in the seventeenth and eighteenth centuries. Following the deductive method, these last regulate all legal spheres down to the minutest detail. Scarcely more than the formal decree of the legislator would be needed to transform them into codes of positive law.

The difference is not to be explained by theological preoccupations, as though it were the part of prudence to restrict the norms in view

1. St. Thomas, *Ethicorum*, I, 3. Cf. Simon Deploige, *The Conflict between Ethics and Sociology*, trans. by Charles C. Miltner, C.S.C. (St. Louis: B. Herder Book Co., 1938), pp. 272–75, for a good treatment of this point and for other pertinent texts of St. Thomas.

2. "It is necessary for anyone who wishes to be an apt student of moral science that he acquire practical experience in the customs of human life and in all just and civil matters, such as are laws and precepts of political life" (*Ethicorum*, I, 4, cited by Deploige, *op. cit.*, p. 274).

of the inability of Old Testament exegesis to explain away certain singular actions of the patriarchs or recorded commands of God which are in seeming conflict with the natural law. But neither is it to be explained on the ground that the natural-law thinking of these theologians, in contrast to the deistic disregard of the positive divine law, had, for what might be called practical reasons, to be limited to a few norms in order to safeguard the positive law.

The real reason for the difference lies elsewhere. There are but few natural-law norms whose intrinsic agreement with justice, with the essential being of human nature, is as self-evident as "Honor thy parents," "Thou shalt not kill," "Thou shalt not steal," "Thou shalt not commit adultery," "Thou shalt not perjure thyself or slander another." Other norms can be obtained only by a thorough consideration of the various circumstances. But the same degree of evidence does not belong to these as belongs to the first principles. This explains not only the diversity of the positive laws according to peoples and times, but also the fact that primitive peoples (*barbari*) hold many things as lawful which are regarded by the legal reason of more mature and more advanced peoples as contrary to the natural law. Normative science definitely requires a more disciplined and more penetrating study, one which perpetually adjusts itself to the being and end of man and rests upon experience and comparison, than do the theoretical sciences.[3]

---

3. Cf. St. Thomas, *Summa theologica*, Ia IIae, q.94, a.4; Deploige, *op. cit.*, pp. 318 ff. It is worth stressing, in view of the widespread confusion which prevails on this fundamental point, that the sociological basis of the doctrine of the natural moral law is a fact, the moral or ethical fact: "All men judge that there is a difference between right and wrong, good and bad in man's free activity. In consequence, therefore, they judge that there are some free actions which man *ought* not to elicit and some which he *ought* to elicit" (Ignatius W. Cox, S.J., *Liberty—Its Use and Abuse*, I, 1; see also nos. 45, 75, and 91). That is to say, wherever we find men, we observe that they attribute to their actions qualities which correspond to what we call the ideas of good and evil, right and wrong. The good or right action is worthy of praise, esteem, approval, whereas the bad or wrongful act evokes disapproval, blame, contempt. The good, the right thing, is to be done; the bad or wrong thing is to be avoided. The good man deserves to be loved, and he who does right merits a reward; on the other hand, the bad man deserves to be hated, and the evil-doer is worthy of punishment. These ideas precise in themselves, and their presuppositions (intelligence and free will) are found among all men, no matter how primitive the latter may be and despite the vague,

Since even St. Thomas had constantly emphasized the value of observation and experience for the normative sciences and especially for the science of law, and since he had expressly demanded extensive studies in comparative law[4] for all who were to occupy themselves with moral science, it was more than a gesture in conformity with the spirit of the nineteenth century when Taparelli wished to construct his systematic exposition of the doctrine of natural law on the basis of experience. Indeed his labors were altogether in line with the whole tendency of the natural-law doctrine of the *philosophia perennis.* Consequently, too, the doctrine of the state of nature has had no importance for it, quite in contrast to the rationalist natural law whose foundation was precisely this state of nature (which for the most part was even viewed as historically existent).

For the same reason a development in the doctrine of natural law is possible. This does not hold good in regard to the first principles of natural law, but it is quite true in the case of the further conclusions. Thus, for example, the institution of private property has, through the teaching of Leo XIII which was occasioned (but not determined) by the situation and problems of his time, without doubt marked a notable advance in its natural-law contents over many a conception of earlier centuries. The same must be said regarding the more exact determination of the relations between the individual and the state. In fact, many matters of a similar nature have received a fuller and more searching treatment in keeping with the growing complexity and maladjustments of contemporary society. Besides, the permanent necessity of the positive law rests on the fact that the positive law gives, in accordance with natural-law norms, its positive organization to the social order. For the social order grows out of historical contingencies: it takes shape in concrete decisions drawn from the unique historical situation in conformity with the special character of the individual people in its capacity as community of persons bound together and united under law.

---

incoherent, and sometimes contradictory ways such ideas are applied. Cf. Jacques Leclercq, *Le fondement du droit et de la société,* pp. 94–96.

4. *In Octo Libros Politicorum Aristotelis Expositio,* II, 5.

This reserve toward rationalist deductions provides the correct explanation of the fact that the natural law of the *philosophia perennis* could never be ousted by positivism, and that within this philosophical system legal positivists like Durandus and Occam have ever remained isolated instances. Furthermore, this same reserve constituted a protection against the danger of embellishing political aims with the dignity, inalienability, and eternity of natural law. Hence this natural law neither could disappear nor did it need to disappear when the political aims were achieved, in contrast to what befell the individualist natural law. On the other hand, this implies no increasingly hollow repetition of traditional, general, and therefore barren formulas. For the distribution of emphasis, conditioned by the dominant problems of the period, brought out of the wealth of inferences and deeper insights, which certainly were not always present to the minds of thinkers, an ever more thorough comprehension of the norms, their interrelations and applications. By natural law, for example, more than one form of state or government is legitimate. Yet a political ideal does exist, as acknowledged by every doctrine of natural law: the reign of the principle of subsidiarity[5] and a sharing in the formation of the collective will that stresses the dignity of the person as well as of the sub-political communities which have proper ends of their own. That is to say, the political ideal peculiar to the natural law of the *philosophia perennis* includes a preference for the mixed form of government, and a repudiation of the attempt to turn the organized people into mere material for rulers or managers of absolutist states. "All should take some share

5. Pius XI, in his Encyclical *Quadragesimo Anno* of 1931, thus enunciates this fundamental principle of social philosophy: "Just as it is wrong to withdraw from the individual and commit to the community at large what private enterprise and industry can accomplish, so too it is an injustice, a grave evil, and a disturbance of right order for a larger and higher organization to arrogate to itself functions which can be performed efficiently by smaller and lower bodies. . . . Of its very nature, the true aim of all social activity should be to help individual members of the social body, but never to destroy or absorb them" (ed. Oswald von Nell-Breuning, § 79). For an adequate understanding of the principle of subsidiarity, cf. Oswald von Nell-Breuning, S.J., *op. cit.*, pp. 206–09; Johannes Messner, *Die soziale Frage*, pp. 517 ff., 651 f., and *Die Berufstaendische Ordnung* (Innsbruck: Verlagsanstalt Tyrolia, 1936), pp. 22 ff. and *passim;* Yves R. Simon, *Nature and Functions of Authority*. The Aquinas Lecture, 1940 (Milwaukee: Marquette University Press, 1940), pp. 46 ff.

in the government, for this form of constitution ensures peace among the people, commends itself to all, and is most enduring."[6]

As self-evident principles, only two norms belong, properly speaking, to the content of the natural law in the narrow sense. These are: "What is just is to be done, and injustice is to be avoided," and the age-old, venerable rule, "Give to everyone his own." These norms of the practical reason are for the latter of the same fundamental importance as the self-evident, indemonstrable principles of the theoretical reason.[7] Moreover, such primary norms of the practical reason, judgments of the primordial conscience, have the same certainty and evidence as the others.

These norms, however, are not purely formal rules devoid of contents. For there exist no merely indefinite justice and one's own, which differ materially at all times. What is just and what is one's own actually exist for everyone. In the case of the *ius naturale*, just as in that of the *lex naturalis*, the proximate and primary cognitive principle is the rational, social nature of man. As the good, so too the just or right (as part of the good) is precisely that which is conformable to rational nature.[8] Thence results a syllogism: What is just, as corresponding to nature, is to be done; but this way of acting corresponds to nature; therefore one must act in this way. Or the matter may be stated with sole reference to cognition: What accords with reason and essence is the just; but this action is in conformity with reason and essence; therefore it is (materially) just.

---

6. St. Thomas, *Summa theologica,* Ia IIae, q.105, a.1.

7. "The precepts of the natural law are to the practical reason what the first principles of demonstrations are to the speculative reason, because both are self-evident principles" (*ibid.,* q.94, a.2). Cf. *ibid.,* q.90, a.1 ad 2; q.91, a.3; Deploige, *op. cit.,* pp. 291–93.

8. "The good of anything consists in this that its action be proportionate to its form. But the proper form of man is that by which he is a rational animal. Hence an action of man must be good in so far as it conforms to reason" (St. Thomas, *Ethicorum,* II, 2, cited by Deploige, *op. cit.,* p. 294). "In human affairs a thing is said to be just from being right, according to the rule of reason" (*Summa theologica,* Ia IIae, q.95, a.2). "Whatsoever has a determinate nature must have determinate actions, becoming to that nature: since the proper operation of a thing is consequent to its nature. Now, it is clear that man has a determinate nature. Therefore there must needs be certain actions that are in themselves becoming to man" (*Summa contra Gentiles,* Bk. III, chap. 129).

In this manner, from the highest principles follow conclusions, of which the first share in the highest degree in the self-evidence of the first primordial norms. They present themselves immediately to human reason either as just and hence to be carried out, or as unjust and therefore not to be done. They are the same ones that have already been mentioned as the contents of the natural moral law. They have received immortal expression in the second table of the Decalogue: Honor thy father and mother; Thou shalt not kill; Thou shalt not commit adultery; Thou shalt not steal; Thou shalt not bear false witness.

These general conclusions share also in the immutability of the first principles. At first sight, however, this appears as anything but immediately evident. "Thou shalt not kill," for instance, certainly does not seem to be valid everywhere and forever. Thus, on the strength of the natural law itself, the state is empowered to put criminals to death, and one who acts in self-defense is entitled to slay an unjust aggressor. But this objection misses the point. The brief statements of the Decalogue are not full and adequate formulations of the respective ethical principles. The humanly exact, and indeed self-evident, meaning of "Thou shalt not kill" is: "Thou shalt not kill an innocent person," just as "Thou shalt not steal" properly means: "Do not take the goods of others against their reasonable will."[9] It is, moreover, the direct killing of an innocent person that is forbidden. This principle holds good always and everywhere.[10] The killing of an innocent person has at all

9. Cf. Stanley Bertke, *op. cit.*, p. 70. Strictly speaking, however, even this formulation is inadequate. Certain Old Testament episodes afford us the occasion of perceiving that we must apparently add the qualification: "save on the absolutely clear and express order of God, supreme Master of human life and property." Yet no such ultimate qualification can be conceived or admitted in the case of such ethical dictates as those against blasphemy, lying, and abuse of the sex functions which are intrinsically connected with the very essence of human nature adequately considered in its constitution, end, and essential relations. After all, not even God can alter the essential properties of a triangle without changing its nature, or do anything else which involves *non-sense*.

10. This absolute prohibition (i.e., at least so far as human authority is concerned) includes, therefore, any form whatever of direct killing of an innocent person for any reason whatever; it includes abortion, therapeutic as well as criminal, and euthanasia or "mercy-killing." But it also includes the grave mutilation—especially direct sterilization—of an innocent person, except where such mutilation is necessary for the good of the whole body or seemingly even where, in general, a person consents to sacrifice an organ for the good of his neighbor. The ethical problem of the *indirect* killing or maiming of an innocent person is governed by the principle of the double effect. For

times been considered a crime. Nor does the attitude of certain primitive peoples toward the killing of the stranger prove anything to the contrary. For the stranger is in their eyes an enemy; he is therefore not innocent, i.e., he is not *non-nocens.*[11]

This norm is of greatest importance for the doctrine of the just war. The strict ethics of war that prevailed in former times conceived even war in ethico-juridical categories and not merely as a non-moral, law-transcending event in the life of Leviathans existing in a state of nature relatively to one another. Only a just war could warrant the killing of enemy soldiers. To be just, a war had (and, of course, still has) to be waged for a just cause, with due measure, and by public authority.[12]

"no one may intend or choose harm to another person, but at most may permit it for just cause; so that every harm to another which follows as a consequence upon a voluntary human act is either entirely unjustifiable, or can be justified only on the principle of the double effect." Now the principle of the double effect may be formulated as follows: It is morally permissible to perform an act (whether of commission or omission) good or indifferent in itself from which follow a good effect and a bad effect, provided (a) that the good effect follows from the act at least just as immediately as the bad effect, and is not obtained by means of the latter; (b) that the good effect alone is intended, the bad effect though foreseen being merely permitted; and (c) that the good resulting from the act outweighs or equals the evil. Killing or maiming a human being in the case of individual or social self-defense is justifiable only to the extent that it is a strictly necessary measure of last resort against an unjust aggressor. The state, in particular, has no blanket, unconditional power over human life and bodily integrity. See T. Lincoln Bouscaren, S.J., *Ethics of Ectopic Operations* (2nd ed., Milwaukee: Bruce Publishing Co., 1944), pp. 25–64; Edgar Schmiedeler, O.S.B., *Sterilization in the United States* (pamphlet, Washington, D.C.: National Catholic Welfare Conference, 1943), pp. 25–34; Joseph B. Lehane, *The Morality of American Civil Legislation Concerning Eugenical Sterilization.* The Catholic University of America Studies in Sacred Theology, No. 83 (Washington, D.C.: Catholic University of America Press, 1944), pp. 63–98; Bert J. Cunningham, C.M., *The Morality of Organic Transplantation.* The Catholic University of America Studies in Sacred Theology, No. 86 (Washington, D.C.: Catholic University of America Press, 1944), pp. 16, 100–06.

11. Cf. Francis P. LeBuffe, S.J., and James V. Hayes, *op. cit.,* p. 45; Regina Flannery, "Nationalism and the Double Ethical Code," *Thought,* IX (1935), 610–22.

12. See John K. Ryan, *Modern War and Basic Ethics* (Milwaukee: Bruce Publishing Co., 1940); John A. Ryan and Francis J. Boland, C.S.C., *Catholic Principles of Politics* (New York: Macmillan Co., 1940), pp. 251–71; John Eppstein, *The Catholic Tradition of the Law of Nations* (Washington, D.C.: Carnegie Endowment for International Peace—Catholic Association for International Peace, 1935), pp. 65–146; Luigi Sturzo, *Les guerres modernes et la pensée catholique* (Montreal: Éditions de l'Arbre, 1942), pp. 31–102; Jacques Leclercq, *Les droits et devoirs individuels,* Part I, *Vie, disposition de soi,* pp. 109–32.

Moreover, "enemy" or "foe" is not primarily and solely an existential concept but a juridical one: hostility, or the state of being an enemy, is a juridical quality. Hence the wounded, defenseless soldier ceases to be in the strict sense an enemy. To slay a wounded, defenseless man is murder; it is the killing of an innocent person. Even though raging passion may at times drive one to do it, the true soldier, the chivalrous warrior will ever regard such an act as contrary to his special type of honor.[13] Besides, the cruelty of civil wars is due to the fact that in this case the adversary takes on the appearance of an actual enemy, without any saving juridical status. For this very reason, however, civil war is not war in the meaning of international law, and the factions involved in civil war are not regarded as belligerent powers. Were they so considered, not war itself but civil war would cease, since two states, and not the citizens of a single state, would then be carrying on a war. In this case the norms of international law would be applied, whereas in a civil war the norms of the state's penal law tend to be applied. This means, as is well known, that each of the factions more or less formally prejudges the prisoners in accordance with the paragraph of the penal code which deals with high treason or according to martial law.

In like manner, the killing of a slave, which the positive law occasionally does not punish because it fails to prohibit it, proves nothing to the contrary. For in the view of such a legal order a slave is not innocent, since only a person can be innocent. As a thing to be held as property, the slave is subject to the *ius fruendi, utendi, et abutendi,* i.e., to the right which an owner possesses of full, free, and exclusive use and disposition of his property.[14] Nor does the "plank of Carneades" create a real difficulty. For, as has been mentioned, the Late Scholastics rightly pointed out that in this extreme instance the order of justice leaves off and the order of charity governs the case.

What radically distinguishes these natural-law norms in their un-

13. All this is true *a fortiori* of the direct killing of innocent non-combatants, even under conditions of total warfare. Cf. John K. Ryan, *op. cit.,* pp. 97–118; John C. Ford, S.J., "The Morality of Obliteration Bombing," *Theological Studies,* V (1944), 261–309.

14. *Abuti* does not mean here to abuse, but to use up. Cf. Jacques Leclercq, *Les droits et devoirs individuels,* Part II, *Travail, Propriété* (Namur: Maison d'Édition Ad. Wesmael-Charlier, 1937), p. 89.

changeableness from the further conclusions is their prohibitive character. They pertain to the prohibitive natural law. When they are fully and precisely formulated, it is impossible to conceive of any situation or circumstance in which they do not bind.

Correct deductive reasoning thereupon yields additional norms; such, for instance, is the rule that what is borrowed must be returned. However, this principle does not apply with the same universality as, for instance, the prohibition against direct killing of an innocent person. For should a weapon be demanded back by the lender because in a fit of rage he is preparing to slay his adversary (*inimicus*, not *hostis*) with it, the borrower's refusal to give it back then and there is justified. That private property must be respected follows from its validity in natural law, which is presupposed in the norm, "Thou shalt not steal." Yet a person who finds himself in dire need may make use of another's relatively surplus property to meet the emergency; by the same token the owner is obliged to suffer this action and may not appeal to the principle of self-defense, since it is not a question of an unjust, unwarranted invasion of property.[15] Even under the old Germanic law of the Frankish period dire need removed the taint of unlawfulness: a wayfarer might cut wood in a strange forest to repair his cart, or he might allow his cattle to graze in a strange meadow. Moreover, the right of self-defense has been recognized at law since the beginning of the historical period. No fine was exacted for an injury inflicted in self-defense upon an aggressor, for the aggressor was *ipso facto* a breaker of the peace (*exlex*, outlaw). But with the progressive development of the positive law, corresponding to the evolution of social conditions, the number of such situations authorizing self-help necessarily grew smaller. The matter underwent a change and with it the application of the natural-law norm, whose validity however remains the same.

From the norm of truthfulness of speech follows the natural-law norm, agreements must be kept. But, as the history of law proves, the correct application of this principle has required a most subtle and

15. Cf. St. Thomas, *Summa theologica,* IIa IIae, q.66, a.7.

careful consideration on the part of reason. It is owing to the discriminating intelligence of wise men that liability for non-fulfillment of a contract arising from malice or negligence is differentiated from the liability which is owing to no fault, which is therefore accidental (such as an "act of God"); accordingly, the two forms of liability are differently dealt with in law.

This example also shows that the farther deductive reasoning descends from first principles and universal norms to particular norms, the more the evidence diminishes; and a keener and more penetrating consideration of all the circumstances is needed for the correct application of the conclusions to facts which become ever more contingent.[16] From this, too, the necessity of the positive law becomes evident. Consideration of these circumstances requires in addition a great deal of experience and wisdom. It is not a matter for everybody, but for the wise: not for the young, but for the old. Among all peoples judges and lawmakers are traditionally the wise old men.[17]

16. "Now since human morals depend on their relation to reason, which is the proper principle of human acts, those morals are called good which accord with reason, and those are called bad which are discordant from reason. And as every judgment of speculative reason proceeds from the natural knowledge of first principles, so every judgment of practical reason proceeds from principles known naturally . . . : from which principles one may proceed in various ways to judge of various matters. For some matters connected with human actions are so evident, that after very little consideration one is able at once to approve or disapprove of them by means of these general first principles: while some matters cannot be the subject of judgment without much consideration of the various circumstances, which all are not competent to do carefully, but only those who are wise" (*ibid.*, Ia IIae, q.100, a.1).

17. Deploige thus sums up the teaching of St. Thomas on this point: "At other times men do not act rightly because they do not see clearly. To guide themselves, all assuredly have certain general precepts of the natural law, supreme norms which are found in the different moralities of peoples, first principles which no human intelligence can be ignorant of. Still, to regulate the details of conduct, the consequences of these precepts must be clearly deduced and they must be applied judiciously.

"Reason, instructed by experience, is the instrument of this work of orientation. But its sharpness of vision is very unequal from one individual to another; and its strength is not exercised in the same way at different moments of life. Youth is ignorant and presumptuous; at a mature age reflection is calmer. Experience is the privilege of those who have lived a long time and have seen much.

"Young or old, hemmed in by ignorance or enlightened by science, all will be able through a bit of attention, if the case is clear, to solve it suitably by recourse to general

Only in these first, self-evident, and unalterable principles and conclusions, do all peoples agree.[18] In the further inferences agreement and unchangeableness cease.[19] St. Thomas would never have taught, as did many exponents of natural law in the eighteenth century, that the oath of two witnesses and the jury system (together with a definite number of jurors) pertain to natural law. The natural-law doctrine of the *philosophia perennis* knew full well that legal reason advances toward true law only slowly, step by step and after following many a wrong path. This, it was clearly aware, is particularly the case in complex social conditions and in view of the uncertainty of judgment which is proper to the practical reason in contrast to the theoretical reason. For the practical

---

principles: each, for example, will spontaneously recognize that he must honor his parent, condemn murder or theft.

"If the situation is complicated, only wise men will be able to take account of all the circumstances. And it will take all the subtlety of their minds to discover, in the series of occasions, the laws of right living" (*op. cit.*, pp. 316–18).

18. Jacques Maritain is altogether correct in his assertion that "natural law is not a written law. Men know it with greater or less difficulty, and in different degrees, running the risk of error here as elsewhere." But he appears to go too far when he adds that "the only practical knowledge all men have naturally and infallibly in common is that we must do good and avoid evil" (*The Rights of Man and Natural Law*, pp. 62 f.). Yet whatever may be the case in regard to individuals, "the peoples of the world, however much they differ as to details of morality, hold universally, or with practical universality, to at least the following basic precepts. Respect the Supreme Being or the benevolent being or beings who take his place. Do not 'blaspheme.' Care for your children. Malicious murder or maiming, stealing, deliberate slander or 'black' lying, when committed against friend or unoffending fellow clansman or tribesman, are reprehensible. Adultery proper is wrong, even though there be exceptional circumstances that permit or enjoin it and even though sexual relations among the unmarried may be viewed leniently. Incest is a heinous offense. This universal moral code agrees rather closely with our own Decalogue understood in a strictly literal sense. It inculcates worship of and reverence to the Supreme Being or to other superhuman beings. It protects the fundamental rights of life, limb, family, property and good name" (John M. Cooper, "The Relations Between Religion and Morality in Primitive Culture," *Primitive Man*, IV [1931], 36). Cf. also Stanley Bertke, *op. cit.*, pp. 73–83.

19. When St. Thomas "finds himself in the presence of different moralities, of contradictory laws, of diversely organized institutions," he neither regards every variation as an anomaly nor attributes all divergences to the same cause. The explanations scattered through his works may be grouped under three heads: "1. the influence of the passions; 2. the unequal development of reason, of insight, and of civilization; 3. the diversity of conditions, of situations, and of circumstances" (Deploige, *op. cit.*, p. 314).

reason concerns itself with the contingent element in human actions.[20] However necessary and certain the universal norms may be, such necessity and certainty grow fainter and fainter as one passes from the general to the particular and the singular. The more uncertain becomes the judgment of practical reason, the greater also becomes the variety of judgments concerning juridical and moral questions. All this shows the great necessity of deciding such matters by means of positive laws and of adjusting the latter to the individual case.[21]

In another respect, too, the danger of error where judgments of the practical reason are concerned is greater than in operations of the theoretical reason. The passions, diverse interests, and selfish appetites disturb the judgment. However correct the knowledge of the theoretical reason may be, and however possible it may be for the practical reason to apply this knowledge to conduct in the judgment of conscience, passions and appetites often bring about in the concrete a blotting out of this knowledge and of the natural law which otherwise is discernible by natural reason.[22] One should not wish to construct a system of natural law by methods proper to geometry; one must, on the contrary, continually consult experience and comparative law. Hence the existing laws and mores, which cannot be totally and in every respect contrary to reason (what would then be left of man?), form the material of experience from which we recognize what is just through reference to rational nature and through knowledge of the being in the laws. This is not the strict, positivist antithesis to the deductive process, but rather the mean: deduction and induction, analysis and synthesis.[23]

This healthy skepticism toward the deductive, arrogant, or naively romantic natural-law doctrine of rationalism, which attempted to set up detailed norms deduced from reason and valid for all men and all times, in no way implies, as has already been remarked, the acceptance

20. "The practical reason is concerned with operable matters, which are singular and contingent, but not with necessary things, with which the speculative reason is concerned. Therefore human laws cannot have that inerrancy that belongs to the demonstrated conclusions of the sciences. Nor is it necessary for every measure to be altogether unerring and certain, but according as it is possible in its own particular genus" (St. Thomas, *Summa theologica*, Ia IIae, q.91, a.3 ad 3).

21. Cf. Deploige, *op. cit.*, p. 313 f., for the pertinent texts of St. Thomas.

22. Cf. St. Thomas, *Summa theologica*, Ia IIae, q.94, a.6; Deploige, *op. cit.*, p. 315.

23. Cf. Deploige, *op. cit.*, pp. 334 ff.

of positivism. The admitted diversity, which leads the positivists to hold that the positive will of the lawmaker, and not agreement with rational social nature, is the foundation of justice, signifies merely that in respect to the more remote conclusions there can be, so to speak, a natural law with a changing content; but this does not hold good for the most general norms and proximate conclusions. For incest (sexual intercourse between ascendants and descendants) remains contrary to the natural law, even though some primitives, in consequence of a corruption of morals, may consider it lawful.[24] Moreover, the natural law does not remain limited to the formal element, in the sense that the principles, "Good or justice is to be done" and "Give to everyone his own," leave always and exclusively to the positive law the determining of what may here and now be good or just, of what may in the concrete be one's own, and in the sense that it is the function of the positive law to fill in the empty form with contents. Such has been the position of Neo-Kantian jurisprudence down to Kelsen. On the contrary, the natural law also includes material, content-filled norms.[25]

The proximate cognitive principle of the natural law (as part of the *lex naturalis*) is the rational, social, essential nature of man,[26] i.e., his

24. Deploige, *op. cit.*, pp. 324–26, gives the various texts of St. Thomas which deal with this type of incest as well as with sexual relations in the collateral lines. Cf. also John M. Cooper, "Incest Prohibitions in Primitive Culture," *Primitive Man*, V (1932), 1–20; "Near-Kin Marriages: the Ethics of Human Interbreeding," *The Ecclesiastical Review*, LXXXVII (1932), 136–48, 259–72.

25. Such formulas as that of the Neo-Kantian Rudolf Stammler, "natural law with a changing content," and that of Georges Renard, "natural law with a progressive content," are consequently altogether unsatisfactory. Much more adequate is the formula, "natural law with changing and progressive applications." Cf. Jacques Leclercq, *Le fondement du droit et de la société*, pp. 45, 57 f. In this sense the natural law is truly dynamic. If man must become what he is, he must continually strive to advance, individually and socially, toward an ever higher degree of human perfection. In other words, the natural law indicates, prescribes, and governs man's basic individual and social duty to make progress, progress that is at once material, intellectual, and moral, and that has no visible earthly limits. Cf. *ibid.*, pp. 148 ff., and, in general, E. Stanislaus Duzy, *Philosophy of Social Change According to the Principles of Saint Thomas*. The Catholic University of America Philosophical Studies, Vol. XCI (Washington, D.C.: Catholic University of America Press, 1944).

26. In this narrow or strict sense, to keep an important point clear, the natural law is the natural "moral law so far as it applies to the regulation of social relations" (Leclercq, *op. cit.*, p. 18).

personal, essential being immanently determined through the concepts of individual and community.[27] The rational substance of the person, endowed with free will, is the bearer, the possessor of rights. Animals have no rights.[28] And whenever, owing to a failure to recognize the native personality of every human being, the slave's character as a person is denied to him (by the positive law),[29] this is a defect in such positive law but no disproof of the fact that all positive law presupposes persons. The individual person is the logically necessary prerequisite of every, even imaginary, legal order, and all the more so of the positive and actual legal order. For the latter is a normative order, an order of oughtness. But a norm logically presupposes a rational being, possessed of free will, as addressee or subject of the norm. Otherwise a distinction between the laws of physical nature and law based on right would be impossible. Moreover, socio-philosophical materialism, as it has taken concrete shape in Russian Communism, is quite absurd for the simple reason that one can indeed understand the masses in a materialist sense but not the elite which directs the masses. For this elite must assuredly view itself as a union of rational beings, as a collective group of social engineers, if only in order to distinguish the masses as a materialist phenomenon.

27. For the ensuing discussion of the weightiest and most fundamental problem of social philosophy in its chief aspects, see in general *ibid.*, pp. 325–39; Hans Meyer, *op. cit.*, pp. 417–54; K. F. Reinhardt, *op. cit.*, pp. 141–47; Jacques Maritain, *The Rights of Man and Natural Law*, pp. 1–19; *Scholasticism and Politics*, pp. 56–88; Charles de Koninck, *De la primauté du bien commun contre les personnalistes. Le principe de l'ordre nouveau* (Quebec: Éditions de l'Université Laval, 1943); Rudolph John Harvey, O.F.M., *The Metaphysical Relation Between Person and Liberty and Its Application to Historical Liberalism and Totalitarianism*, The Catholic University of America Philosophical Studies, Vol. LXIV (Washington, D.C.: Catholic University of America Press, 1942); James H. Hoban, *The Thomistic Concept of Person and Some of Its Social Implications*, The Catholic University of America Philosophical Studies, Vol. XLIII (Washington, D.C.: Catholic University of America Press, 1939); Franz Mueller, "Person and Society according to St. Thomas," in Theodore Brauer and others, *Thomistic Principles in a Catholic School* (St. Louis: B. Herder Book Co., 1943), pp. 184–263; Wilhelm Schwer, *Catholic Social Theory*, trans. by Bartholomew Landheer (St. Louis: B. Herder Book Co., 1940), pp. 115 ff.

28. Cf. Jacques Leclercq, *op. cit.*, pp. 15 f.; Francis P. LeBuffe, S.J., and James V. Hayes, *op. cit.*, pp. 140 f.

29. But also in Aristotle's slave-by-nature doctrine. Cf. *Politica*, I, 4–7, 1253b 23–1255b 40.

The personal being of man exists as a datum prior to all positive law, at least for the formation of the legal community. But this means that it also exists as a datum for the positivist theory of law. For precisely this state of being a person, this state of being an end in oneself, is the first fact, and in it lies the original germ of right. At the beginning, as Jhering has noted, stands not right itself, but one's right. No European positivist would now maintain that the state of being a person and the rights which flow immediately therefrom (first of all, the right to be regarded even legally as a person) originated through the will of the state. Rather, as Dernburg has said, "the state regulates private rights, but it does not invent them; it safeguards them, but it did not first create them." Or, like Cosack, positivists speak of subjective rights as being guaranteed (hence not given or "granted"). Prior to the state, then, there exist rights of the person. Yet these rights are not mere facts, to which the state thereupon attaches legal effects, as asserted by the latest form of positivism, the normative school. They appear rather as claims against the positive law, claims that demand recognition. In 1878 the German Imperial High Court of Justice rightly spoke of the natural right which an author has to his name. Here it is really a question of a natural right. For this reason, too, the *suum cuique* is not simply dependent upon material realization through the positive law. There exists a *suum*, a right, which comes into existence with us.

This is, in the first place, the right to life and property. Upon this all exponents of natural law, Aristotle and St. Thomas, Hobbes and Rousseau, and even all positivists are in agreement. The *conservatio sui ipsius seu membrorum suorum* is not peculiar to Hobbes; on it rests the right of self-defense. The latter is grounded in the natural law, and it excludes unlawfulness purely and simply, not merely that which is contrary to the positive law. The integrity of this sphere of personal being, this first circle of right of one's own individual life, is an absolute presupposition of the legal order. The safeguarding or guaranty of this first *suum* of the person is exactly what essentially differentiates the legal order from the order of love. Personality, i.e., the state of being a person, is likewise the root of honor, of one's good name. For what else do honor and good name signify than the radiation of one's personality into the world of law? They are simply the special form of fellowship under law. Their negation is the negation of fellowship under law, of the basis of social life. They are consequently a presupposition of every positive legal order. The latter does not confer them; it protects them with the power proper to law. This legal good, by the way, is so prepositive that it always obtains recognition even in spite of the positive law, which pays too little heed to injuries inflicted upon a person's honor.

In the same way, personality carries with it personal liberty, which in the positive legal order finds expression in guaranteed rights to liberty. This holds good for all legal orders, and all natural-law systems recognize it. Such rights also outline the sphere of right that is "given" with the nature of a person. In the course of history, indeed, they may expand or contract. Yet they cannot so contract that all freedom whatever comes to an end. In such a case human personality would cease effectively to exist. The person would then become a means, would existentially vanish and become an impersonal "thing," an inherent contradiction. Varied as may be the expansions and contractions of the sphere of freedom that are encountered in the history of law, there still exists a real legal difference between the serf (bound to the soil) under the feudal system and the slave of Greco-Roman antiquity.

Materially this freedom is closely bound up with the institution of private property. "The conception of property is the direct outcome of the conception of the ego. Just as the expression 'mine' and 'thine' occur in every language to indicate ownership, so the consciousness of self contains the consciousness of property. . . . Hence property is no arbitrary idea, but is founded in man's natural impulse to extend his own personality." So wrote Heinrich von Treitschke, although shortly beforehand he had observed that without the state and its law "there could be no property or security of property."[30] This is an evident, typically positivist contradiction, unless this last statement is taken to mean merely that the institution of property can in the long run be maintained only if the state protects it, so that for the sake of natural-law ownership itself man was compelled to pass from the *status naturalis*

---

30. *Politics*, trans. by Blanche Dugdale and Torben de Bille (2 vols., New York: Macmillan Co., 1916), I, 390 f. and 388 f.

to the *status civilis*. According to St. Thomas, "that which is ordered to a man is what is said to be his own."[31] In other words, one's own is an extension of the ego. Definite things are not of their very nature and forthwith ordered by natural law to this person. On the other hand, it is self-evident that the person has a right to the products created by his labor (with, of course, the proper reservations) and to have these pass into his ownership.[32] The institution of private property is of natural law. In the long run man cannot exist, cannot make good his right to marriage or to a family or to security of life, and cannot maintain his sphere of individual right to a life of his own, unless he is entitled to ownership through the acquisition of goods. The right to private property follows from the physical, ontological make-up of the individual person, from the body-spirit nature of man. "With reason, therefore, the common opinion of mankind, little affected by the few dissentients who have maintained the opposite view, has found in the study of nature, and in the law of nature herself, the foundations of the division of property, and has consecrated by the practice of all ages the principle of private ownership, as being pre-eminently in conformity with human nature, and as conducing in the most unmistakable manner to the peace and tranquillity of human life."[33]

31. *Summa theologica*, Ia, q.21, a.1 ad 3.

32. Other major or original titles of acquiring ownership are the effective first occupation of unclaimed property and natural increase or accession; minor and more or less derived titles are carnal intercourse, gifts and bequests, hereditary succession, prescription, contracts of various kinds. Cf. Oswald von Nell-Breuning, *op. cit.*, p. 120; Charles C. Miltner, C.S.C., *The Elements of Ethics*, pp. 227–31; Ignatius W. Cox, S.J., *Liberty—Its Use and Abuse*, II, 93–108.

33. Leo XIII, *Rerum Novarum* (1891), § 8, ed. by Oswald von Nell-Breuning, *op. cit.*, p. 370. The question of whether and in what precise sense private ownership, or the institution of private property, is a positive and strict dictate of the natural law or is rather merely in eminent accord with the natural law is not an easy one. It has numerous facets, and it must be viewed from many angles. In the thought of Aristotle and St. Thomas, observes Jacques Leclercq, "*property is an institution necessary to man, and it must be established to the extent that it is necessary or useful. But it is not one of those institutions which, like the family, flow directly from nature. It is natural in the sense that it is natural for man to live in society and that property is an institution indispensable to the social order*, but *its immediate establishment comes from society and the latter*, in consequence, *regulates its forms*. Furthermore, *the use of property must be directed above all toward the common good*" (*Les droits et devoirs individuels*. Part II, *Travail*,

In ownership lies the guaranty not only of security of the material conditions of existence, but also of the specifically human perfection, greater personal freedom.[34] To state the matter negatively, whoever has no property all too easily becomes property, a mere means in the hands of one who possesses a superabundance of property.[35] This right of private property, already shown to be suited to the needs of the individual person, follows also from the need of the family. "That right of property, therefore, which has been proved to belong naturally to individual persons must also belong to a man in his capacity of head of a family; nay, such a person must possess this right so much the more clearly in proportion as his position multiplies his duties.

"For it is a most sacred law of nature that a father must provide food and all necessaries for those whom he has begotten; and, similarly, nature dictates that a man's children, who carry on, as it were, and continue his own personality, should be provided by him with all that

---

Propriété, pp. 93 f.). For an excellent and full treatment of the right of private property in the light of the natural law, see *ibid.*, pp. 81–170. Cf. also William J. McDonald, *The Social Value of Property according to St. Thomas Aquinas*. The Catholic University of America Philosophical Studies, Vol. XLVIII (Washington, D.C.: Catholic University of America Press, 1939); John A. Ryan, *Distributive Justice* (rev. ed., New York: Macmillan Co., 1927), pp. 57–66; Ignatius W. Cox, S.J., *op. cit.*, II, 66–86; Charles C. Miltner, C.S.C., *op. cit.*, pp. 218–31; Oswald von Nell-Breuning, *op. cit.*, pp. 94–122.

34. "*Property is an essential guaranty of human dignity.* For, in order that a man may be able to develop himself in a human fashion, he needs a certain *freedom* and a certain *security.* The one and the other are assured him only through property. . . . If man has the right to dispose of himself, he has the right of property, not only in the sense that the property of those who are owners in consequence of fortuitous circumstances must be respected, but in the sense that *the state has the obligation of organizing society in such a way as to render as easy as possible the acquisition of a minimum of stable property according to a rule of equality*" (Jacques Leclercq, *op. cit.*, pp. 130 f.).

35. Such persons become proletarians, urban or rural, "owning no property, possessing no land or tools or any capital of their own, dependent exclusively on daily wages, and living in rented rooms" (Carlton J. H. Hayes, *A Political and Cultural History of Modern Europe* [2 vols., New York: Macmillan Co., 1932–36], II, 47). Cf. also Goetz A. Briefs, *The Proletariat* (New York: McGraw-Hill Book Co., 1937). In this respect it makes little or no difference whether the masses of people are completely dependent economically upon wealthy individuals, great corporations, or the state itself. Moreover, the natural-law defense of the right to private property is essentially the defense of well-distributed property, not of an abstract right that can in practice be exercised only by the few.

is needful to enable them honorably to keep themselves from want and misery in the uncertainties of this mortal life. Now, in no other way can a father effect this except by the ownership of profitable property, which he can transmit to his children by inheritance."[36] The truth of this line of thought is established also by the fact that all social utopias which reject the very institution of private property, as well as Russian Communism with its juridical rejection of private ownership of productive property, tend equally to reject the family as a permanent community.

However, only the legal institutions of private property and inheritance are of natural law. That is to say, the natural law requires only that there be private ownership and the right of inheritance. It does not demand the property and inheritance institutions of feudalism, or of liberalist capitalism, or of a system in which private, corporate, and public forms of ownership exist side by side. These are positive-law determinations which spring from the diversity of peoples and which change with the socioeconomic evolution.[37]

But individual personality does not exhaust the essential nature of man, even if in itself it may provide the basis of an original sphere of right. Sociality is just as constitutive of the essential nature of man as is his rationality. Sociality, indeed, so pertains to man's nature that a definition which omits this constitutive element must be considered incomplete. It is therefore nothing superadded; it is equally original. The individual person and the community are ontologically so related

36. Leo XIII, *Rerum Novarum*, §§ 9 f., ed. by Oswald von Nell-Breuning, *op. cit.*, pp. 370 f. Cf. Jacques Leclercq, *op. cit.*, pp. 133–40.

37. "Since the right to life is primary and paramount, the natural law ordains that the organization of property must be such as to provide all who claim membership in the human species with a reasonable opportunity for the adequate satisfaction of their needs. In the present order the institution of private property, in its essentials, is best calculated to serve this purpose. But the basic institution itself is not to be confused with particular forms it may assume in different ages or regions. These will be justified according as they continue to show that they are achieving the general aim of ministering to the good of human life. The decrees of nature oppose any attempt at complete collectivization but natural right may also be violated under a regime in which a great number, although theoretically free, are in practice excluded from the possibility of acquiring property" (William J. McDonald, *op. cit.*, p. 183).

to each other that they can have no existence independently of each other. Even though the individual person may always have genuine self-subsistence and hence a unique kind of being, he has at the same time a limited existence that does not yet realize perfectly the idea of man. For man is perfected only in the community. It is essential for him to be a member of enduring communities. "Man comes into existence as fruit of these communities, and only by becoming a member *in* them does he experience full incarnation. . . . But because 'being a member' denotes uniqueness and differentiation from all others, the individual as person is not submerged but rather expands his personality from a cramping, impoverishing state of isolation and self-sufficiency into the full man. Wherefore all shutting of oneself off from the fullness of life in communities means for the individual a personal atrophy and mutilation, a failure to realize one's being."[38] In the concrete, of course, a person is always a member of his family, his nationality, his occupational group, his state, and lastly of mankind. The individual, as Max Stirner conceived him,[39] simply does not exist.

Moreover, Hugo Grotius and Leibnitz, as well as the entire past in company with the adherents of the Christian natural law, still held fast to the principle that the union of men with God carries with it the union of men among themselves. The ultimate metaphysical principle of the order of communities was thereby strikingly expressed. For it affirms the unity of the ontological and teleological orders that extend from the individual through the communities of persons, which serve to perfect the idea of man and thereby to preserve their super-individual partial ends, on up to God as the supremely perfect Person and the highest End and Good of all creation; and then down again from God to the individual, to whom the communities are prior in the sphere of ends. The necessary communities or societies that are grounded in the nature of man, without which man cannot live, have thus at any given time partial ends of their own which cannot be permanently absorbed by the higher community.[40] And throughout them all there remains

38. August Pieper, *Organische und mechanische Auffassung des Gemeinschaftslebens* (3rd ed., M.-Gladbach: Volksvereins-Verlag, 1929), pp. 20 f.

39. Cf. W. W. Willoughby, *op. cit.*, pp. 36–39.

40. For an illuminating discussion of necessary societies, see Jacques Leclercq, *Le fondement du droit et de la société*, pp. 278–322.

intact the primordial personal goal of man, his eternal happiness or the salvation of his soul in the beatific vision and in the union of love with God.

This ultimate metaphysical foundation, which enters the domain of theology, does not need to be considered now. As a matter of fact, not only metaphysics but every deeper social and moral science reaches into the realm of theology. But thought can stop short of ultimates and yet grasp the natural-law existence of communities and their orders. For the ontological necessity of, say, the family, nationality, occupational group, and state clearly results from the idea of man, not from the idea of the state. The family and its basis, marriage, are prior to the state. The national community, which is built up through community of blood, language, and culture (national spirit) out of families (basically therefore upon biological being, and not upon the *nomos*), is also prior to the state, even though it may tend toward the form of statehood and may be on the way to becoming a state. But nation and state do not coincide conceptually: as there is a national state, so there is a non-national or multinational state. Furthermore, inside the national economy and culture the members of the nation are organized according to their professional function into occupational groups, and according to locality into political groups, for the complete achievement of the common good. These necessary societies are always present, at least in rudimentary forms. Their essential characteristic is by no means merely their super-individual goal or their juridical organization, but precisely their necessity derived from the idea and end of man. They are consequently distinguished by their permanence: in the domain of the earthly and temporal they are everlasting societies. Besides these, however, men form numerous other societies for particular purposes. The latter societies belong to history and to it alone, not to the idea of man, whereas the former are the very medium of history.[41]

41. Indeed, as Jacques Leclercq has succinctly pointed out, "if the particular societies within the state are not necessary, each one taken by itself—if the commune is not necessary, or the province, or the professional group—*what is necessary is that there be some particular societies,* and indeed in every political society as soon as it exceeds the stage of a village community." Imperfect, dependent or non-sovereign as such societies may be, they are yet genuine societies, i.e., permanent unions of men formed

The family is prior to the state. The state may never take over entirely the end and functions of the family, even though it may have the duty, in virtue of its right of guardianship, to intervene in case this or that family is delinquent in its own duty.[42] It is likewise competent and obligated to re-establish, whenever necessary, the natural foundation of the family in economic life and in legislation through such measures as housing projects, a family wage, tax exemption or alleviation, reform of marriage legislation, protection of parental rights. Such necessity is present whenever a general failure in their essential functions on the part of concrete families is due to a faulty economic or juridicoethical evolution (e.g., in the case of the propertyless, proletarian family of modern capitalist society).[43]

This essential structure of the family, which exists prior to the state, signifies also that the family is an autonomous sphere of right. Parents, especially the father, have natural rights which the positive law does not confer upon them, but which, as already existent, it protects and guarantees. From the marriage contract spring the natural rights of the husband and wife to each other's person, so that the breach of such rights (adultery) is accounted unjust in itself and therefore unjust independently of the positive law. Otherwise why should people have waxed indignant at the early marriage legislation of Soviet Russia? The fact of the matter is that the end or meaning of marriage and the family is independent of the will of the state as well as of the will of the parties to the marriage contract.[44] Marriage and the family produce rights and duties that are grounded in the very nature of these institutions. The recognition and juridical relevance of these rights and duties, and not the fiat of the state, make it possible to decide whether in a concrete case marriage or concubinage is present.

In the same way, a national community comprising a number of

for the purpose of achieving a common end. *Le fondement du droit et de la société*, pp. 284 f.

42. Cf. Jacques Leclercq, *Marriage and the Family. A Study in Social Philosophy*, pp. 358 ff.

43. Cf. *ibid.*, pp. 243–46.

44. Marriage involves the special type of contract known as contract of adherence. Cf. *ibid.*, pp. 29–33.

families is a necessary and true society. It is this essential being that gives meaning to the assertion of the natural rights of a nationality, as these rights, in the national state or in the state which includes national minorities, become a concrete problem with regard to language, schools, and national culture. The treaties about minorities did not invent or create this right; it existed before them. No one will question that the betrayal of one's nationality is a crime. This is true even if no penal code of a state which includes minorities expressly defines the actual case of treason to one's nationality and threatens it with punishment.

For the application of the principle of *suum cuique,* there exists inside these communities of family and nation a material *suum* of the member as well as of the subordinate society in relation to the higher community.

The social process of perfecting the idea of man reaches its fulfillment in the state, which since the time of Aristotle has been termed perfect society, i.e., a society which is genuinely self-sufficient, because in it the natural tendency to live in society finds its completion. The family, even the large patriarchal family or clan, requires a higher social form for secure and permanent existence, for earthly happiness, for genuine self-sufficiency. Political life is a third necessary domain, specifically distinct from household economy. Individuals are not free to unite or not to unite to form a state. On the contrary, the natural moral law imposes such union upon them in conformity with the goal of perfecting their social nature. On this necessity, then, is based the authority of the state and of its head. The *suum* which the state or the public authority is entitled to demand rests on the realization of the idea of the state as a necessary society. This *suum,* moreover, is not the sum of the rights which individuals transferred to the state, to the sovereign, in some supposed social and governmental contract. It is a specific *suum* which is grounded in the essential function of the state, namely, the establishment, maintenance, and promotion of the common good, of the *ordo rerum humanarum.* All this is more than a mere legal order. It involves the promotion of the welfare of families and individuals in their various spheres of life: economic, occupational, cultural. It is a question of promoting, not of creating. The state as such does not produce culture. This is done by persons in the family as well as in their national and religious communities.⁴⁵ For this reason, too, the common good is not really separated from the good of the individual members. Rather, a coincidence takes place, just as the health of an organism is indeed predicated of the entire organism, yet consists in the fact that the organs are sound and in good order.⁴⁶

Nevertheless, though the idea of man is thus perfected in the state, the individual state is not the final form of community. For the nation-states, the nations and their states, form in their totality the international community, mankind as a whole, whose supernatural counterpart is the world Church, the Church of the nations. And in this international community or great society individual rights and rights of the community recur in an analogous sense. As a result, the personified states and nations as values in themselves possess natural rights of their own to their existence, to freedom (i.e., the right to self-determination for the concrete realization of the common good), and to their honor as the basis of their legal partnership in the international community, whose object is order and peace. The tragic conflicts which are inevitably bound up with the rise and decay of individual states and nations as a biological and ethical life-process arise because the positive law exerts itself more vigorously here to uphold permanently the *status quo* than it does in the individual state. These conflicts must be settled on the basis of justice, on the basis of the common good of the international community. The positive international law also has its foundation in the natural law.⁴⁷

45. A good summary statement of the proper functions, primary and secondary, of the state is found in John A. Ryan and Francis J. Boland, C.S.C., *Catholic Principles of Politics*, pp. 127–39; cf. also *ibid.*, pp. 108–26, for a trenchant discussion of erroneous theories about the functions of the state.

46. What is the meaning of the pregnant phrase "common good"? The beneficial objects denoted by the term "good" "are all the great classes of temporal goods; that is, all the things that man needs for existence and development in this life. They comprise all these orders of goods, spiritual, intellectual, moral, physical and economic; in other words, all the external goods of soul and body. The *common* good means not only the good of all in general, or as a whole, but the good of every class and, so far as practicable, the good of every individual. To put the matter in summary terms, the State is under obligation to promote the welfare of its citizens, as a whole, as members of families, and as members of social classes" (*ibid.*, pp. 104, 106 f.).

47. For an illuminating and cogent natural-law discussion of state and national sovereignty with its limitations and inadequacies as well as of the imperative material

In view of all this, it is impossible to speak purely and simply either of a primacy of the individual person or of a primacy of the community. For none of these societies is absolute, however much it may have its own end-values in the order of ends and its autonomy in the social process. None of them is in an absolute sense an end-community in which the individual person would be merged and would become a mere means. His eternal goal, the salvation of his soul, imparts to the person an ultimate transcendence.[48] Thence result certain natural rights for the individual person in relation to the state. These rights are not first conferred upon him by the positive law; they are at most explicitly recognized by it. Thus it is not in virtue of this recognition that such rights have force; they are recognized because they are valid absolutely.[49]

---

and moral necessity of an organized world society, see Jacques Leclercq, *Le fondement du droit et de la société*, pp. 285–322. Cf. also the admirable "Preliminary Recommendation on Post-War Problems" formulated by the Inter-American Juridical Committee at Rio de Janeiro, September 5, 1942, in *Bulletin of the Pan American Union* (April, 1943), pp. 212–24; Thomas R. Hanley, O.S.B., "Some Interpretations of the Present World Crisis," *The National Benedictine Educational Association Bulletin*, XXV (1943), 159–75; Luigi Sturzo, "The Influence of Social Facts on Ethical Conceptions," *Thought*, XX (1945), 101–10; Guido Gonella, *A World to Reconstruct. Pius XII on Peace and Reconstruction*, trans. by T. Lincoln Bouscaren, S.J. (Milwaukee: Bruce Publishing Co., 1944), especially pp. 246–78; John J. Wright, *National Patriotism in Papal Teaching* (Westminster, Md.: Newman Bookshop, 1943), in particular pp. 195–323; Emery Reves, *The Anatomy of Peace* (New York: Harper and Brothers, 1945)—with certain reservations, particularly with regard to the chapter entitled "Failure of Religion" which, for all the justice of some of its criticisms and strictures, must be set down as altogether sophomoric. Of great value, likewise, are the pamphlets prepared by specialists and issued by the Catholic Association for International Peace, Washington, D.C.: *The World Society* (1940); *International Ethics* (4th ed., 1942); *A Peace Agenda for the United Nations* (1943). Lastly, for certain sobering, though perhaps not entirely convincing, reflections upon the problem of a world state, see Heinrich Rommen, "Realism and Utopianism in World Affairs," *The Review of Politics*, VI (1944), 193–215.

48. In the final analysis, the person is a rational substance, a substantial reality, whereas any society whatever is but an accidental reality, a reality of order, of the category of relation, not a super-person. Cf. Jacques Leclercq, *Le fondement du droit et de la société*, pp. 325–28, 360–64.

49. However, even though man's natural rights are commonly termed absolute and inviolable, they are limited by the requirements of the universal order to which they are subordinated. Absolute, in the sense in which it is here used, does not mean unlimited. Specifically, the natural rights of man are limited intrinsically by the end for which he has received them (self-development within order) as well as extrinsically by the equal rights of other men, by his duties toward others. Cf. Jacques Leclercq, *op. cit.*, pp. 329–33.

They are precisely those rights which at bottom are always presupposed: the rights of the individual person and of the necessary societies, the family and the nation, which exist between the person and the state. Whenever the state demolishes these rights to material justice, it does away with its own juridical being. For justice is the foundation of the state.[50]

The natural law contains the necessary structural laws of societies. Hence also the close relationship between natural law and social philoso-

50. John A. Ryan and Francis J. Boland, C.S.C., *op. cit.*, pp. 13–27, deal very ably with the subject of natural rights; cf. also Hans Meyer, *op. cit.*, pp. 474–93; Jacques Maritain, *The Rights of Man and Natural Law*, pp. 64–68, 73–114; K. F. Reinhardt, *op. cit.*, pp. 154–58. Thomas P. Neill nicely sums up the whole matter: "It is from natural law, and from it alone, that man obtains those rights we refer to as inalienable and inviolable. Man's only right, in the last analysis, is the right to be a man, to live as a human person. Specific human rights, then, are all based on man's right to live a human life. Some of these rights belong to man simply as a man and therefore are above and beyond the reach of the State. His right to existence, for example, the right to perfect his moral nature, his right to personal freedom, the right to be treated as a free, intelligent, responsible human being in no way depend upon the state. But there are other rights that man enjoys as a member of political society: freedom of expression, freedom of association, equal access to the law. And there are still others that he derives from his particular position in society, rights without which he could not properly perform his social functions: the right to form vocational groups, to a living wage, to human working conditions, to be treated as a responsible person rather than as a unit of labor energy.

"Each of these rights, of course, involves an obligation on the part of all others to respect it. But each of these rights, it should be remembered, is also founded on a corresponding duty on the part of its possessor. The right to freedom of religion, for example, is based on the duty to worship God, just as the right to work is based on the duty of self-preservation and self-perfection. Each of these human rights, moreover, is limited by the rights possessed by all other men. No right is, properly speaking, an absolute right. Even freedom of religion is limited by the human rights of all others within the state. Thus the state has the right, based on its duty of protecting its citizens, to forbid a religious group from practicing infanticide or polygamy.

"Human rights can have no foundation other than natural law. Legally, of course, they come from the state, but if a legal 'right' is truly to be a right it must be based on natural law—which is only another way of saying that it must be based on man's very nature. And since they are based in human nature they are really inalienable and morally inviolable. Only the Creator of human nature can take them away, and God could do that without contradicting Himself only by changing human nature itself. Thus the soundest, the only foundation of those human rights so flagrantly violated today is natural law. The only foundation for a sound structure of government and of all social institutions is natural law" (*Weapons for Peace* [Milwaukee: Bruce Publishing Co., 1945], pp. 155 f.).

phy: natural law is social philosophy for the practical reason. A science of pure law is consequently unsatisfying. For law is at bottom founded on the essentially teleological character of social being, and in practice its concrete contents are always social life which requires the form of law. But this is not to assert that sociologism is alone warranted in law. For the sociological school of law is indeed able to explain the origin and effect of positive legal norms from the actual sociological facts, but it cannot explain law itself. The two schools of thought constitute a positivist cleavage of the natural-law doctrine. Natural law, of course, implies an ultimate unity of essential being and oughtness.

To the natural law corresponds a genuine pluralism, from which the principle of the subsidiarity of the state takes its origin. The natural-law sub-political spheres in which the individual person lives his life (the family, the local community, the nation in its occupational groups) are autonomous partial or imperfect societies with ends of their own. These societies combine organically for the ordering of the common good in the same way as the persons and communities which never lose their proper being are joined together in the organic unity of the state. Such societies are not, consequently, mere genetico-historical rudiments of the state. They are not stages of the social process that gradually wither away. On the contrary, they are enduring institutions, and their specific functions can never by wholly and permanently taken over and fulfilled by the state.[51] The opposite view rests upon the inherently false antithesis between individual and state. It either removes social life entirely from the political sphere (liberalism), or it makes all community life a matter of complete state control (Russian Communism, Italian Fascism, German National Socialism).

There exists a true economy of the social virtues. Communities do not live through law, although they do live in the law. They live through

---

51. No one has made this point more lucidly or more strongly than Leo XIII: "Particular societies, then, although they exist within the State, and are each a part of the State, nevertheless cannot be prohibited by the State absolutely and as such. For to enter into 'society' of this kind is the natural right of man; and the State must protect natural rights, not destroy them; and if it forbids its citizens to form associations, it contradicts the very principle of its own existence; for both they and it exist in virtue of the same principle, namely, the natural propensity of man to live in society" (*Rerum Novarum*, § 38, ed. by Oswald von Nell-Breuning, *op. cit.*, pp. 388 f.).

specific virtues correlated with their being. The family is the natural nursery of the virtues of obedience, self-sacrifice, loyalty, and mutual responsibility and care. All succoring love, too, is stamped with the family spirit. Economic and occupational life is founded upon the exercise of the virtues of social justice, fidelity to one's given word, and social solidarity in action. The total emptying or sabotage of the idea of the state which occurred at the hands of individualism rests ultimately upon the individualist belief that the sole source from which the community lives is law, and that its order alone is needed. For the rest, the free individuals, through short-term contracts corresponding to their selfish interests of the moment, would create of themselves and almost automatically the social harmony that is here and now fitting.

No, neither individuals in their selfishness nor a bureaucratic industrial state which hinders the free unfolding of personality and the functioning of imperfect societies can act creatively. Creative action belongs to the person as well as to the national community in its capacity as the imperishable ground and native soil of the state. Yet, since the state regulates and promotes the continuous life of the communities and individuals; since, in accordance with distributive justice, it guides the stream of moral, intellectual and material goods, which constitute the common good and concomitantly the good of its members, back to these members; since it fashions a true human order: dignity, honor, and a high degree of sovereignty belong to the state and must be accorded to it.

Positivism is incapable of a correct view of these things which form the basis of the life of the state. The doctrine of the natural law, on the other hand, can give to the state a true ethical foundation through the morality in law.

CHAPTER XIV

❧❧

Natural Law and Positive Law

Legal positivism, that is, the theoretical rejection of the natural law according to form (as non-positive source of valid law) and content (as law contained in no positive norm), maintains that the natural-law doctrine represents a dualism which is inimical to legal security; or that for fixed objective norms it substitutes subjective opinions concerning a juridical oughtness; or that in a dualistic fashion valid legal norms are drawn from a system of norms which is set in contrast to the positive law (ethics, law of reason, reform proposals for new legislation, Roman law as written reason). Hence positivism regards the natural law as a non-law in the proper sense of the word. It refers, instead, to ethics, to fabricated ideal norms for new legislation, to politico-legal aims, and so on.

Law, according to positivism, is only positive law, that is, statute law and such customary law as is recognized by the state. More precisely, positivism characterizes as law to be applied by the judge and alone to be considered by jurisprudence those norms only which are enacted as such by the factual and published will of the legislative organ in due conformity with constitutional law or which are explicitly or tacitly admitted by it. The positivist is ever seeking for the written or actually enforced factual decision of the will which converts a potential norm into an actual norm. Moreover, he is concerned solely with this formal origin of law, with the source of the norm and its manner of formation, not with its content. *Auctoritas facit legem*, law is will. The question of whether something can be wrong in itself is meaningless for him. To him, right and wrong are not material qualities of norms; they merely denote the presence or absence of agreement with the factual will of the lawmaker. In contrast, for instance, to the Roman jurist, the positivist does not search for justice by way of the positive norm in which it is contained materially; he inquires rather for the norm which is derived from the will of the legislator. The establishing of this fact settles for him the question whether a legal norm lies before him. He presumes its justice, or he asserts that the question of justice is an ethical question, not a juridical one.

In constitutional states, however, the typical positivist runs into difficulties. Particularly when it comes to applying the law, he must inquire not only whether the path of legislation prescribed by the constitution has been followed, but also whether the law (including customary law) is not in conflict with the higher norms of constitutional law. And there the legal positivist readily runs afoul of natural law. To the positivist, many constitutional provisions are not genuine legal norms but rather programmatic utterances of the constituent or constitution-making power. Take, for instance, such a constitutional provision as "Property imposes obligations; its use must at the same time be a service of the common weal." The positivist characterizes this provision as a mere guiding rule, not as a binding norm for either lawmaker or citizen. He insists upon taking such a view even though this provision is aimed directly at the individualist concept of property, and though property and obligation obviously are juridical concepts. Here, in our view, lies the typical positivist short circuit. The positivist, who for that matter does not know what to do with such highly important constitutional preambles, perceives in these cases invasion points for natural law to be applied by the judge. In the United States the judge, by referring to the natural-law foundation of man's rights to liberty, has set himself not only above the lawmaker but in theory even above the framers of constitutional law. For the real lawmaker is not the one who enacts the laws, but the one who sovereignly expounds them. But the interpreter refers precisely to natural law and justice. This formalist method makes positivism possible even for Catholic thinkers, when they regard ethics and the moral law as norms derived from God's will. Such norms do not indeed have legal validity, but they do have the moral force of oughtness.

It is generally acknowledged today that positivism is inadequate from the standpoint of both legal theory and legal philosophy. One of its bases, the theory of the completeness of the law or absence of gaps in the law, has been given up. The theory of legal monism has likewise been widely abandoned. For good faith, the principles of morality and the carefulness of the ordinary merchant are often used by the judge as valid norms not only beyond or in addition to the positive law, but even contrary to the positive law. That is, they are used contrary to the factual will of the lawmaker, even if generally on the basis of the unwarranted fiction that the lawmaker could have willed no wrong.

To look more closely into the matter, we may note several phenomena as sources of legal positivism. In periods of philosophico-ethical uncertainty and barrenness the jurist, who is of course concerned with the practical settlement of legal questions, rightly holds to the positive law that is sure because it is enforced and applied. This is all the more true when the abstract speculations of rationalism have split into increasingly subjective views of various schools.[1] At times when no natural order obtains, but, as in Communist Russia, even the national community is viewed as a social mechanism to be organized along engineering lines, positivism may well be congenial.

The predominance of positivism or of the natural law is likewise connected with types of state or forms of government. Royal absolutism provides in itself a more favorable environment for positivism than do liberal democratic states in which the judge is more or less sovereign. Even forms of government are determined by the antithesis of reason and will, for governmental types are differentiated also by their types of legislation.

But the natural law need not stand diametrically opposed to the positive law, nor has such an opposition always existed in history. Natural law and positivism are, indeed, directly opposed to each other. But natural law and positive law are, as the Christian doctrine of natural law expresses it, directed immediately to each other. The natural law calls imperatively for specification by positive enactments, even though

---

1. Cf. Jacques Leclercq, *Le fondement du droit et de la société*, p. 57.

it is at the same time the measure and guideline of the positive law. It requires the positive law; or, as the Christian tradition affirms in an apt distinction, it requires human law, i.e., enactment by earthly authority. In this question of the relationship between natural law and positive law the schools of natural law differ as much as they do over principles. For the Sophists as well as for Rousseau's individualist natural law the positive law was the direct opposite of the law of nature. The positive law, since it served to secure the interests of the ruling class, was even materially opposed to the natural law. The democratic revolution was the first to make its natural law the exclusive law. The natural law of rationalism believed that, from principles that varied from time to time, a materially complete system of law could be deduced, which thereupon needed but the formal legal decree to become also positive law.

The natural law of the *philosophia perennis,* on the other hand, contains but a few universal norms and forgoes deductive extremes. It states explicitly that in the normative sciences certainty and necessity decrease in proportion as deduction moves farther away from the first self-evident principles. It has so strong a feeling for the great blessing of a secure and reliable legal order, which it considers a most essential element of the common good, that it regards as non-binding only that positive law which has been changed into non-law by the prohibitive norms of the natural law. Of course, it accords the permissive natural law and equity their proper place. It is revolutionary only in respect to the law that has become materially immoral. Its attitude toward the imperfections of the positive law is merely reformist. It may with some exaggeration be called a skeleton law. It determines what positive arrangements, in themselves capable of being willed in given historical circumstances, can be right. Thus it does not affirm that private ownership of capital is wrong, or that the attainment of just wage claims by means of a strike (break of contract) is wrong when state protection of labor is lacking. Nor does it assert that dictatorship is intrinsically wrong, since dictatorship becomes wrong only through the misuse of the dictatorial power that for the time being is historically necessary, just as it does not pronounce parliamentary democracy to be inherently wrong. Nor, finally, does it declare every war unjust. Yet it does say that, where no fault of the owner exists, complete expropriation without compensation is unjust. It does declare that the general strike for the illegitimate achievement of the rule of the proletariat is wrong. And it does say that disregard of the natural rights to life and to the necessary liberties of the person is wrong, irrespective of by whom and under what circumstances they are infringed.

The natural law calls both for the positive law and for the lawmaker. To begin with, only the first principles and proximate conclusions (Decalogue) are immediately evident and epistemologically necessary. The theoretical reason proceeds from the particular, which is given in sense perception, to the general. Therefore its knowledge bears the stamp of certainty and necessity far more than does that of the practical reason. The practical reason proceeds from the general principle to the singular, to the contingent, to the multiplicity of possible means and intermediate ends in a world which is incessantly changing in virtue of the actions of others and one's own development, although the higher end, e.g., the common good, remains ever the same. Consequently the more the practical reason descends from the principles to the further conclusions and comes to apply them to increasingly more concrete situations of fact, its knowledge becomes more uncertain, variable, and questionable in application.[2] St. Thomas rightly observes that "to

2. This is the true meaning of certain passages of Aristotle (*Ethica Nicomachea*, I, 3, 1094b 11–26; II, 2, 1103b 26–1104a 9) and St. Thomas (*Ethicorum*, II, 2) which are sometimes cited to show that even these weighty authorities did not regard ethics as a science that yields conclusions which are certain. Summarizing what has been said on this subject in the preceding pages, we may affirm that the primary principles and proximate conclusions of ethics, together with their applications to the simplest problems of human living, enjoy a degree of certainty that is either absolute or borders on the absolute. This is evidenced, too, by the agreement between the fundamental prescriptions or presuppositions of the moral codes of primitive and civilized peoples alike. There exists, moreover, a much larger area of human activity in which developed practical reason can attain at least moral certitude, i.e., certainty of a kind that will satisfy the mind of a prudent man, and this area of more remote conclusions includes all the basic and common duties of ordinary life, individual and social. Finally, there is a peripheral area of considerable and elastic dimensions, an area of very remote conclusions consisting of involved, complex, and extremely contingent cases and relationships with which especially the human lawmaker has largely to deal. It is in part with the second category of ethical conclusions, but especially with the third one, that the remarks of Aristotle and St. Thomas have to do. If it is nonsense to hold that the

suitably introduce justice into business transactions and personal relations is more laborious and difficult to understand than the remedies
in which consists the whole art of medicine."³ Owing to this very
uncertainty, men stand in great need of the positive norm which derives
and determines what is to be inferred from the general principle, regard
being had for the national character and the concrete historical situation.
Without such a positive norm no certainty and no order at all could
arise in view of the number and diversity of the deductions. Above all,
everyone who has not succumbed to rationalism and does not regard
men as purely thinking and inferring beings knows how great a danger
reason runs of being misled by passions when it comes to applying
norms to one's own as well as to opposing interests. He also knows
how easily the voice of conscience is drowned out by the tempestuous
demands of selfishness. An authoritative determination of the conclusions is plainly needed in order that these, as norms which emanate from
authority and demand obedience, may be able to support conscience and
reason.

For the same reasons the natural law as well as what is derived from
it requires also a positive, earthly sanction, which it does not of itself
immediately possess. Indirectly, of course, it does have a sanction. Every
people that disregards the laws of moral living is doomed to deterioration
and to destruction. Justice remains the foundation of the state, and world
history continues to be world judgment. Yet an immediate sanction is
needed, a direct threat of force. The menace to order is inherent in
the imperfection of all that is human, in the disordered vital impulse
and immoderate instinctive drives of individuals and their groups and

---

findings of ethics are no more than mere opinions, it is quite as impossible to accept,
without the most serious qualifications and reservations, the view of John M. Cooper
(except perhaps in the matter of private ownership) that "ethics is not an exact science.
Its major conclusions are woven of probabilities. Moreover, in all ethical discussions
of larger problems, such, for example, as the right or desirability of life, of truthfulness,
or of property ownership, our final practical ethical judgments must be arrived at after
a careful weighing of the prospective or actual gains to welfare as compared with the
prospective or actual losses" ("Contraception and Altruistic Ethics," *The International
Journal of Ethics*, XLI [1931], 459). Cf. Charles C. Miltner, C.S.C., *op. cit.*, p. 7; Stanley
Bertke, *op. cit.*, 63–73; Michael Cronin, *The Science of Ethics*, I, 21–25, 127–74.

3. *Ethicorum*, V, 15, cited by Deploige, *op. cit.*, p. 314.

communities.[4] The propensity to disorder which is found in man and his associations is just as strong as, nay even stronger than, the rational longing for *ordo*. All this calls for a positive ordering and safeguarding of human existence and welfare at the hands of a concrete power. The *philosophia perennis* does not subscribe to the unfounded optimism of Rousseau's idea of natural law. It is aware of the demonic element in

4. Cf. in general Miriam Theresa Rooney, *Lawlessness, Law, and Sanction.* The Catholic University of America Philosophical Studies, Vol. XXXIV (Washington, D.C.: Catholic University of America Press, 1937). It is important to note, in connection with the intrinsic sanction attached to the natural moral law, that neither ignorance nor good faith on the part of either individuals or entire societies suffices to ward off the harmful psychological, moral, social, and often physical consequences of actions that are in themselves bad that are violations of the natural moral law. The invincible ignorance, good faith or sincerity of individuals and groups provide the basis for the weighty and often disconcerting distinction between objective wrong and subjective guilt, between material sin and formal sin and hence they serve to excuse one from formal guilt in the sight of God. Yet certain consequences of evil acts are inexorable; they lie in the nature of things. They are the inescapable penalties for the want of deep and correct insight into, and faithful adherence to, the conditions fixed by nature, and ultimately by nature's Author, for human individual and social development and happiness. Furthermore, they are the needed spur to a reconsideration of the moral quality of actions hitherto regarded as good; they constitute necessary and salutary incentives to moral reform as the indispensable means to genuine and rounded human progress; and they give the lie to the senseless but oft-heard saying, "There is nothing wrong or bad but thinking makes it so." An excellent illustration of this point is furnished by the widespread practice of positive contraception or artificial birth control, which, objectively, as a deliberate perversion whereby the essential order between the sex act and its primary end is destroyed (as in final analysis nothing but mutual masturbation), is intrinsically immoral and therefore justifiable under no circumstances whatsoever. Now, even if we largely grant invincible ignorance and good faith to the non-Catholic masses and their moral leaders regarding this rather remote conclusion from the primary principle of the natural moral law (on the possibility of the invincible ignorance of some Catholics in this matter, cf. Stanley Bertke, *op. cit.*, pp. 97 ff.), will the wedge-principle in ethics cease to operate? Will birth rates cease to fall or populations to decline? Will the various and complicated untoward economic, social, political, international, and interracial consequences of a widespread practice of artificial birth control be avoided? Will men more readily master the sexual part of their nature and more easily subject it to reason? Will the consequent small family really promote the moral growth of parents and the moral education of children? Will the moral fiber of individuals and societies be strengthened? Will the mounting pleasure complex be checked? Will the principle that the end justifies the means, the implicit assumption mostly underlying the acceptance and defense of positive contraception (as also of eugenic sterilization, therapeutic abortion, artificial insemination as usually practiced,

man's nature, of the dark forces which produce disorder and destruction. Even though, for example, the natural law forbids theft, there is need of the positive penal law which attaches the penalty as a legal consequence to the actual fact of theft. Justice determines what this penalty is in the light of the principle of proportionateness; and prudence aids in its determination by drawing upon the principle of suitableness of means to the end and upon the requirements of education. For punishment is not an end in itself: its object is requital (*iustitia vindicativa*) as well as deterrence and education.[5]

The special form of the virtue of prudence for the lawmaker consists not only herein, but also in deriving the positive norm from the principles with due regard for concrete circumstances. St. Thomas, it will be recalled, repeatedly mentions the function of circumstances in determining the reasonableness of a law. "The execution of justice, in so far as it is directed to the common good, which is part of the kingly office, needs the guidance of prudence. Hence these two virtues—prudence and justice—belong most properly to a king," i.e., in his principal function of lawmaking.[6] For prudence combines the knowledge of general principles with the knowledge of particulars which are the matter of action, since it governs the right choice of means for attaining the end.[7] The prudence of the lawmaker is the most perfect species of

---

euthanasia, and the like), be restricted in its applications to this single case? To ask these and other pertinent questions is to answer them. Whether in good faith or in bad faith, a society addicted to artificial birth-control practices will inexorably pay the terrible penalties of its contravention of the natural moral law, first indeed in subtle ways, and then more and more openly and upon an ever vaster scale. It is a mere question of time.

5. For a thorough and severe criticism of the notion of punitive justice, apparently accepted here, as confused, sentimental, irremediably obscure, and unnecessary, see Jacques Leclercq, *Les droits et devoirs individuels.* Part I, *Vie, disposition de soi,* pp. 82–96: social self-defense and emendation of the guilty person provide a sufficient basis for the legitimacy of punishment, which may be reparational, repressive (personal and exemplary), and educational. For an exposition of the dominant scholastic view of punishment in terms, rightly or wrongly, of the philosophy of St. Thomas, cf. George Quentin Friel, O.P., *Punishment in the Philosophy of St. Thomas and among Some Primitive Peoples.* The Catholic University of America Philosophical Studies, Vol. XLVII (Washington, D.C.: Catholic University of America Press, 1939).

6. St. Thomas, *Summa theologica,* IIa IIae, q.50, a.1 ad 1, 3.

7. Cf. *ibid.,* q.47, a.6, 15.

prudence, and it is compared to the prudence of subjects as mastercraft to handicraft.[8]

It is thus sufficiently established that all positive laws should in some way be derivations from the natural law or determinations of it. But this does not mean that every positive law which is not a correct derivation or determination of the natural law is therefore not binding and is devoid of obligation. Only those positive laws are purely and simply non-obligatory which command one to do something that in itself is immoral and unjust. To this category belong laws that are at variance with the prohibitive precepts of the natural law. There is nothing revolutionary about this; it is something self-evident. Scarcely anybody will regard as right a law which allows assassination, adultery, or perjury. Few will call the early Christians contemners of law because they refused obedience to the pagan laws which prescribed sacrifices to idols.

On the other hand, an unjust law (e.g., a tax law which is in conflict with the principle of justice and proportionateness) is not solely on that account devoid of obligation. An unjust law is not forthwith an immoral law in the strict sense, that is, a law which prescribes a sinful action. In cases of this kind the maintenance of even an imperfect *ordo* takes precedence over resistance to a particular unjust law. The natural law is, of course, a norm for the lawmaker. Such a view has been held by nearly all philosophers of law, including the founders of the modern theory of sovereignty, Bodin and for a time even Hobbes. Yet a positive law which is certainly unjust but does not contradict the natural law in its prohibitive norms does not give to judges and other public officials, whom the constitution obliges to apply and execute the law, or to the subjects of the law a right to consider the law non-binding and invalid. Even a tax law which agrees neither with distributive justice nor, say, with the principle of expenditure in the general interest does not justify a person in defrauding the revenue. The natural-law principles of obedience and truthfulness here again take precedence. The proper remedy is not disobedience but use of the means provided by the constitution. Since, however, the prohibitive precepts of the natural law have precisely

8. Cf. *ibid.,* q.50, a.1 f.

the function of protecting the social order in its deepest foundation, a positive law that commands something which is in itself unjust and immoral must be regarded as non-law.[9] When little or no respect any longer exists for any authority; when marriage generally ceases to be differentiated from concubinage and promiscuity; when the honor of one's fellow citizen is no longer respected and oaths no longer have force, then the possibility of social living, of order in human affairs, vanishes altogether.

So far as the other norms of the natural law (*ius naturale permissivum vel praecipiens*) are concerned, the positive law is free in its efforts to give effect to these precepts. For in this case questions of national character, suitableness of means, circumstances, and forms of government are decisive. Here, in other words, the prudence of the lawmaker is the decisive factor. This prudent reserve of the traditional natural law (*ius naturale perenne*) also implies that there are no points of irreconcilable opposition between the natural law and the historical school of law: the two can and should complement each other.

Some examples may serve to illustrate this. The institution of private property is at the very least in accordance with the natural law. But this does not mean that severe restrictions on the use of property, or even expropriations for reasons of general welfare, are absolutely contrary to the natural law. Nor does it mean that the Roman law idea of property or the feudalist or capitalist systems of ownership pertain to the natural law. It involves merely the directive to the lawmaker to fashion the actual order of ownership in such a way that property may here and now be qualified to perform (for the individual person, for the family in general, and for most of the members of the nation) its natural-law social function in keeping with the national character and the stage of economic development. The property system of private capitalism with its unrestrained freedom of ownership, with its mobilization of all real

9. Why may society never demand from one of its members an action that is unjust, immoral, sinful? Because "the reason for the existence of society is to aid in developing men in accordance with their human nature, and because sin is that which is contrary to the requirements of human nature. To sin is to act as though one were not a man, to go counter to one's nature as a reasonable being, to deny one's humanity" (Jacques Leclercq, *Le fondement du droit et de la société*, p. 335).

property, with its tendency toward giant corporations and trusts, and with its division of each people into a relatively few "haves" and a great many "have-nots," has been for a long time in no position to perform this function. Taking their stand on the natural law, and often enough in prophetic loneliness, Catholic social reformers since Bishop von Ketteler (1811–77), and even since the romantic movement, have been making this clear in their struggle against economic liberalism. They have also been at pains to point out that the liberty of the propertyless is largely a fiction. To save the family they have demonstrated its right to property as a material substratum of its biological and moral existence. Furthermore, it was owing to its individualism that the Roman people fashioned its positive institutions of property along individualist lines. It was in accordance with the corporative spirit of the German people, however, to fashion in Germanic law a substantially different system of property, one which imposed heavy obligations upon owners, and included specific forms of joint ownership (e.g., in the apportionment of the returns of property among many joint claimants), and especially to treat personal and real property according to separate forms. Hence Bishop von Ketteler, the adherent of natural law, in his proposals for social reform significantly called for the restoration of Germanic law. The positive institutions of property do not have the character of something holy. On the contrary, the common good requires of the lawmaker that he prudently introduce changes into the system of property and adapt it to new economic conditions. A complex commercial and industrial economy obviously calls for a different system of property than is required by a simple natural economy.

The rationalist school of natural law had inferred from its own view of natural law that either absolute monarchy or pure democracy, according to the preferences of the writers and the supposed needs or trends of the times, is alone authorized by natural law. The older natural-law doctrine had never advocated sharply defined ideal governments of this sort. Its ideal government was the system of mixed government, which in any event included the participation of the people.[10] St. Thomas

10. In a long and temporarily discontinued series of penetrating and diffuse (and also somewhat confusing) articles on "The Theory of Democracy" in *The Thomist* (Vol. III, July, 1941-Vol. VII, January, 1944), Mortimer J. Adler and Walter Farrell, O.P., challenge some of the traditional conclusions of natural-law political thinking. The

holds that the constitution must be suited to the character of the people and to its moral vigor. An earnest, moderate, and responsible people which cherishes the general welfare may with full right govern itself through republican institutions and freely elected officials.[11] Here indeed the natural-law principle, *salus populi* (taken concretely in the sense of an individual people in its historical peculiarity) *suprema lex*,[12] is valid, and not the positivist axiom which declares that the will of the prince is the supreme law. Thus the Christian natural law has never indulged in the mania for deduction which characterized rationalism. On the contrary, it has been able to take into account the peculiarity of individual peoples and their legal genius, the course of their historical development, and their economic evolution. For only the eternal structural laws of the social life of man as such are of natural law, not the concrete architectural form. The stylistic variation of the art-forms of individual peoples is no disproof of the eternal laws of beauty in art.

The natural law calls, then, for the positive law. This explains why the natural law, though it is the enduring basis and norm of the positive law, progressively withdraws, as it were, behind the curtain of the positive law as the latter achieves a continually greater perfection. This is also why the natural law reappears whenever the positive law is

---

authors are wholly intent upon establishing their proposition that "democracy is, on moral grounds, the best form of government," and in reformulating the basic problem of the classification of states. Cf. *ibid.*, III (1941), 398.

11. Cf. St. Thomas, *Summa theologica*, Ia IIae, q.97, a.1, quoting St. Augustine. "All should take some share in the government, for this form of constitution ensures peace among the people, commends itself to all, and is most enduring. . . . Accordingly, the best form of government is in a state or kingdom, wherein one is given the power to preside over all, while under him are others having governing powers. And yet a government of this kind is shared by all, both because all are eligible to govern, and because the rulers are chosen by all. For this is the best form of polity, being partly kingdom, since there is one at the head of all; partly aristocracy, in so far as a number of persons are set in authority; partly democracy, i.e., government by the people, in so far as the rulers can be chosen from the people, and the people have the right to choose their rulers" (*ibid.*, q.105, a.1).

12. This principle has, however, been all too frequently interpreted and applied in the sense of *raison d'Etat*, the canon of political non-morality, Machiavellianism, power politics. Cf. Jacques Leclercq, *Le fondement du droit et de la société*, pp. 295 ff.

transformed into objective injustice through the evolution and play of vital forces and the functional changes of communities.

For the same reason the practical jurist is generally satisfied with the theory and exclusive application of the positive law. "Our quarrel does not turn on the thing, but on a word: on the meaning in which we use the word 'law.' We term law only the positive norm which emanates from the will of the state. What you call natural law we consider ethics, the moral foundations of law which we also acknowledge" (H. Ermann). Natural law is viewed simply as non-applicable law, as devoid of force in the legal sense. But such a view is altogether inadequate. In the first place, it mistakenly presupposes the completeness of (the lack of gaps in) the positive law. Next, it does not square with all legal systems. It stems rather from a politico-legal conviction that, since the judge is bound to apply the positive law, he should not meddle with the function of the legislator whose express duty it is to realize justice. In states where judicial supremacy prevails (in ancient Rome, in medieval German law, in countries of the Anglo-Saxon common law)[11] the judges' ruling is directly creative of law. Certainly these judges appealed and still appeal precisely to the natural law or natural justice. Finally, as has already been indicated, even the positive law frequently refers to the natural law, especially under the form of equity.

It seems that, with regard to the matter of validity, two things have to be distinguished: the validity of law which is related to the order of mere existence (practical and historical factuality) and the validity of law which is related to the order of essence (the metaphysical order). The positive law has validity to the extent that it is promulgated by the duly constituted lawmaker as his factual will. The natural law has validity independently of its embodiment in a factual volitional act. It is thereby valid at least for the lawmaker. Whether and to what extent it binds the judge or has validity for him is more a question of the constitution of the state: it depends rather upon the public-law principle of the division of powers. According to this principle the judge, i.e.,

13. This is scarcely true of modern England itself, where parliament is, at least in theory, legally omnipotent.

the judicial power, has only to apply the laws or the law of the land. Yet it would be decidedly narrow and illogical to exclude natural law from the laws, and to contend that only such laws are meant as are duly enacted in conformity with the formal legislative procedure established by the constitution without any regard to matter and content, to what is intrinsically just or unjust, i.e., without regard to the natural law. Under constitutional government bulwarked by a bill of rights there exists indeed a strong presumption of law and of right that all laws enacted in keeping with constitutional procedure are not out of harmony with the natural law. It is from this assumption that such laws derive not only their factual enforceability but also their ultimate validity before conscience. Nevertheless this presumption is precisely what it means, a practical device which in particular circumstances does not exclude the duty of the judge to invalidate or not to apply a certain positive law which is clearly at variance with the natural law. In any event the prohibitive precepts of the natural law bind even the judge.[14]

Under constitutional, free government with the added safeguard of a bill of rights there thus exists a strong presumption that the positive law is a determination and derivation of the natural law. For this reason and also because of the consequent *de facto* legal peace, which enables and permits men to accept without further scrutiny the order of positive law, the idea of natural law remains as it were latent. But it makes itself felt whenever the positive law, in itself or in the eyes of a large number of people, appears to be in conflict with the natural law. Then the primordial rights of the person, the family, and the national group stand forth with elemental force against the power of the state, which develops into tyranny by denying the foundations of political community, its own moral root: the natural law. But this is juridically permissible and can meet with ethical approval only if the natural law is real, valid law; otherwise such disobedience toward the positive law could not be approved of. If the old distinction between unlawful sedition

14. Caution is especially imperative, however, where the remote conclusions of the natural law, where borderline cases are concerned. Is a judge, e.g., bound to condemn a defendant who, though known to the judge to be innocent, is judicially proved guilty? St. Thomas answers yes, but St. Bonaventure teaches the contrary. Cf. Stanley Bertke, *op. cit.*, p. 73.

and justifiable resistance to the power of the state (i.e., revolution)—a distinction which played such a vital role in medieval legal thought in the form of the common subjection of people and ruler to the law[15]—has progressively disappeared in the modern age, this is due to several factors. First, the people take an increasingly greater part in the development of the positive law, in lawmaking as well as in administering and applying the law. Thus is produced a greater unity of law with the spirit of the people. Secondly, interpretation of the written law in accordance with justice and equity is achieved through the ethos of the true judge. Lastly, the world of positive law has been progressively penetrated by the principles and prestige of Christian ethics.[16]

15. Carlyle and Carlyle point out that the general political principles of the Middle Ages were "the supremacy of law, the community as the source of political authority, the limited authority of the ruler, and the contractual nature of the relations between the ruler and the community," and they rightly insist that the development of these principles was not more than incidentally related to the frequent conflicts which occurred between the temporal and spiritual powers. *A History of Mediaeval Political Theory in the West*, V, 438; see especially pp. 441–74.

16. It is a pleasure to recommend to the law student, and to practicing lawyers as well, the mature and balanced volume of William Francis Clarke, *The Soul of the Law* (Boston: Bruce Humphries, 1942).

CHAPTER XV

Conclusion

Modern totalitarianism with its depersonalization of man, with its debasement of man to the position of a particle of an amorphous mass which is molded and remolded in accordance with the shifting policy of the "Leader," is of its very nature extremely voluntaristic. *Voluntas facit legem:* law is will. How seldom the theorists and practitioners of totalitarianism mention reason, and how frequently they glory in the triumph of the will! The will of the Leader or of the Commissar is not bound by or responsible to an objective body of moral values or an objective standard of morality revealed in the order of being and in human nature. The will is not bound by the objective, conventional meaning of words or by the relation of these to ideas and things. Ideas, as well as the words which express them, are mere tools for the will: they are to be remolded whenever this is expedient. Accordingly an appeal from decisions of this will to natural law, to intrinsic right, to justice and equity, to ideas, must appear as "treason" which stems from democratic decadence or from bourgeois prejudices. The defense against totalitarianism cannot plead greater efficiency, more economic productivity, which are the categories in which the totalitarian "social engineer" thinks. Such a defense must appeal to justice, to the rule of reason; it must plead in the name of the natural law and of the natural rights of human persons and their free associations. Natural law is not only an ideal for the positive law, for legislation to realize; it is also a critical norm for the existing positive law.

Natural law, however, is essentially a framework law, a skeleton law. It does not ordinarily give us a concrete norm directly applicable to action here and now in the involved situations of actual life. It does not, for instance, tell us which of the many possible forms of laws about property is right in the abstract. Neither the capitalistic nor the feudal system of property is imposed by the natural law. But it judges each and every existing system of property in terms of justice. Moreover, natural law does not condemn the wage contract as such or the socio-economic order of which the wage contract is so important a part, but it makes clear that a social order in which the so-called iron law of wages rules the labor market violates justice and equity. Further, natural law does not proclaim that democracy as a form of government is the sole admissible mode of political organization; yet it does tell us that any form of government, even one that is decked out in the trappings of democracy, which does not recognize the fundamental rights of the person and of the family is tyrannical and may, therefore, rightly be resisted. Natural law, finally, does not say that the Security Council of the United Nations is, in its concrete form, good and efficient; but it does forbid the independence of a small nation to be sacrificed out of mere expediency for the sake of the "security" of a great power. This quality of the unvarying natural law, which elevates it above the changing historical positive law, which makes it both the ideal for lawmakers and the critical norm for existing laws, renders it possible for the natural law to govern the acquisition and exercise of political power itself.

Politics is and remains a part of the moral universe. For it is inexcusable to view politics merely as the technique or art of achieving and retaining social power for some selfish end through the skillful exploitation of human weaknesses, by deceit or by terrorist methods. Politics is rather the great architectonic art by which men build the institutions and protective forms of their individual and communal life for a more perfect realization of the good life. Its main function is to establish an order and unity of cooperation among free persons and free associations of persons in such a way that these, while they freely pursue their individual and group interests, are nevertheless so coordinated that they realize at the same time the common good under the rule of law. But the rule of law is the natural law which justifies the use of political power and before which power itself as well as resistance to arbitrary acts of those in authority must establish its legitimacy: through the natural law alone can we solve the crucial political problem of the legitimacy of power and the duty of free persons to obey. Thus the rule of law, the paramount law binding both the ruler and the ruled, necessarily implies the idea of natural law as the critical norm for the existing positive legal order and for the demand to change it, if it has become unjust. The hope of a peaceful change of the legal *status quo* within each nation as well as in the community of nations depends on the acceptance of such a higher law that measures both the legal rights of the *status quo* and the claims of those who would alter it; and it measures them because it is based on natural reason, in which all men participate. For the natural law, ultimately of divine origin but revealed in the very order of being, is but the rule of reason founded upon the rational and social nature of man. *Veritas facit legem:* law is truth.

"All men are born natural-law jurists." This fact, which Bergbohm notes at the beginning of his great attack on the natural law, should surely have shown an unbiased person that the very essence of man as a moral, social being points to the nature of law. For all men are born natural-law jurists because in the human soul lies the ineradicable demand that the law must live in morality. All law must be just: only then can it obtain that power which primarily holds together and continually renews every community, and in particular every political community, the power to bind in conscience. But the proper function of the natural-law doctrine is precisely to show forth the connection between morality and law. Consequently it must, for the sake of the very existence of man and his concrete legally ordered communities, ever recur, and it does in fact always return whenever the genius of law seeks out its own foundations.

The foundation of law is justice. "Truth grants or refuses the highest crown to the products of positive legislation, and they draw from truth their true moral force" (Franz Brentano). But truth is conformity with reality. And just as the real and the true are one, so too the true and the just are ultimately one. *Veritas facit legem.* And in this profound sense of the unity of truth and justice the words, "And the truth shall make you free,"[1] are applicable to the community of men under law. True freedom consists in being bound by justice.[2]

1. John 8:32.

2. But the most important lesson of this entire study of the history and philosophy of the natural law may be succinctly stated in a paraphrase of a law of philosophical experience formulated by Etienne Gilson (*The Unity of Philosophical Experience*, p. 306): "The natural law always buries its undertakers." Or, as Horace has expressed it (*Epistles* I, x, 24): *Naturam expellas furca, tamen usque recurret.* "You may drive out nature with a pitchfork, yet it will always return!"

Select Bibliography

Because the subject of natural law touches at least five disciplines in the modern academy—law, philosophy, theology, politics, and history—the literature is extraordinarily diverse. The best single source is the *American Journal of Jurisprudence* (formerly the *Natural Law Forum*), which publishes articles, reviews, and bibliographies reflecting the entire spectrum of natural law themes and methods. See, for example, the recent bibliography by Schall.

Schall, James V. "The Natural Law Bibliography." *American Journal of Jurisprudence* 40 (1995): 157–98.

GENERAL STUDIES

Historical summaries and interpretations of natural law vary considerably. The book by Rommen's Italian contemporary, d'Entrèves, is still useful, but one should get the 1994 edition, which includes new appendices reflecting changes in the author's thinking. The encyclopedia entry by Leo Strauss is perhaps the best summary of Strauss's approach to the problem of natural law. Simon's book, based on his 1958 lectures at the University of Chicago, is a remarkably clear exposition of the philosophical problems that attend theories of natural law.

d'Entrèves, A. P. *Natural Law.* 2d rev. ed. London: Hutchinson University Library, 1972. Reprint, with new Introduction by Cary J. Nederman. New Brunswick and London: Transaction Publishers, 1994.

Gierke, Otto. *Natural Law and the Theory of Society.* 2 vols. Cambridge: Cambridge University Press, 1934.

Simon, Yves R. *The Tradition of Natural Law: A Philosopher's Reflections.* Ed. Vukan Kuic. 1965. Reprint, with an introduction by Russell Hittinger. New York: Fordham University Press, 1992.

Strauss, Leo. "On Natural Law." In *Studies in Platonic Political Philosophy,*

137–46. Chicago: University of Chicago Press, 1983. Originally published in the *International Encyclopedia of the Social Sciences,* ed. David L. Sills, 2:80–90.

ANCIENT

Systematically developed theories of natural law are the work of medieval and modern minds. But the problem of natural justice was addressed by Plato, Aristotle, and the Greek and Roman Stoics. Works by Barker, Miller, Maguire, Spanneut, A. Watson, and G. Watson treat the concept of justice by nature in the philosophers of antiquity; Novak studies its development in Jewish thought. In *The Natural Law,* Rommen depicts the transition from classical to medieval theories as being smooth and cumulative. The essay by Koester, however, suggests that the transition was more abrupt. He argues that the introduction of biblical ideas of creation and law into the Graeco-Roman world is chiefly responsible for the concept of "natural law." The essay by Mahoney traces some of the early theological formulations and uses of natural law.

Barker, Ernest. "Aristotle's Conception of Justice, Law, and Equity in the Ethics and the Rhetoric." In *The Politics of Aristotle,* 362–72. Oxford: Oxford University Press, 1958.

Koester, Helmut. "The Concept of Natural Law in Greek Thought." In *Religions in Antiquity,* ed. Jacob Neusner. Leiden: E. J. Brill, 1968.

Maguire, G. P. "Plato's Theory of Natural Law." *Yale Classical Studies* 10 (1947): 151–78.

Mahoney, John, S.J. "Nature and Supernature." In *Natural Law and Theology,* ed. Charles E. Curran and Richard A. McCormick, 413–63. New York: Paulist Press, 1991.

Miller, Fred D. "Aristotle on Natural Law and Justice." In *A Companion to Aristotle's Politics,* ed. David Keyt and Fred D. Miller. Oxford: Basil Blackwell, 1991.

Novak, David. "Natural Law, Halakhah and the Covenant." *Jewish Law Annual* 7 (1988): 43–67.

Spanneut, M. "Stoicism: Influence on Christian Thought." In *New Catholic Encyclopedia.* Vol. 13, 719–21. New York: McGraw-Hill, 1967.

Watson, Alan. "The Legacy of Justinian Natural Law." In *Roman Law and Comparative Law,* 214–20. Athens: University of Georgia Press, 1991.

Watson, G. "The Early History of Natural Law." *Irish Theological Quarterly* 33 (1966): 65–74.

MEDIEVAL AND SCHOLASTIC

Today, the work of Thomas Aquinas is widely regarded as the preeminent example of medieval natural law theory. For general studies on Thomas Aquinas, see the books by Chenu and Torrell. By no means, however, is contemporary Thomism a united front. Adler, Brock, and Grisez provide three very different interpretations of Thomas's natural law theory. The essays and books by Bourke, Davitt, Dewan, and McInerny treat various Thomistic themes and issues. While not being explications of Thomas's texts, the books by Maritain, Simon, and Messner represent some of the best neo-scholastic work on natural law in Rommen's generation. Murray's influential collection of essays tries to reconcile the scholastic tradition with American institutions. Finally, the essay by Alasdair MacIntyre reflects upon the papal use of natural law in the recent encyclical *Veritatis Splendor.*

Historically, Thomas was only one tributary of medieval natural law thinking. Works by Berman, Gilby, Gratian (new edition by Thompson and Gordley), Kuttner, Pennington, Post, and Ullmann explore the political and jurisprudential themes that formed the institutional context and background of the philosophical and theological debates in the medieval schools. Works by Oakley, McDonnell, Gewirth, and Tuck examine the non-Thomistic channels of medieval natural law thinking, some of which proved very influential for the development of modern theories of law and rights.

Adler, Mortimer. "A Question About Law." In *Essays in Thomism,* ed. Robert E. Brennan, 207–36. New York: Sheed and Ward, 1942.

Berman, Harold J. *Law and Revolution: The Formation of the Western Legal Tradition.* Cambridge: Harvard University Press, 1983.

Bourke, Vernon. "The Background of Aquinas' Synderesis Principle." In *Graceful Reason,* ed. Lloyd Gerson. Toronto: Institute for Mediaeval Studies, 1983.

———. "The Synderesis Rule and Right Reason." *Monist* 66 (1983): 71–82.

Brock, Stephen L. "The Legal Character of Natural Law According to St. Thomas Aquinas." Ph.D. diss. University of Toronto, 1988.

Chenu, Marie-Dominique. *Toward Understanding Saint Thomas.* Trans. A. M. Landry and D. Hughes. Chicago: Henry Regnery, 1964.

Davitt, Thomas E. *The Nature of Law.* St. Louis: B. Herder, 1951.

Dewan, Lawrence. "St. Thomas, Our Natural Lights, and the Moral Order." *Angelicum* 67 (1990): 285–308.

Donagan, Alan. "The Scholastic Theory of Moral Law in the Modern World."

In *Aquinas,* ed. A. Kenny, 328–29. Notre Dame: University of Notre Dame Press, 1969.

Gewirth, Alan. *Marsilius of Padua: The Defender of Peace.* Vol. 1 of *Marsilius of Padua and Medieval Political Philosophy.* New York: Columbia University Press, 1951.

Gilby, Thomas. *Between Community and Society: A Philosophy and Theology of the State.* London: Longmans, Green and Co., 1953.

———. *The Political Thought of Thomas Aquinas.* Chicago: University of Chicago Press, 1958.

Gratian. *The Treatise on Laws (Decretum DD. 1–20), with the Ordinary Gloss.* Trans. Augustine Thompson, O.P., and James Gordley Washington, D.C.: Catholic University of America Press, 1993.

Grisez, Germain. "The First Principle of Practical Reason: A Commentary on the *Summa Theologiae* 94.2." *Natural Law Forum* 10 (1965): 168–201.

Kuttner, Stephen. "The Natural Law and Canon Law." *Proceedings of the University of Notre Dame Natural Law Institute* 3 (1950): 85–116.

MacIntyre, Alasdair. "How Can We Learn What *Veritatis Splendor* Has to Teach." *Thomist* 58, no. 2 (1994): 171–94.

Maritain, Jacques. *La loi naturelle ou loi non écrite.* Fribourg: Éditions universitaires Fribourg Suisse, 1986.

McDonnell, K. "Does William of Ockham Have a Theory of Natural Law?" *Franciscan Studies* 34 (1974): 383–92.

McInerny, Ralph. "The Basis and Purpose of Positive Law." In *Lex et Libertas,* ed. L. J. Elders and K. Hedwig, 137–46. Vatican: Pontificia Accadmia Di S. Tommaso E Di Religione Cattolica, 1987.

Messner, Johannes. *Social Ethics: Natural Law in the Western World.* Trans. J. J. Doherty. St. Louis: B. Herder, 1965.

Murray, John Courtney. *We Hold These Truths.* New York: Sheed and Ward, 1960.

Oakley, Francis. "Medieval Theories of Natural Law: William of Ockham and the Significance of the Voluntarist Tradition." *Natural Law Forum* 6 (1961): 65–83.

Pennington, K. *The Prince and the Law.* Berkeley: University of California Press, 1993.

Post, Gaines. *Studies in Medieval Legal Thought.* Princeton: Princeton University Press, 1964.

Simon, Yves R. *Philosophy of Democratic Government.* Chicago: University of Chicago Press, 1951.

Torrell, Jean-Pierre. *The Person and His Work.* Vol. 1 of *Saint Thomas Aquinas.*

Trans. Robert Royal. Washington, D.C.: Catholic University of America Press, 1996.

Tuck, Richard. *Natural Rights Theories.* Cambridge: Cambridge University Press, 1979.

Ullmann, Walter. *Jurisprudence in the Middle Ages.* London: Variorum Reprints, 1980.

ENLIGHTENMENT

Although there are family resemblances between premodern and modern theories of natural law, the Enlightenment era theorists reworked natural law in the light of new philosophical vocabularies and under the pressure of new political and institutional forces. Ruby and Rapaczynski investigate how the new sciences changed the logic of predicating "law(s)" of "nature." Windolph and Bobbio examine the most important figure in that change, Thomas Hobbes. Leo Strauss's book recommends itself. Strauss emphasized the discontinuity of ancient and modern theories of natural right. There is much disagreement, however, about how this discontinuity applies to John Locke. Different readings of Locke are to be found in the books by Grant, Andrew, and Haakonssen. Haakonssen examines the Enlightenment generally, and Scottish tradition in particular. Buckle, Schneewind, Waddicor, and Windolph take up the issue of natural law in various Enlightenment philosophers.

Andrew, Edward. *Shylock's Rights: A Grammar of Lockian Claims.* Toronto: University of Toronto Press, 1988.

Bobbio, Norberto. *Thomas Hobbes and the Natural Law Tradition.* Chicago: University of Chicago Press, 1993.

Buckle, Stephen. *Natural Law and the Theory of Property: Grotius to Hume.* Oxford: Oxford University Press, Clarendon Press, 1991.

Chroust, Anton-Hermann. "Hugo Grotius and the Scholastic Natural Law Tradition." *New Scholasticism* 17, no. 2 (1943): 101–33.

Grant, Ruth. *John Locke's Liberalism.* Chicago: University of Chicago Press, 1987.

Haakonssen, Knud. *Natural Law and Moral Philosophy: From Grotius to the Scottish Enlightenment.* Cambridge: Cambridge University Press, 1996.

Rapaczynski, Andrzej. *Nature and Politics: Liberalism in the Philosophies of Hobbes, Locke, and Rousseau.* Ithaca: Cornell University Press, 1987.

Ruby, Jane E. "The Origins of Scientific 'Law.'" *Journal of the History of Ideas* 47 (1986): 341–59.

Schneewind, J. B. "Kant and Natural Law Ethics." *Ethics* 104 (October 1993): 53–74.

Strauss, Leo. *Natural Right and History.* Chicago: University of Chicago Press, 1953.

Waddicor, Mark H. *Montesquieu and the Philosophy of Natural Law.* The Hague: Martinus Nijhoff, 1970.

Windolph, F. Lyman. *Leviathan and Natural Law.* Princeton: Princeton University Press, 1951.

ANGLO-AMERICAN

The Atiyah-Summers volume compares English and American legal cultures, including their respective attitudes toward natural law. For the English situation, see the works of Hart (1958), Postema, and Stanlis; for the American, see Brownson, Corwin, Hittinger (1990), and Tiedeman. The famous debate of a generation ago, between Fuller and Hart, exemplifies many of the differences between the English and American minds on natural law.

Concerning the role of natural law in judicial review, see my remarks in the Introduction on the books by Corwin, Cover, Haines, and Wright. For the Fourteenth Amendment and the jurisprudence of due process see Arkes (1994), Ely, Nelson, and Stevens. The Barnett volume includes essays on the Ninth Amendment. Arkes (1990), Dworkin, and Richards agree that the Constitution requires a moral interpretation but differ considerably on both the substance and the logic of the morality that ought to guide jurisprudence. The essay by Hittinger explores natural law grounds for judicial restraint. Ely argues that theories of natural law provide no such restraint.

Arkes, Hadley. *Beyond the Constitution.* Princeton: Princeton University Press, 1990.

———. *The Return of George Sutherland: Restoring a Jurisprudence of Natural Rights.* Princeton: Princeton University Press, 1994.

Atiyah, P. S., and R. S. Summers. *Form and Substance in Anglo-American Law.* Oxford: Oxford University Press, Clarendon Press, 1987.

Barnett, Randy E., ed. *The Rights Retained by the People: The History and Meaning of the Ninth Amendment.* Fairfax: George Mason University Press, 1989.

Brownson, Orestes A. "The Higher Law." In *Essays and Reviews, Chiefly on Theology, Politics, and Socialism,* 349–67. New York: D. and J. Sadlier, 1880.

Corwin, Edward S. *The "Higher Law" Background of American Constitutional Law.* Ithaca: Cornell University Press, 1955.

Cover, Robert M. *Justice Accused: Antislavery and the Judicial Process.* New Haven: Yale University Press, 1975.

Dworkin, Ronald. " 'Natural' Law Revisited." *University of Florida Law Review* 34 (1982): 165–88.

Ely, John Hart. *Democracy and Distrust.* Cambridge: Harvard University Press, 1980.

Fuller, Lon. *The Morality of Law.* Rev. ed. New Haven: Yale University Press, 1969.

Haines, Charles Groves. *The Revival of Natural Law Concepts.* Cambridge: Harvard University Press, 1930.

Hart, H. L. A. "Positivism and the Separation of Law and Morality." *Harvard Law Review* 71 (1958): 593–629.

———. *The Concept of Law.* Oxford: Oxford University Press, 1961.

———. "Review of Lon L. Fuller, *The Morality of Law.*" In *Essays in Jurisprudence and Philosophy*, 343–64. Oxford: Oxford University Press, Clarendon Press, 1983.

Hittinger, Russell. "Liberalism and the American Natural Law Tradition." *Wake Forest Law Review* 25, no. 3 (1990): 429–99.

———. "Natural Law in the Positive Laws: A Legislative or Adjudicative Issue?" *Review of Politics* 55, no. 1 (1993): 5–34.

Nelson, William. *The Fourteenth Amendment.* Cambridge: Harvard University Press, 1988.

Postema, Gerald. *Bentham and the Common Law Tradition.* Oxford: Oxford University Press, 1986.

Richards, David A. J. *Toleration and the Constitution.* Oxford: Oxford University Press, 1986.

Stanlis, Peter J. *Edmund Burke and the Natural Law.* Shreveport: Huntington House, 1986.

Stevens, Richard J. *Frankfurter and Due Process.* Lanham, Md.: University Press of America, 1987.

Tiedeman, Christopher G. *The Unwritten Constitution of the United States.* New York: G. P. Putnam's Sons, 1890.

Wright, Benjamin Fletcher. *American Interpretations of Natural Law.* Cambridge: Harvard University Press, 1931.

CONTEMPORARY DEBATES

In addition to the issue of judicial review, contemporary debates about natural law often crystalize around two other problems: first, the ongoing debate over legal positivism; second, the role of subjective rights in natural law theory.

The book by John Finnis is a good place to begin in understanding both of these problems. A professor at Oxford, Finnis has developed an influential theory of natural law that has affinities to both the scholastic and analytical traditions. Finnis also systematically develops a theory of natural rights. The works by George, MacCormick, and Raz indicate that debates between natural lawyers and positivists are more refined today than they were a generation ago. On the problem of natural rights, see the two works by Fortin, who questions the compatibility between the older natural law tradition and the modern notion of personally possessed (i.e., subjective) rights. McInerny and Veatch also explore philosophical problems of welding together the two traditions. Maritain's book is a famous example of the effort by some neo-Thomists to affirm the modern notion of inalienable rights. Hervada, on the other hand, develops an older conception of natural rights, not unlike Rommen. Writings by Tierney, Tuck (above), and Villey take different positions on the historical question of whether modern natural rights are rooted in the medieval scholastic tradition. Books by Gewirth, and Rasmussen and Den Uyl are recent efforts to make sense of natural or human rights completely apart from the scholastic tradition. Finally, Shapiro provides an intellectual history of the evolution of modern rights theories.

Finnis, John. *Natural Law and Natural Rights.* Oxford: Oxford University Press, Clarendon Press, 1980.

Fortin, Ernest. "The New Rights Theory and the Natural Law." *Review of Politics* 44 (October 1982): 590–612.

———. " 'Sacred and Inviolable': *Rerum Novarum* and Natural Rights." *Theological Studies* 53 (1992): 202–33.

George, Robert P., ed. *Natural Law Theory: Contemporary Essays.* Oxford: Oxford University Press, Clarendon Press, 1992.

———. *The Autonomy of Law: Essays on Legal Positivism.* Oxford: Oxford University Press, Clarendon Press, 1996.

Gewirth, Alan. *Reason and Morality.* Chicago: University of Chicago Press, 1978.

Hervada, Javier. *Natural Right and Natural Law: A Critical Introduction.* Trans. Alban d'Entremont. Pamplona, Spain: University of Navarra, 1987.

MacCormick, Neil. "Natural Law and the Separation of Law and Morals." In *Natural Law Theory: Contemporary Essays,* ed. Robert P. George, 105–33. Oxford: Oxford University Press, Clarendon Press, 1992.

Maritain, Jacques. *Man and the State.* Chicago: University of Chicago Press, 1951.

McInerny, Ralph. "Natural Law and Human Rights." *American Journal of Jurisprudence* 36 (1991): 1–14.

Rasmussen, Douglas B., and Douglas J. Den Uyl. *Liberty and Nature: An Aristotelian Defense of Liberal Order.* La Salle, Ill.: Open Court, 1991.

Raz, Joseph. *The Morality of Freedom.* Oxford: Oxford University Press, Clarendon Press, 1986.

Shapiro, Ian. *The Evolution of Rights in Liberal Theory.* Cambridge: Cambridge University Press, 1986.

Tierney, Brian. "Villey, Ockham and the Origin of Individual Rights." In *The Weightier Matters of the Law,* ed. John Witte and F. S. Alexander. Atlanta: Scholars Press, 1988.

———. "Aristotle and the American Indians—Again." *Christianesimo Nella Storia* 12 (Spring 1991): 295–322.

Veatch, Henry B. *Human Rights: Fact or Fancy?* Baton Rouge: Louisiana State University Press, 1985.

Villey, Michel. *Le droit et les droits de l'homme.* Paris: Presses universitaires de France, 1983.

Index

This book was set in Caslon, an English type designed in 1722 by William Caslon. It is often used in body text because the individual letters have a simple charm and are interesting and legible.

Printed on paper that is acid-free and meets the requirements of the American National Standard for Permanence of Paper for Printed Library Materials, Z39.48-1992. ∞

Book design by Betty Palmer McDaniel, Athens, Georgia
Composition by Monotype Composition Co., Inc., Baltimore, Maryland
Printed and bound by Edwards Brothers, Inc., Ann Arbor, Michigan